# Introducing
# Medical
# Anthropology

# Introducing Medical Anthropology

## A Discipline in Action

*Second Edition*

MERRILL SINGER AND HANS BAER

A division of
ROWMAN & LITTLEFIELD PUBLISHERS, INC.
*Lanham • New York • Toronto • Plymouth, UK*

Published by AltaMira Press
A division of Rowman & Littlefield Publishers, Inc.
A wholly owned subsidary of The Rowman & Littlefield Publishing Group, Inc.
4501 Forbes Boulevard, Suite 200, Lanham, Maryland 20706
http://www.altamirapress.com

Estover Road, Plymouth PL6 7PY, United Kingdom

British Library Cataloguing in Publication Information Available

Library of Congress Cataloging-in-Publication Data

Singer, Merrill.
  Introducing medical anthropology : a discipline in action / Merrill Singer and
Hans Baer.
      p. cm.
  Includes bibliographical references and index.
  ISBN 978-0-7591-2088-4 (cloth : alk. paper) —
  ISBN 978-0-7591-2089-1 (pbk. : alk. paper) —
  ISBN 978-0-7591-2090-7 (ebook)
  1. Medical anthropology. I. Baer, Hans A., 1944- II. Title.
GN296.S57 2011b
306.4'61—dc23                                                      2012032142

Printed in the United States of America

# Contents

# Preface

The second edition of *Introducing Medical Anthropology: A Discipline in Action* reflects the continued broad interest in health in social, cultural, and environmental contexts. As medical anthropologists active in fieldwork, we wrote this introductory text with three goals in mind: First, we want to show the wide applications of medical anthropology. As a social science, medical anthropology addresses specific health issues but also seeks to build a broad, theoretically based understanding of what health is, how culture and health interact, the role of social relations in shaping disease, the importance of the health/environment interface, and a range of other issues. In other words, this book is designed to help students new to medical anthropology gain an initial understanding of the subdiscipline's approach to health in light of the importance of interacting culture, social, environmental, and political economic contexts.

As we hope to demonstrate on the pages that follow, in addition to increasing the fund of knowledge about health, illness, and treatment, medical anthropology is actively and productively engaged day to day in addressing pressing health problems of diverse types around the globe through research, intervention, and policy-related initiatives. Strong involvement in diverse health issues and application is seen as well in the careers of the two authors of this book. Merrill Singer, a professor of anthropology and community medicine at the University of Connecticut, has helped develop, implement, and evaluate a number of projects designed to prevent the spread of HIV/AIDS, projects that have contributed to a measurable drop in local HIV incidence. He also has been quite active in environmental health issues and the adverse impacts of climate change on human health. He has carried out health-related research in several locations around the United States, as well as in China, Haiti, the Virgin Islands, and Brazil. Hans Baer, who has a joint appointment in the Development Studies Program, School of Social and Environmental Enquiry, and in the Centre of Health and Society, University of Melbourne, has carried out studies of complementary and alternative healing systems in the United States, Britain, and Australia as part of a broader project designed to understand the processes of health care system integration. Elsewhere in this book, we present many additional real-world examples of the ways medical anthropologists are tackling health-related issues and the impact their work is having on health.

One of the goals of this book is to affirm that medical anthropologists are very involved in the process of helping, to varying degrees, to change the world around them through their work in applied projects, policy initiatives, and advocacy. Not all medical anthropologists teach—many are involved full time in applied work—and not all of medical anthropology involves application. Medical anthropology both addresses specific health issues and analyzes them in their broader context. In other words, medical anthropology seeks to understand health-related issues and to use this knowledge in improving human health and well-being.

A second goal of this book is a presentation of the fundamental importance of culture and social relationships in health and illness. Through a review of the key ideas, concepts, methods, and theoretical frameworks that guide research and application in medical anthropology, the book makes the case that illness and disease involve complex biosocial processes and that resolving them requires attention to a range of factors beyond biology, including systems of belief, structures of (often unequal) social relationship, and environmental conditions.

Finally, through an examination of the issues of health inequality, such as exposure to pesticides among farmworkers on the one hand and environmental degradation and environment-related illness on the other, the book underlines the need for going beyond cultural or even ecological models of health toward a comprehensive medical anthropology. Such an approach integrates biological, cultural, and social factors in building unified theoretical understandings of the origin of ill health while contributing to the building of effective and equitable national health care systems (e.g., Rylko-Bauer and Farmer 2002). In this manner, medical anthropologists seek to be part of a collective process aimed at creating a healthier world for both humanity and the biosphere, thereby prevailing over widespread patterns of health and social injustice and environmental destruction.

# 1

# Introduction to Medical Anthropology

Healing requires a legitimated, credible and culturally appropriate
system.

—*Mildred Blaxter (2004:43)*

People who encounter the term "medical anthropology" for the first
time often are puzzled by what the term means. Is it the study of how
medicine is practiced, what doctors, nurses, or traditional healers from
other health care systems actually do? Or is it the study of what it means and
feels like to be sick? Perhaps it is the study of folk illnesses in different societies? Might it be the application of cultural knowledge to the actual treatment
of diseases? All these questions, in fact, can be answered in the affirmative.
Medical anthropology addresses each of these issues—and far more. A starting premise of medical anthropology is that health-related issues, including
disease and treatment, how and why one gets sick, and the nature of recovery,
are far more than narrow biological phenomenon. These processes are all
heavily influenced by cultural and social factors as well. Consequently, medical anthropology has developed a *bio-sociocultural approach* in its effort to
address health as an aspect of the human condition.

To take one example, medical anthropologists ask questions such as the
following: Could we really understand the AIDS epidemic and respond to it
effectively simply by studying the human immunodeficiency virus, its impact
on cells of the body, and medical interventions designed to stop the virus
from destroying the immune system? Would we not also need to know how

1

to reach and effectively engage those who are at greatest risk for infection, to figure out the structural and situational factors that contribute to their involvement in risky behaviors, to know how much they know and what they feel about AIDS and how these factors influence their behaviors, and to determine whether the ways we go about interacting with them in the community and in the clinic draws them closer or pushes them away from our treatment programs? In other words, beyond biology it is clear that there are critically important areas of knowledge in the fight against the AIDS epidemic. Now, if we think about the AIDS epidemic as a global problem, with different routes of infection, different populations at risk, different beliefs and behaviors associated with HIV/AIDS in diverse settings, and different health care systems in different parts of the world or even different parts of a single country, we begin to get an initial sense of why a social science like anthropology might—as it certainly has—have a significant role to play in addressing the AIDS epidemic. This is of no small importance as we know from available research showing that HIV/AIDS is destined to take a greater toll on our species, proportionately and in terms of absolute numbers, than the bubonic plague, smallpox, and tuberculosis combined. Consider the epidemic in South Africa. As Didier Fassin (2007:261) points out, "In one decade, the rate of HIV infection went from less than 1 percent to over 25 percent of the adult population and AIDS became the main cause of death for men and women between 15 and 49 years of age," with an expected drop in average life expectancy in the country of as much as twenty years. Moreover, the global pandemic has helped to shape the social, cultural, and health worlds of people all over the planet, whether or not they are always aware of it. Within the broader story of the devastating impact of HIV/AIDS, however, there are many differing local narratives that together comprise the complex mosaic of the pandemic. The work of medical anthropologists has been part of that story in many places and the same is true for a vast array of other health issues.

## THREE CASE STUDIES IN APPLIED MEDICAL ANTHROPOLOGY

### Coping with Cystic Fibrosis

The Reynolds family has two children. Carl is five, and Stuart is seven. The younger of the two boys has cystic fibrosis (CF), the most common fatal genetic disease in the United States. Cystic fibrosis causes the body to produce a thickened form of mucus that clogs the lungs, leading to repeated bacterial infections and increasing lung damage. While the median age of survival among CF sufferers has been rising, most people with the disease do not live very far into adulthood before they succumb. Day-to-day care of a child with CF commonly falls on family members who must learn to cope with both a painful prognosis and the demands of responding to the patient's menacing symptoms, including pounding on the sufferer's chest and back for at least thirty-five to forty minutes at a time, two to four times a day, to dislodge mucus. Some burdens fall particularly hard on the siblings of children with CF. Deana Reynold, Stuart's mother, notes one of these burdens that he must endure: "When Carl's sick, all the phone calls are, 'How's Carl?' Everybody who sees Stuart [says], 'How's your brother doing?' And all the presents. Carl gets all the presents. It has to have some kind of effect on him [Stuart]." How (and how well) do families with a child with CF cope? What toll does the disease take on family relations and on the emotional well-being of family members? How are siblings affected by growing up with a chronically ill brother or sister? How can health care providers most effectively communicate with families at various stages in the natural history of CF progression? Having previously studied children with cancer, medical anthropologist Myra Bluebond-Langner (1996) set out to answer these critically important questions. For nineteen months, in the clinic and in their homes, she repeatedly interviewed and observed families that were recruited from the patient rolls of the Cystic Fibrosis Center of St. Christopher's Hospital for Children in Philadelphia. She also interviewed attending physicians and reviewed patients' medical charts. Like most anthropologists, she immersed herself in the lifeworlds of the people she was studying. Her field notes and taped interviews filled thousands of pages and numerous three-ring binders. In the end, after many months of data collection and careful analysis, she was able to answer the key questions that motivated the study. Additionally—and tellingly—she was able to use her findings to develop a set of useful guidelines for physicians to use in clinical intervention with families with a CF sufferer. As a result, physicians now have a clearer idea of how best to communicate with families and to assist them in coping with the difficult challenges they face and the weighty burdens they must bear. Like the work of many other medical anthropologists, this work by Bluebond-Langner has helped to make a positive impact in the tangled and often confusing world of health and illness. Addressing conflicts, miscommunications, and other problems in doctor-patient relationships as well as patient access to high-quality, culturally appropriate health care are central issues in medical anthropology. But there are many other concerns as well.

**The Bone Crusher**

   Dengue is a mosquito-borne viral disease found in more than one hundred countries and territories around the world, primarily in tropical and subtropical environments of Latin America, the Caribbean, and Southeast Asia, although a U.S. outbreak occurred in Hawaii in 2001. Current estimates are that each year fifty million to one hundred million people are infected with dengue when they are bitten by either the *Aedes aegypti*, the mosquito that also transmits yellow fever, or *Aedes albopictus* mosquitoes. Mosquitoes become infected when they bite people who are infected, and, in turn, they subsequently transmit the infection to other people that they bite. In Southeast Asia and in most of Latin America and the Caribbean, the disease is pandemic, meaning that it is now firmly entrenched in the population and spreading. Malaysia has been particularly hard hit; thousands of people fall victim each year to this disease colloquially known—because of the fearsome joint pain it causes—as the "bone crusher." Other symptoms include stomach pain, headaches, nausea and vomiting, pain behind the eyes, and body flushes. In a more intense and even more frightening form, known as hemorrhagic fever, the sufferer's gums, nose, and internal organs bleed.

   A number of medical anthropologists have worked on preventing the spread of dengue. Karl Kendall (1998), for example, developed a strategy that involves studying and utilizing local health beliefs and practices in the development of community health campaigns about dengue in El Progreso, Honduras. In Kendall's approach, the first step in raising community awareness of effective prevention involved conducting in-depth interviews and surveys with community members to assess what they think and believe about dengue, its routes of infection, and the strategies they use to prevent becoming sick with the dreaded disease. This information was used to frame a locally meaningful education campaign designed to raise community awareness of the insects that transmit dengue, including effective pest control measures. This culturally sensitive project proved to be effective in reducing the populations of dengue-carrying mosquitoes, lowering rates of infection.

   Sara Crabtree and colleagues (2001) built on this approach in the prevention of dengue in two communities in Malaysia. Like Kendall, Crabtree and coworkers began their work with a study of community knowledge, attitudes, and behaviors related to the disease. They also conducted focus groups with four different subgroups—women, youth, men who were heads of families, and village leaders—in an area that had not yet been hard hit by dengue. Through this research, it was found that the communities lacked much awareness of mosquito-borne disease transmission; they did not associate getting sick with being bitten by mosquitoes. Consequently, while they were available, people did not make much use of mosquito nets or spray repellents. The team then organized a set of three-day workshops that were designed to train volunteers to conduct a needs assessment on how to prevent dengue in their local communities. Under the guidance of the researchers, these individuals then carried out a door-to-door survey in their local communities. Researchers then worked with the needs assessment staff in translating findings into a strategic set of recommendations for practical, achievable activities to reduce mosquito populations. With the support of local leaders, actions based on these recommendations, such as burning accumulated rubbish, cleaning water containers, and identifying and eliminating breeding sites, were implemented to lower mosquito populations, a goal that was achieved in both participating communities. The medical anthropologists involved in this project believed that this success was due in large part to the initial assessment to ascertain community concerns, mobilize locally generated prevention ideas, and involve community members in all phases of the prevention initiative.

Despite the efforts described here, dengue continues to spread in the world, as do a range of old, new, and renewed diseases that were once controlled but are again spreading out of control (see chapter 6). From the fight against AIDS to the reduction of venereal diseases, medical anthropologists, with their unique approach to understanding health and disease in terms of the interaction of human biology with social and cultural factors, are often on the front lines of infectious and other disease prevention as well as of the development of culturally appropriate and hence often more effective approaches to care. Although not all medical anthropology projects are effective and success might be achieved at a much lower level of effect than would be desired, medical anthropologists can point to a strong track record of making useful contributions to improving health, usually at the local level but sometimes even more broadly.

### Pesticide Poisoning

The World Health Organization, a technical agency of the United Nations, estimates that there are more than a billion agricultural workers in the world, most in developing countries. Various studies have shown that one of the health problems commonly faced by agricultural workers is poisoning due to exposure to dangerous pesticides; indeed, they are the sector of society most likely to suffer health consequences from the powerful commercial poisons sprayed on food and ornamental crops to limit plant pests. Not only are those who work in agriculture at risk, but so are their spouses and children. Poisoning occurs because pesticide sprays are caught in the wind and drift into adjacent fields where people are working or into areas where they and their families live, because workers are sent to work in fields in which pesticide has recently been applied, and because workers pick up pesticides on their clothing and other possessions, including their food containers, and bring them home unaware of potential risk. Even if exposures are limited, pesticides accumulate in the body, so that repeated contact increases risk for health-threatening outcomes. One of the most commonly used groups of pesticides, organophosphates (OPs), can be taken into the body through breathing, through ingestion, and through skin exposure. Organophosphates are known to damage nerves by reducing the availability of acetylcholinesterase, a necessary enzyme found at nerve endings. Organophosphate poisoning can produce rashes, nausea and vomiting, body fatigue, loss of consciousness, shock, and even death.

Existing protections for farmworker health are limited. In 2002, for example, the Pesticide Action Network North America and a group of collaborating organizations issued a report called *Fields of Poison* based on data on pesticide poisoning collected by the California Department of Pesticide Regulation. The report found that farmworkers face a two-sided threat from pesticides: first, the existing set of regulations designed to protect them from harmful exposure to toxic chemicals is woefully inadequate to really provide safeguards against acute pesticide exposure, and, second, even the existing laws are weakly enforced. To address this issue, Thomas Arcury, Sara Quandt, and a team of colleagues (2005) recruited a group of nine farmworker households in North Carolina and Virginia for participation in an intervention study called ¡La Familia! Reducing Farmworker Pesticide Exposure, which was funded by the National Institute of Environmental Health Sciences. The research team conducted in-depth interviews with agricultural landowners and agricultural extension workers, completed interviews on beliefs about pesticide exposure and safety among primarily Latino farmworkers, collected samples in the homes of farmworkers to detect the presence of OP pesticides on household furnishings, and carried out urine tests of farmworker adults and their children to assess body metabolite levels, which reveal whether OPs are present in the bodies of study participants.

These researchers found high levels of OP metabolites, which are the by-products of OP exposure, in the members of all of the households they studied, and all households had at least one member with especially high levels. Moreover, families that had carpeted homes but lacked a vacuum cleaner had higher-than-average OP metabolite levels. Bathing patterns also were linked to OP metabolite levels. As a result of their findings, this research team was able to identify specific policy changes that were needed to reduce farmworker exposure to OPs, including ensuring that all rented farmworker dwellings have shower facilities and working vacuum cleaners, that all farmworker dwellings are built at a safe distance from agricultural fields, and that all farmworkers receive training in pesticide risks and handling. Reflecting on the ultimate goals of their study, they conclude,

> Providing farmworker families (as well as all Americans) with safe and affordable housing will reduce their exposure to pesticides. This is not an instance of "blaming the victim" for exposure to pesticides, and attempting to address a systematic health disparity by educating those exposed to pesticides. Rather, it is an effort to build the capacity of farmworkers to defend themselves and to demand safe housing for their children. (Arcury et al. 2005:50)

Notably, most farmworkers live in countries with far fewer resources and weaker laws to protect workers than is the case in the United States. Pesticides produced in the United States, however, are shipped around the world, and anthropologists have observed them being applied by hand by workers who had received little or no information about how deadly they can be if not handled properly. For medical anthropologists who work with agricultural populations, there is much work to do to help them protect themselves from occupational threats to their lives and well-being. In this instance, part of the problem is social inequality and the prevailing structure of power relations in society, such as the making and enforcing of laws that favor one social class, ethnic group, or gender over another. Indeed, medical anthropologists have found that social relationships, such as those between ethnic groups, and social structures that determine access to resources and other things of value are a fundamental factor in health generally.

Although pesticide poisoning is a significant threat to the health of farmworkers, it is neither the only one nor the only one that has been effectively studied by medical anthropologists. For example, Sarah Horton and Judith Barker (2010) have examined the issue of severe dental caries among the children of farmworkers in the Central Valley of California. They report that poor early oral health can have enduring effects both on children's physical development, including malformation of oral arches and crooked adult teeth, and on their emotional development, as a result of social stigmatization as young adults. This research examined the role played by inadequate diet as well as other anthropogenic environmental factors in the development of what they refer to as *stigmatized biologies*. For example, these researchers present the case of Jorge, a young man who has "borne the marks of his lack of insurance as a child all his life. A star athlete and popular high school senior, Jorge feels his one social vulnerability is his stained and crooked smile" (Horton and Barker 2010:213).

Moreover, they reveal how market-based dental health insurance systems—and lack of access to insurance coverage among many farmworkers—contributes to enduring negative health effects. For this analysis, they use Margaret Lock's concept of *local biology* and recognition of the plasticity of biology to show how biology, rather than being a static or uniform phenomenon, in fact differs across groups as a result of factors like culture, diet, and the impress of a human-made environment and as consequence of differential social access to prevention care and treatment. Thus, they argue that market-based health care systems create embodied differences between groups of people in society that both reflect and reproduce a structure of social inequality. Investigations of this sort affirm the value of a bio-sociocultural model in medical anthropology.

## PRACTICAL AND THEORETICAL CONTRIBUTIONS OF MEDICAL ANTHROPOLOGY

The cases described here suggest an answer to the question, why have a medical anthropology? The answer is this: because medical anthropologists, using anthropology's traditional immersion methods for studying human life up close and in context, as well as the discipline's holistic picture of the human situation, a traditional disciplinary concern with understanding things from the insider's point of view and flow of experience, and an applied orientation to human problems, can make an important difference in the world. Revealing the nature of this difference is, as noted in this chapter, one of the main goals of this book.

While a primary emphasis of this book is on the practical contributions of medical anthropology, the theoretical contributions of the discipline are equally important and guide the application of medical anthropology in addressing particular health-related issues. Theory in medical anthropology addresses questions such as the following: What determines health and illness? How and why do societies vary in their health care systems, illness beliefs, and illness experiences? What role does culture play in treatment outcome? These questions are also addressed in this book.

### Clarifying the Culture of Health and Illness

Beyond its initial goal, a second goal of this book is a presentation of the fundamental importance of culture and social relationships in health and illness. Through a review of the key ideas, concepts, methods, and theoretical frameworks that guide research and application in medical anthropology, the book makes the case that illness and disease involve complex biosocial processes and that resolving them requires attention to a range of factors beyond biology, including systems of belief, structures of (often unequal) social relationship, and environmental conditions.

### Health Inequality

Finally, through an examination of the issues of health inequality, such as exposure to pesticides among farmworkers on the one hand and environmental degradation and environment-related illness on the other, the book underlines the need for going beyond cultural or even ecological models of health toward a comprehensive medical anthropology. Such an approach integrates biological, cultural, and social factors in building unified theoretical understandings of the origin of ill health while contributing to the building of effective and equitable national health care systems (e.g., Rylko-Bauer and Farmer 2002). In this manner, medical anthropologists seek to be part of a collective process aimed at creating a healthier world for both humanity and the biosphere and thereby prevailing over widespread patterns of health and social injustice and environmental destruction.

## DEFINING MEDICAL ANTHROPOLOGY

There is no simple definition of medical anthropology because medical anthropologists are involved in so many different issues and kinds of work. Because of this range, any easily crafted definition falters because it leaves out as much as it holds in. In effect, this whole book is designed to define medical anthropology. Generally, however, medical anthropologists are engaged in using and expanding many of anthropology's core concepts in an effort to understand what sickness is; how it is understood and directly experienced and acted on by sufferers, their social networks, and healers; and how health-related beliefs and practices fit within and are shaped by encompassing social and cultural systems and social and environmental contexts. In this multifaceted task, medical anthropologists take a page out of Shakespeare's comedy *The Merry Wives of Windsor* in defining their domain of research: "Why, then the world's mine oyster, / Which I with sword will open." In other words, medical anthropology is concerned not with a single society or with a particular health care system but rather with health issues throughout the whole world and even through time. Their sword, so to speak, are strategies of research, that are based on fieldwork and related methods that are close to the experience being studied.

While recognizing the fundamental importance of biology in health and illness, medical anthropologists generally go beyond seeing health as primarily a biological condition by seeking to understand the social origins of disease, the cultural construction of symptoms and treatments, and the nature of interactions between biology, society, and culture. Similarly, they tend not to accept any particular health care system, including Western biomedicine, as holding a monopoly on useful health knowledge or effective treatment; rather, they see all health care systems—from advanced nuclear medicine or laser surgery to trance-based shamanic healing or acupuncture—as cultural products, whatever their level of healing efficacy and however efficacy is defined within particular healing traditions.

**Culture and Biology**

Medical anthropologists seek to understand and to help others see that health is rooted in (1) cultural conceptions, such as culturally constituted ways of experiencing pain or exhibiting disease symptoms; (2) social connections, such the type of relations that exist within the family or within society and the encompassing world political and economic system generally; and (3) human biology, such as the threat of microscopic pathogens to bodily systems and the body's immune responses to such threats. In pursuing these lines of inquiry, medical anthropologists are especially concerned with linking patterns of disease, configurations of health-related beliefs and behaviors, and healing systems with cultural systems, social hierarchies, and biosocial relationships. Consequently, medical anthropologists have tended to look at health as a "biocultural and biosocial phenomenon," based on an understanding that both physical and sociocultural environments in interaction determine the health of individuals and of whole populations.

Some medical anthropologists, those who call themselves critical medical anthropologists (including both authors of this book), stress what they call a critical biocultural model, one that is especially concerned with investigating the role of social inequality in shaping health, health-related experience and behavior, and healing, issues we will explore throughout this book. Whatever their theoretical perspective (and several alternative perspectives exist within the discipline), however, medical anthropologists tend to have an applied orientation; they are concerned with putting their work to good use in

## BIOCULTURALISM

*Bioculturalism* refers to the significant interactions that take place between biology and culture in health and illness. Consider the issue of pain. In childbirth, a baby with a comparatively large head pushes its way through a small birth channel, a process that often produces "intense labor pains" among women giving birth in the United States. While these pains are expected, they are not accepted as tolerable, and the medical administration of painkillers is commonly demanded, sometimes vehemently so. In Poland, by contrast, labor pains are not only expected but also accepted, and painkillers are not normally requested. What accounts for these differences? While pain on one level is biological, part of a bodily communication system composed of nerves that ensures urgency in limiting bodily damage (e.g., pulling one's stray finger from the fire), medical anthropologists have argued that pain expression and experience can be understood only in a cultural context. Culture teaches us how to think about, experience, and respond to the sensation of pain. At the same time, in assessing a disease, it is important to consider how biology and culture interact. For example, it is likely that a devout Jew or Muslim could be made violently ill by being forced to eat pork, while consuming this meat is considered very satisfying among most people in New Guinea. The same could be said of monkey brains, worms, or hamburger, depending on the cultural traditions of the people involved. Cultural beliefs and practices are very involved as well in the spread and reaction to many infectious diseases, such as sexually transmitted diseases. Disease rarely acts as an independent biological force whose health impact is everywhere the same. Rather, disease expression is shaped by cultural values, beliefs, and expectations. Cultural practices may inhibit or promote disease spread, and, conversely, disease can significantly mold culture.

addressing real and pressing health-related problems in diverse human communities and contexts (e.g., Rylko-Bauer et al. 2006).

## HISTORY OF MEDICAL ANTHROPOLOGY

### The Straits Expedition

Interest in health-related issues within anthropology dates to the very origins of the discipline as a field-oriented social science. In 1898, three British researchers—W. H. R. Rivers, fellow physician C. G. Seligman, and Alfred Haddon—initiated the historic Cambridge University Torres Straits (Australia) expedition, one of the earliest anthropological research projects. Various kinds of data on indigenous Australian peoples were collected during this expedition, including information on traditional healing beliefs and practices. Rivers, who some see as the father of medical anthropology, used data from the expedition to refute the popular notion among Western physicians and other worldly observers of the era that the ethnomedical practices of non-Western societies were "a medley of disconnected and meaningless customs" (Rivers 1927:51). Instead, he argued, ideas and practices around health and healing found in preliterate societies constitute internally coherent structures of cultural beliefs about the causes of disease. Now more than eighty years old, this perspective on healing systems around the world has been abundantly supported by subsequent research in medical anthropology and has guided numerous examinations of the nature of the relationship of health beliefs and practices to the encompassing cultural context in which they are found, such as faith healing in the context of folk Christianity, as in the case of El Santuario de Chimayó, a Catholic healing church in New Mexico, shown in Figure 1.1. This pattern is not limited to folk traditions but includes the dominant healing system, biomedicine, within modern Western society and globally. For example, in the 1989 book *The Woman in the Body: A Cultural Analysis of Reproduction*, an influential text in medical anthropology discussed in chapter 3, Emily Martin shows that the dominant metaphors in biomedicine for the delivery of babies come from the arena of industrial production. In her examination of medical textbooks, Martin found that reproduction is talked about and taught to students using analogies and concepts borrowed from factory production. In this biomedical cultural model of birth, (1) the doctor is portrayed as the manager of the laboring process, much like a factory foreman who oversees and regulates the production process; (2) the uterus is portrayed as the machinery of reproduction; (3) the mother is talked about as a kind of laborer, and hence she is said to be "in labor" during the birthing

FIGURE 1.1
Crutches left behind at El Santuario de Chimayó Church in New
Mexico, where pilgrims come to get "healing soil" from a hole in
the church floor. Photo by Pamela Irene Erickson.

process; and (4) the baby is the product. This way of viewing reproduction,
Martin found, is often in conflict with the views held by women who have
given birth or who are about to give birth, creating the potential for misun-
derstandings and conflicts in childbirth.

## W. H. R. Rivers and Beyond

In Rivers's book on ethnomedicine, *Medicine, Magic, and Religion* (1927),
a volume that has been called the "symbolic totem of medical anthropology"
(Landy 1977:4) because it incorporates health-related issues into the agenda

of anthropology, Rivers also maintained that non-Western ethnomedical traditions and biomedicine constitute completely separate entities. Indigenous healing, he asserted, is characterized by manipulation, through the use of spells and other ritual, of assumed magical connections among objects and beings in the world as well as by beliefs about the actions of supernatural beings (e.g., spirits) in causing and curing illness. Biomedicine, by contrast, is grounded in natural laws and scientific principles. Ever since, medical anthropologists have grappled with understanding similarities and differences in healing systems cross-culturally. The distinctiveness of biomedicine has been intensely debated within the field. While some medical anthropologists have accepted it as a standard by which to assess the efficacy of other healing systems, other medical anthropologists have sought to show the following:

- Biomedicine in its understandings and practices reflects its culture of origin no less than any other ethnomedicine.
- Folk healing systems around the world incorporate practices (e.g., bone setting) that are based on observation and practical reason as well conceptions and protective behaviors that are believed to be derived from natural laws, such as the hot and cold properties of foods or other elements in nature, and not just on magical or religious belief.
- Many of the ideas and practices found in biomedicine are not, in fact, based solely on natural laws and scientific principles.

Pearl Katz, in her 1999 book *The Scalpel's Edge: The Culture of Surgeons* (which is described in greater detail in chapter 2), portrays modern surgery as an elaborate set of rituals that function to limit ambiguity, uncertainty, and error. The process of "scrubbing," for example, involves very strict behaviors, within precisely designated time periods, such as washing each hand in particular ways for a specified amount of time. While it is possible to significantly reduce the presence of pathogens on one's hands and arms through careful cleaning, the precisely defined rules of scrubbing appear to serve also to reduce anxiety about not being sufficiently germ free to avoid infecting the internal organs of the patient. By closely adhering to the rituals of surgery, the confidence doctors and nurses need to undertake a very delicate and potentially disastrous activity, such as cutting open and in some way changing a patient's internal environment, is heightened.

As a result of such studies, biomedicine is now analyzed within medical anthropology as one among many ethnomedical systems around the world, though a rather distinctive one because of its global reach, broadly recognized efficacy in handling many health problems, and ties to the international scientific community and dominant social classes worldwide. One consequence of this shift in perspective is that the medical anthropological perspective "helps us step back from medicocentrism by refusing to take [bio]medical categories and their various meanings as givens" (Saillant and Genest 2007:xxvii), including the biomedical tendency toward biological reductionism. As a result as well, diversity within biomedicine is more apparent, varying in its practice and perspectives across countries and within different medical specialties.

### Rudolf Virchow

Returning to the origin of medical anthropology, Otto von Mering (1970:272) contends that the emergence of the field dates to the late 1800s when Rudolf Virchow, a renowned German pathologist who is often regarded as the father of social medicine because of his interest in how the distribution of health and disease mirrors the distribution of wealth and power in society, helped establish the first anthropological professional society in Berlin. Virchow was an important early influence on Franz Boas, the father of American anthropology, while he was affiliated with the Berlin Ethnological Museum from 1883 to 1886.

### Erwin Ackerknecht and William Caudill

During the 1940s and 1950s, Erwin Ackerknecht, a German émigré, emerged as an important figure in the evolution of medical anthropology. Using field accounts from anthropologists working in various societies, Ackerknecht sought to develop a systematic understanding of healing beliefs and practices that emphasized that (1) healing behaviors and ideas tend to reflect the wider cultural traditions of the society in which they develop and that (2) whatever their ability to improve the health of patients, healing systems reinforce core cultural values and structures and contribute to maintaining the status quo by controlling social conflict and deviance.

### The Postwar Period

After World War II, a growing number of anthropologists began to turn their attention to health-related issues, especially applied ones. Thus, the very first review of what we now call medical anthropology was produced by William Caudill eight years after the end of the war and was titled "Applied Anthropology in Medicine" (Caudill 1953). Caudill's paper marked two important developments in the evolution of medical anthropology: (1) the entry of a number of anthropologists after the war into international health development work and (2) the hiring of anthropologists to work in medical schools and clinical settings as teachers, researchers, administrators, and, in some cases, clinicians. Involvement in the international health field actually began during the 1930s and 1940s within the context of British colonialism—an era during which the delivery of Western health services was seen as central to a larger effort to administer and control indigenous peoples.

### Medical Anthropology and National Development

Cora DuBois became the first anthropologist to hold a formal position with an international health organization when she was hired by the World Health Organization in 1950. Within a few years, Edward Wellin at the Rockefeller Foundation, Benjamin Paul at the Harvard School of Public Health, and George Foster and others at the Institute for Inter-American Affairs had joined the pool of anthropologists involved in seeking to address health-related aspects of technological development around the world, including the negative health consequences of ill-planned development projects. Another set of anthropologists became involved in efforts to facilitate the delivery of biomedical care to people in developed nations and underdeveloped sectors of technologically advanced nations. Alexander and Dorothea Leighton, for example, became involved in the Navajo-Cornell Field Health Project. This applied initiative created the social role of "health visitor," a Navajo paramedic and health educator who acted as a "cultural broker" or community liaison between the white-dominated health care system and the Navajo people.

### The Discipline Is Born

Whatever its diverse roots, as a distinct and labeled subdiscipline of anthropology, medical anthropology has a relatively short history that can be traced to the period after World War II (Roney 1959). Organizationally, medical anthropology began with the formation of the Group for Medical Anthropology in 1967, with Hazel Weidman, an applied anthropologist, as chair. Ultimately, this fledging organization became the now quite-robust Society for Medical Anthropology, a formal section of the American Anthropological Association since 1972, with Dorothea Leighton, a psychiatrist-anthropologist, serving as its first president. As the field continued to grow and diffuse, medical anthropology associations formed subsequently in other nations as well. Today, as described throughout the rest of this book as well as in several others that bring together the range of work done in the field (e.g., Brown 1998; Sargent and Johnson 1996), medical anthropology continues to grow in size and diversity of work as well as in terms of the impact of the efforts of medical anthropologists on a wide range of health-related issues internationally. As in any field, there have been disagreements and debates as well as frustration about structures that sometimes restrict the influence of medical anthropology on health-related policy making, and there have been worries about how to have a bigger role in shaping public health discussions to include issues of culture, social organization, and the voices of socially marginalized populations.

## THE RELATIONSHIP OF MEDICAL ANTHROPOLOGY TO ANTHROPOLOGY AND TO OTHER HEALTH-RELATED DISCIPLINES

### Health Research and the Subfields of Anthropology

Traditionally, anthropology in the United States has comprised four subfields—social and cultural anthropology, biological anthropology, archaeology, and linguistics—although in other countries, such as the United Kingdom and Australia, the discipline has focused more narrowly on social and cultural anthropology. While some have proposed that medical anthropology constitutes the fifth subdiscipline of anthropology, others see it as sitting on the cusp between cultural and biological anthropology and incorporating elements of each in its understandings of health, illness, and healing. An alternative perspective places medical anthropology on the cusp between general or theoretical anthropology and applied anthropology. In this book, as we have stressed, a primary focus is on the applied side of medical anthropology.

Medical anthropology has become one of the largest topical interest areas beyond the four primary subfields of the discipline. One of the current debates within medical anthropology is the degree to which it has had an impact in shaping the ideas and orientation of the wider field of anthropology, including to what degree medical anthropology has developed its own theories and to what degree it has merely borrowed and applied those found elsewhere in the discipline.

### Medical Anthropology and Paleopathology

Medical anthropology has developed an important interface with archaeology. In that archaeology in the United States is often defined as part of sociocultural anthropology or at least as part of one of the four subfields of anthropology, the bridging nature of medical anthropology is particularly apparent in the field called "paleopathology," which is the study of diseases in the past and, in particular, in prehistoric times. This research is accomplished through the study of human fossil remains recovered through archaeological excavations. Buikstra and Cook (1980) delineate four stages

## APPLIED ANTHROPOLOGY

Medical anthropology straddles the line between theoretical and applied anthropology. Applied anthropology is the application of anthropological theories, concepts, and methods to solving problems in the world. Applied anthropologists work in many different areas, from A for aging, such as solving problems in the isolation aging people often feel in Western society, to Z for zoos, as seen in work done to determine how to use zoos to educate visitors about pressing environmental issues. While it is sometimes asserted that applied anthropology grew out of theoretical anthropology, the reverse is in fact the case. In the United States, for example, some of the individuals who first found employment as anthropologists worked for the Bureau of American Ethnology (BAE). The BAE was set up in 1879 as a policy research arm of the federal government to provide research needed to inform congressional decisions about the American Indian population. The bureau's first director, W. J. McGee, proposed that the organization focus on what he called "applied ethnology," which led to a series of descriptive reports that were prepared for policymakers. Despite this fact, there have been strong tensions at times between applied and theoretical anthropology. Some theoretical anthropologists identify the discipline's mission as understanding diverse pathways in human social life. They assert that to use anthropology to formulate planned social change violates two basic disciplinary principles: cultural relativism, which proscribes judging any given society by the values of any other, and avoidance of research bias, which includes, among other concerns, the scientific standard of minimizing opportunities for data contamination because of the value commitments of the researcher. Both of these principles suggest that intervention is, by definition, not anthropology. Applied anthropologists counter that science does not exist in a social vacuum and that its fundamental purpose is to apply its findings to solving human problems and improving the quality of human life. Because we live in a world of cultural contact and resulting social change that often leads to pressing problems and extensive human suffering, applied anthropologists feel obliged to apply their skills and understandings to solve real-world challenges. In recent years, these divisions have begun to break down, and older animosities about what is the proper role of anthropologists in society have begun to fade into history. An example of one kind of work that applied medical anthropologists do is seen in the work of Alayne Unterberger through a community-based organization that she heads called the Florida Institute for Community Studies in Tampa. This organization addresses the health problems of migrant and nonmigrant farmworkers in the Tampa area. One of the projects is called Pocos Hijos. This is a family planning education and referral effort that focuses on identifying and meeting the health and service needs of farmworkers and their families. The project is guided by an advisory committee comprised of current and past clients. It seeks to ensure that the project successfully identifies and helps to meet pressing community-identified needs. Originally begun as a needs assessment research project, Pocos Hijos now delivers culturally, linguistically, and gender-appropriate community outreach, radio programming, and youth outreach.

in the development of paleopathology: (1) the descriptive period during the nineteenth century, focusing on bone abnormalities; (2) the analytical period during the early twentieth century, when an attempt was made to interpret bone abnormalities; (3) the period between 1930 and 1970, when the field became more specialized, drawing on fields such as radiology, histology, and serology; and (4) the current phase beginning around 1970, when the field became considerably more interdisciplinary and incorporated genetic studies, including examination of microbial DNA in bone and soft tissue in order to diagnose disease in past humans.

As Roberts and Manchester (1995:9) point out, one of the important limitations of this endeavor is that the populations being studied are long dead, and consequently the number of cases being studied from any population are limited, a mere "sample of a sample of a sample." As a result, it is difficult to generalize to the whole population from which the cases are drawn.

Despite this limitation, paleopathology has much to teach us about diseases and related health problems of antiquity, including congenital defects, traumatic injuries, infectious diseases, metabolic and nutritional disorders, degenerative diseases, circulatory problems, caries, and even cancer. For example, bone spurs in the knees, toes, and spines of ancient Mesoamerican women strongly suggest that they spent long hours grinding maize in order to make flour.

Paleopathology can also contribute to the solving of medical mysteries. A case in point is the cause of death of Pharaoh Tutankhamun, more popularly known as King Tut, a relatively minor ruler historically but today the best-known member of ancient Egypt's dynastic line. On November 4, 1922, archeologists discovered and began excavating King Tut's thirty-three-hundred-year-old subterranean royal burial tomb in Valley of the Kings, the royal necropolis of Egypt's eighteenth through twentieth dynasties, located on the west bank of the Nile River opposite the modern city of Luxor. The richness of the funerary artifacts in the tomb, and the discovery of the pharaoh's mummy, led to extensive press coverage and the rapid rise of King Tut in the popular imagination worldwide. A subsequent autopsy of the Tutankhamun mummy concluded that the pharaoh had died around the age of nineteen years old. Speculation soon developed about the cause of death of the young ruler. Initial conjecture focused on the king's skull because of a small dense spot, suggesting the possibility of brain trauma inflicted by a murderous blow to the back of the head. According to Bob Brier, author of the popular book *The Murder of Tutankhamen* (1998), in light of the "violent, unstable times Tutankhamun ruled in, and [based on] forensic evidence . . . murder and intrigue emerged as the best explanation" (xix) of the pharaoh's untimely death. Additionally, based on several peculiar features of statues, paintings, and other ancient depictions of King Tut and members of his family (e.g., suggesting androgynous characteristics among males as well as notably elongated heads and fingers), numerous speculative reports have been published about various diseases allegedly suffered by King Tut. Among these are Marfan syndrome, a genetic disorder that leads to above-average height, long slender limbs, and long fingers and toes; Wilson-Turner X-linked mental retardation syndrome, a congenital disease characterized by mental disabilities, childhood obesity, and enlarged male breasts; and Fröhlich syndrome, a disease caused by tumors of the hypothalamus that produces mental retardation and retarded sexual development. In part to test these various hypotheses, Zahi Hawass, an archaeologist and Egypt's secretary general of the Supreme Council of Antiquities, led an international team that carried out a set of now widely publicized anthropological, paleopathological, radiological, and genetic analyses of a group of mummies as part of the King Tutankhamun Family Project. While discounting various earlier hypotheses about King Tut's death, this study concluded that a likely cause of death was the occurrence of multiple health problems including malaria (based on findings of ancient malaria DNA in King Tut's mummy), juvenile aseptic bone necrosis or Köhler disease II (involving loss of blood to the king's left foot, causing bone death and collapse), and a fracture of his left femur that was unhealed at the time of death. King Tut's death, in other words, was a consequence neither of intrigue and ancient rivalry nor of a rare and disforming genetic disorder, but rather was caused by the adverse interaction of several diseases and trauma-induced infection (Hawass et al. 2010). Most important, this study suggested the possibility that malaria, alone and in interaction with other diseases and conditions, was an important factor in the health of all sectors of ancient Egyptian society.

## Medical Anthropology and Epidemiology

### The AIDS Connection

Beyond its ties to subfields within anthropology, medical anthropology also has an important connection with epidemiology, a discipline concerned with the patterns and spread of disease, including containing outbreaks of disease. At the U.S. Centers for Disease Control and Prevention (CDC), a branch of the national Public Health Service, scientists monitor the appearance and spread of disease all over the country and beyond. In the AIDS epidemic, for example, CDC researchers attempted to understand what was causing the disease, how it was spread, and how the AIDS epidemic could be stopped. There has been a long but in some ways not always deep collaboration between epidemiologists and medical anthropologists. Well over 250 medical anthropologists, for example, have worked on some aspect of the global AIDS epidemic, often in close partnership with epidemiologists and other researchers and interventionists (Bolton and Orozco 1994). In this work, as Patricia Whelehan notes in her 2009 book *The Anthropology of AIDS: A Global Perspective*, medical anthropologists have addressed various bio-sociocultural factors, ethical issues, cultural factors and social reactions, gender roles and relations, sociopolitical and socioeconomic influences, and transnational and intergroup differences in the nature of the impact and range of responses that have developed to the pandemic. Medical anthropologists have played various roles in the global AIDS pandemic. To cite one example, they have worked closely with outreach workers who locate and recruit hard-to-reach at-risk individuals, such as injection drug users, for interviews by the anthropologists on patterns of HIV risk and/or for participation in prevention interventions. Research of this sort has led to discoveries by medical anthropologists and their colleagues of a range of behaviors beyond direct syringe sharing that can spread the virus that causes AIDS as well as sexual risk associated with injected and noninjected drug use (such as the use of crack cocaine). In addition, medical anthropologists were involved in identifying social and behavior contexts in which risky behavior is most frequent, assessing the role of social networks in the spread of HIV infection and the importance of exposure to violence in risk behavior, and have played key roles in prevention research on syringe exchange.

Broader social and political issues have also been addressed by anthropologists in the AIDS pandemic. In her work in South Africa, for example, Ida Susser (2009) focused on women's avenues of hope, sources of resilience, and mounting community activism in response to the toil of AIDS. Central to Susser's objective was the development of a detailed account of women's on-the-ground responses to the entwined effects of disease, gender discrimination, and the world economic system through which wealthy countries promote deprivation, social suffering, and the spread of disease in poorer nations.

Notably, Melissa Parker (2003:179), who studied unsafe sex among gay-identified men in the backrooms of pubs, clubs, and saunas in London, has argued that anthropologists should "draw upon their ethnographic expertise and help to design interventions which target people and places with the explicit intention of promoting social change and saving lives."

*Cultural Epidemiology*

In his 2005 book *Epidemiology and Culture*, James Trostle, an anthropologist long concerned with building collaboration between epidemiology and anthropology, has argued for the creation of a "cultural epidemiology" that would integrate the anthropological concept of culture into the set of explanatory variables used by epidemiologists to explain disease. Cultural beliefs and practices about condom use, for example, have contributed to the spread of HIV infection. Because many people link condom use to casual intercourse with people other than their main partner, it is difficult to convince them to use condoms with their primary partners. Another example of how culture can impact HIV prevention is provided by Alexander Rödlach (2006) in his study of AIDS-related beliefs in Zimbabwe in sub-Saharan Africa. Rödlach found that many people in Zimbabwe wonder if the disease is spread either by sorcery or as a result of a conspiracy, such as a plot by the U.S. government to punish people of color. Importantly, he argues that studying such beliefs, which are widespread in the world, is not an attempt to contribute to the construction of an *exotic other* (i.e., viewing people who are culturally different as bizarre or less intelligent). Rather, he emphasizes that developing a better understanding of cultural beliefs about the nature and spread of AIDS "yields theoretical insights into how people explain and react to health problems, [which] in turn benefits health programs" (2006:13). Sorcery and conspiracy beliefs, he notes, are prevalent in social groups that have endured suffering, through poverty, discrimination, and disempowerment, at the hands of outsiders. Such beliefs, in other words, are culturally constituted *idioms of distress* that express the harmful experience of feeling helpless and unable to control much about one's life (and hence suspecting a nefarious outside agent as the source of one's painful lived experiences). Medical anthropologists use the term "idioms of distress" to describe the culturally specific and symbolically rich frameworks of understanding through which people both experience and articulate social discontent and suffering. In addition, they have come to recognize that even standard biomedical terms like diabetes can come to be used popularly as idioms of distress when they refer to health conditions that reflect health and social disparities and express the lived experience of social suffering (Mendenhall et al. 2010).

### Health Transitions

Within epidemiology, the term "health transition" is used to label broad changes that have occurred within particular historic phases in the health profile of populations and the primary causes of mortality. The first health transition in human history began about ten thousand years ago when the development of agricultural modes of food production and more sedentary communities led to a marked increase in acute infectious diseases (often involving the adaptation of the disease-causing pathogens of domesticated animals like cattle to human hosts and resulting in human epidemics). A second health transition occurred between the late eighteenth and early twentieth century with the rise of industrial economies. This economic and social transformation, involving the restructuring of environments, industrial pollution of the environment, and changes in life conditions, resulted in the growing importance of chronic diseases like heart disease, stroke, cancer, and diabetes and what are termed "behavior problems," such as substance abuse. Ultimately, a drop also occurred in many developed nations in rates of lethal infectious diseases as well. However, one effect of the second health transition is that poorer countries now suffer from what has been called the "triple burden" of acute disease, such as diarrheal disease; chronic disease, such as cancer; and behavioral pathology, such as the global spread of illicit drug injection. At the same time, health care systems have been changing. One force pushing such changes is the imposition of what are called "neoliberal reforms" by international lender institutions (i.e., banks that loan money for development to poorer countries), such as the World Bank. In poorer nations, such as Mongolia, as medical anthropologist Craig Janes (Janes and Chuluundorj 2004) found during his research there, lender-endorsed steep cuts in government investment in the health sector and the transformation of health services from a government-provided benefit to a purchasable commodity resulted in a significant drop in the quality and quantity of health services available in rural areas while restricting access to services that were still in operation. Janes discovered that women in particular were vulnerable to these changes, leading to increasing rates of both poor reproductive health and maternal mortality. Similar negative health effects of what has been called "structural adjustment" (i.e., changes in government policies and structures demanded by international development loan providers like the World Bank and International Monetary Fund) have been described by medical anthropologists working in various locations around the world. As Mark Nichter indicates in his 2008 book *Global Health: Why Cultural Perceptions, Social Representations, and Biopolitics Matter*, structural adjustment has led to a proliferation of service-providing nongovernment organizations (NGOs) in underdeveloped nations. One result is that in places like Haiti there are multiple, uncoordinated, and competing health programs governed by the dictates of foreign funding institutions. This change has contributed "to the undoing of government services" (Nichter 2008:139) and the weakening of governments in developing nations, pushing them, as has occurred in places like Haiti, Peru, El Salvador, and several countries in southern Africa, beyond the ability to meet the basic public health needs of their citizens (M. Singer 2010a, Smith-Nonini 2010). A study that reviewed a decade of the effects of structural adjustment policies in eight Latin American countries, for example, found that, in an effort by lender banks to make interest from the development loans they had made, health and social expenditures designed to meet human needs were cut drastically, leading to ever-widening disparities between the health and well-being of the rich and that of the poor (Petras and Vieux 1992).

In the last decades of the twentieth century, a third health transition began, and it continues into the twenty-first century. This transition involves the rapid appearance and global spread of new infectious diseases like HIV/AIDS, SARS, and avian influenza and the development of new levels of virulence and drug resistance in older infectious diseases like tuberculosis. In the third health transition "poverty combines with urbanization and the dissolution of traditional family structures to intensify [health] challenges" from infectious agents, processes of globalization (e.g., rapid travel and the global shipment of commodities) enable the brisk movement of infectious diseases around the world, and microbial adaptation to medicines weakens the effectiveness of drugs like antibiotics to control all infectious diseases (Barret 2010). At the same time, adverse synergistic interaction among diseases (infectious, chronic, behavioral) has promoted the appearance and adverse health impact of disease "syndemics" that further increase the total health burden of affected populations (Bulled and Singer 2010, M. Singer 2010b). These factors are significantly shaping contemporary global health and appear likely to do so well into the future.

### Illness and Help-Seeking Behavior

One of the important issues medical anthropologists have focused on is how local sociocultural factors come into play in "monitoring the body, recognizing and interpreting symptoms, and taking remedial action . . . to rectify the perceived abnormality" as well as "adherence to therapeutic advice, changes in treatment regimens [e.g., switching healers], and evaluation [and reevaluation over time] of therapeutic efficacy and outcome" (Christakis et al. 1994:277). In short, medical anthropologists are interested in the ways that culture helps to shape the "illness behavior patterns," including help-seeking actions, found in a society. Of note, illness behavior is mediated by a sufferer's subjective interpretations of the meaning of experienced symptoms. However, these interpretations are not solely idiosyncratic but rather are influenced by wider cultural understandings of illness and the comments and actions of the sufferer's social network. For example, Nichter (2008:74) observes that in "several areas of Africa where malaria is endemic, seizures [which in biomedicine are recognized as symptoms of malaria infection] are viewed as a 'folk illness' largely unrelated to malaria and are often attributed to supernatural causes." Illness behavior is impacted by various factors, including gender (thus men and women often "get sick" differently) and socioeconomic status. Also, illness behavior in a society is not static; as a society changes, illness behaviors change as well, including patterns of use of health services. The global distribution of pharmaceutical drugs, for example, has contributed to the use of these commercial laboratory remedies in ways that go far beyond their intended purposes and patterns of use, such as crushing antibiotic capsules and applying them to wounds or the emergence of folk healers who administer individual antibiotic injections. Documenting and assessing emergent patterns of illness behavior and their causes is a role that medical anthropologists are playing in the realm of epidemiology. More broadly, medical anthropologists seek to move beyond the examination of individual suffering to social suffering,

**Medical Anthropology and Public Health**

Closely related to epidemiology is the discipline of public health, a field that is concerned with assessing and improving the quality of health of the general populations as well as that of especially vulnerable and at-risk sub-groups therein. In the past, medical anthropologists have contributed to public health by ethnographically examining disease-promoting behaviors in social context. As Peter Brown and colleagues (1996:198) point out, "As interpreters of human behavior who elucidate how and why people do what they do," medical anthropologists have been able to contribute to disease prevention and control.

There have been a number of methodological and conceptual develop-ments in public health in recent years that have created new opportunities for medical anthropology to play a part in public health discussions and interven-tions. Among these new developments are (1) the growing public health and medical concern with health inequities, (2) the increasingly recognized need to enhance the cultural competence of health care providers, (3) the emer-gence and growing influence of the community-based participatory research model, (4) the diffusion of and increasing funder emphasis on evidence-based interventions in public health, (5) the mounting demand for translational research that allows the findings and knowledge produced by health-related studies to shape health intervention efforts, and (6) the spiraling interest in what have come to be called complementary and alternative medicines. At the same time, a research method developed within anthropology—rapid ethnographic assessment—has spread into public health, creating additional opportunities for medical anthropology to have an impact on health issues. Each of these increasingly important arenas of public concern in which medi-cal anthropology directly or indirectly has played a role is described next.

*Health Inequity or Disparity*

Health inequity or disparity refers to the significant differences in the health profiles (i.e., the distribution of diseases) across human populations, social strata such as social classes, or other segments of the population, such as rural areas compared to urban settings. Additionally, health disparities researchers are concerned with why disparities in health exist. In the United States, for example, as Grace Budrys (2003:39), in her book *Unequal Health: How Inequality Contributes to Health and Illness*, observes, from a health standpoint "being at the top of the [social class] heap is a lot better than be-ing on the bottom. . . . There has been an explosion of research indicating that social class is a powerful, and arguably the most powerful, predictor of health." The nature and importance of health inequities will be examined in greater detail in chapter 6. Suffice it to note here that it is an important health arena in which a number of medical anthropologists have become quite active, such as Sabina Rashid who works among the poor of Dhaka, Bangladesh (Figure 1.2).

### Community-Based Participatory Research

There are various approaches to research on health issues in specific populations and communities. In the "unilateral research model," researchers based at universities or research centers design a research project based on their understanding of the key issues and questions. The research agenda in this approach is almost completely if not completely determined by the researchers in terms of their conceptions and interests. After a project is largely designed, the researchers may contact and subcontract with a community organization to recruit participants from the community who will be interviewed in the planned study. Often strapped for funding, community organizations accept such subcontracts even though they may at the same

FIGURE 1.2
Children from poor families in an urban slum in Dhaka, Bangladesh. Photo by Sabina Faiz Rashid.

time resent not having much voice in planning the study, including a say in what from the community's perspective are the key health issues in need of research. Another approach to research is called the "collaborative model." In this approach, while researchers initially conceptualize a study, they then contact one or more organizations based in the community of concern and invite them to participate in fleshing out the details of the study. While the community organization(s) participates at some level in the study, the bulk of project direction, decision making, and funding is still centered in the university or research institute. Both unilateral and collaborative research projects are very common and can be found on most university campuses, often funded by federal research grants or private health foundations.

As contrasted with both of these approaches to research, community-based participatory research (CBPR) is based on a full partnership between researchers and community representatives and organizations, from project conception to completion, including publication of findings. Community-based participatory research grew out of recognition that traditional population-based biomedical research methods lack authentic community involvement and often result in community alienation from research and researchers. In some cases, researchers have come to be defined as exploiters of communities rather than as their natural allies. Consequently, in CBPR-guided projects, the community plays a key role in setting the research agenda. In this, communities are guided by their pressing need for specific health-related knowledge, which can be put to use in addressing community health problems and in making ongoing decisions about the direction of the research. As the concept of CBPR has developed and its value recognized, various efforts have been made to establish guidelines for successful and mutually satisfying participatory research projects.

The community-based organization known as Community-Campus Partnerships in Health, for example, which has as its mission the creation of healthier communities and the overcoming of complex societal problems, has identified the following principles and best practices in CBPR (see www .ccph.info/):

- Research partners should establish the mission, values, goals, and measurable outcomes for the partnership.
- The relationship between partners is best characterized by mutual trust, respect, genuineness, and commitment.
- The partnership should balance power and share among partner organizations.

- There should be open communication between partners, making it an ongoing priority to listen to others.
- Partners should share the credit for the partnership's accomplishments (e.g., publications).

Medical anthropologists have contributed to the development of this alternative orientation to research. For example, the Institute for Community Research in Hartford, Connecticut, a community-based organization that has been led by anthropologists since its founding, has established the Youth Action Research Institute to promote the use of a participatory action research model among youth. Central to the institute's work have been projects that involve minority youth in ethnographic research on issues of concern to the youth (e.g., AIDS and substance abuse), including the primary health and social problems faced by their communities. Anthropologists train youth in ethnographic methods and help them identify problems for action research. The goals of this project are personal growth among the youth participants, the development of positive peer norms, and the assessment of community health needs.

### Diffused Evidence-Based Intervention

There has been a strong effort in recent years to accelerate the movement of scientifically proven (i.e., evidence-based) intervention models, such as training programs to assist people in avoiding HIV infection. Rather than funding organizations to implement intervention models that have not been evaluated, funder institutions, such as the CDC, are increasingly requiring the use of models that have proven to be effective. The CDC's Diffusing Effective Behavioral Interventions project, for example, has helped implement eighteen different research-based HIV prevention models through community-based organizations, health departments, and other prevention providers across the United States. These were designed for specific populations, such as injection drug users, sexual and romantic partners of injection drug users, men who have sex with men, heterosexuals at high risk, people living with HIV/AIDS infection, and homeless and runaway adolescents. To prepare community organizations to successfully implement these intervention models in their respective communities, the researchers or those they have trained are called in to provide guidance and technical assistance to the frontline people who would use the models in day-to-day prevention work.

*Translational Research*

Translational research is a specialized type of research that is carried out with the intention of improving the flow of knowledge from research into action in public health or some other arena of social intervention. AIDS practitioners and policy advocates, for example, have complained that the findings of behavioral research are slow in finding their way to public prevention efforts. For example, anthropologists and others who conduct ethnographic research with injection drug users have observed that they engage in a number of behaviors during the consumption of drugs that might lead to HIV infection. One of these behaviors involves several drug users pooling their money to purchase a packet of an illicit drug, such as heroin or cocaine, and then mixing it with water, using one of the participant's syringes and the unit gauge on its barrel to measure the right amount of water to allow an equal distribution of the dissolved drug. If the syringe that is used for this purpose contains HIV, the virus that causes AIDS, then the virus may be flushed into the container (such as a bottle cap) that is being used for drug mixing and drawn up by all the individuals who are sharing the drugs from that container. In this way, all these individuals may be exposed to HIV infection. An examination of the messages given by prevention programs to drug injectors to protect themselves, however, often urges them only not to "share needles." Because individuals who share drugs may never share a needle, they may falsely believe that they are protected from HIV infection when in fact other behaviors in the drug preparation and use process are causing disease transmission.

As a result of examples like this, those involved in translation research have urged social scientists not only to publish their findings in professional journals, most of which are not widely read outside of academic and research settings, but also to take specific steps to ensure that their research is readily accessible to, relevant for, and understood by those who work in HIV/ AIDS prevention programs or who make health policy decisions. As Sloboda (1998:203) has written, a "key issue that faces the field of intervention in general is how to translate the research findings for more widespread practice." The need for readily accessible and usable knowledge is particularly great in intervention efforts targeted to populations that are harder to reach and harder to retain, such as injection drug users and commercial sex workers, a task that has been taken on by a number of medical anthropologists. At the same time, interventions models proven effective at the local level, if they are to have a significant impact on the epidemic, must be scaled up beyond the pilot level. For example, with regard to AIDS prevention programs in Africa, Binswanger (2000:2173) argues, "In most of Africa, there are examples of excellent HIV/AIDS prevention, mitigation, and care projects. These projects reach only a small fraction of the population however. Like expensive boutiques, they are only available to a lucky few." This too is a type of work that is well suited to the skills and interests of medical anthropologists because "translating recent research advances into communities at risk . . . requires thoughtful adaptation to meet the needs of the community effectively with emphasis on social, economic, and cultural heterogeneities" (McGarvey 2009:242). It also requires creativity and a keen awareness of the cultural life and social context of target populations (Figure 1.3).

### Complementary and Alternative Medicine

There has been a fairly dramatic shift in recent years in the way policymakers, health care providers, and the general public view healing systems beyond the dominant biomedical approach. One indication of this change is the remaking of the American pharmacy. Today the shelves of the average major chain pharmacy in the United States and Australia (although not everywhere

FIGURE 1.3
AIDS educators in Havana, Cuba. Photo by G. Derrick Hodge.

in the world; see Figure 1.4) are filled with over-the-counter alternative medicines, such as St. John's wort, echinacea, and black cohosh, that in the past could have been found only in specialty health food stores or alternative markets. Moreover, in 1992 the U.S. Congress established the Office of Alternative Medicine, which in 1999 became the National Center for Complementary and Alternative Medicine, one of the twenty-seven research institutes and centers that make up the National Institutes of Health. The mission of the center is to promote scientific exploration of promising nonbiomedical healing practices and to disseminate research-based information on these practices to the public and health professionals. While some have argued that the new interest in complementary and alternative healing systems is driven, at least in part, by a desire to subordinate them to the dominant biomedical system (Baer 2004), there clearly has been a significant change in the way they are viewed and their place in Western societies if not globally. We will return to the issue of complementary and alternative medicine later in the book as we explore alternative health approaches. Here, suffice it to say that the rise

FIGURE 1.4
Modern pharmacy in Cuba lacks the many over-the-counter commercial "folk medicines" now found in U.S. pharmacies. Photo by G. Derrick Hodge.

in interest in complementary and alternative medicine rests on and grew out of a long history of anthropological study of nonbiomedical healers and their approaches to the treatment of illness.

### Rapid Ethnographic Assessment

The rapid ethnographic assessment approach to research, which has now been adopted by health promotion institutions around the globe, was first fully described in the late 1980s and early 1990s by anthropologists Susan Scrimshaw and Elena Hurtado. Rapid ethnographic assessment is designed to bridge the gap between science and public health practice and policy by allowing the swift movement from community-based research on health or other pressing social issues to interventions that are based on research findings. While ethnographic research traditionally was both a labor- and time-intensive approach, Scrimshaw sought a methodology that would take advantage of close-up ethnographic insight in a community of concern without requiring the customary year or more of social immersion and extensive documentation of behaviors and events characteristic of traditional anthropological fieldwork. Rapid approaches allow researchers to build on existing knowledge of a target community and to implement several strategies for the rapid development of rapport, such as the use of local staff to collect information in their own communities and collaboration with local community organizations, in the assembly of highly focused data on narrow issues and problems. For example, in Project RARE (Rapid Assessment, Response, and Evaluation), anthropologists and other researchers used focus groups, quick-intercept interviewing, concentrated field observation, and social mapping to identify and describe gaps in the existing array of AIDS prevention programs and services in several dozen cities across the United States. In the Hartford RARE project, for example, the research team, which consisted of people from the local community who were led by several community-based medical anthropologists, found that late-night (midnight to 4:00 A.M.) sexual and drug use behavior was not being addressed by AIDS prevention efforts, resulting in a continued spread of HIV in the local population. As a result, the city health department began to require late-night prevention efforts by some of the organizations that it funded to prevent the spread of AIDS in the city. The value of rapid research methods has been recognized in other fields as well, leading to the development of other types of accelerated assessment and evaluation models, such as rural rapid appraisal, rapid epidemiology, rapid disaster assessment, and rapid assessment of biomedical conditions. All these present emergent arenas of employment for medical anthropologists.

## Medical Anthropology and Bioethics

Bioethics emerged as a new academic field during the 1970s and has quickly become an important force in science and medicine and, through the setting of health-related social policies and the rise of institutional review boards (IRBs), in medical anthropology as well. The term "bioethics" can be defined as a branch of the field of ethics that is concerned with the establishment and application of standards and principles by which human actions within the arenas of health care, health-related decision making, and health research can be judged morally right or wrong. Many hospitals, for example, employ experts on bioethics to provide consultation on the treatment of terminally ill patients and to inform decision making regarding issues such as organ transplant, abortion, euthanasia, in vitro fertilization, and the allocation of scarce clinical resources. As Everett (2006:46–47) points out, while it is likely that, because of the kinds of research they do, medical anthropologists would have something important to offer, "they have found it especially difficult to find a place within bioethics debates" that tend to be dominated by the fields of philosophy, law, and biomedicine. Medical anthropologists, in fact, have sometimes been critical of bioethics because of a lack of sensitivity to cultural differences. Rayna Rapp (2000:44), a medical anthropologist who does ethnographic research on genetic counseling, for example, argues that bioethics is "self-confidently unaware of its own sociocultural context" and fails to consider whether the standards it develops reflect the values of non-Western populations. Thus, bioethics has emphasized the importance of respecting individual autonomy, free will, and self-determination and thus has opposed forcing patients or research participants to do things against their will or without their full consent. The problem, medical anthropologists point out, is that the values emphasized in bioethics reflect the Western celebration of individualism, a moral stance that is not shared by cultural systems that emphasize collectivist models or rigid social hierarchies. The narrow application of Western ethical standards without sensitivity to alternative norms may be construed as ethical imperialism.

Moreover, bioethics has been used in the effort to set standards for ethical research in light of a past history of gross violations of the rights of human subjects in research. All universities and research centers now have IRBs that apply standards established for medical research to all forms of research involving human subjects. According to these standards, all research that has potential risks for human participants, including research by medical anthropologists, must be reviewed and approved by an IRB. A number of anthropologists have questioned the appropriateness of IRB review of ethnographic research on the grounds that it commonly involves the misapplication of standards that were established for biomedical and experimental research where life and death risks are not uncommon (Marshall and Koenig 1996). Further, there has been some concern that IRBs may require anthropological researchers to engage in behaviors that create rather than avoid ethical dilemmas, such as mandating that research participants sign informed consent forms that result in participants' names being part of a project's records. In the study of illegal behaviors, such as illicit drug use or prostitution, this may contradict the researcher's commitment to protect the confidentiality of study participants. Medical anthropologists recognize that the kind of research they conduct commonly encounters perplexing ethical dilemmas and recognize the need for ethical principles to guide their research activities. Whether bioethics is the appropriate source for such principles is an issue of debate. Whatever the challenges, there is little doubt that medical anthropology will continue to engage and develop in relationship with the field of bioethics.

## MEDICAL ANTHROPOLOGY AROUND THE WORLD

Medical anthropology first coalesced into a named subfield of anthropology in the United States, but it subsequently has developed in other countries as well, further underlining the vitality and diversity of this field of research and application. Although medical anthropologists participate in a global discourse (through conferences, journal publications, visiting professorships, and cross-national collaborative research), to a degree, as Saillant and Genest (2007:xviii) stress, the field is "fragmented by its myriad national traditions." In Brazil, for example, Annette Leibing (2007) notes that the term medical anthropology (anthropolgia médica) is not commonly used, but rather the preferred term is "the anthropology of health." The reasons for this involve a desire to clearly define the field and the issues of its concern as beyond the narrow frameworks of biomedicine. Additionally, within the Brazilian anthropology of health, there is an "aversion to a perceived American hegemony in the field" (Leibing 2007:58), although Leibing acknowledges that the studies of American anthropologists are the most often cited in Brazilian publications. Both of the issues Leibing raises are quite valid concerns that should be cause for reflection for the field as a whole. How is it possible to create a truly world medical (or health)

anthropology and to insure the field is not overly influenced by the un-
deniable dominance of biomedical ways of thinking about health and
illness? As another example, in Italy, as Mariella Pandolfi and Gilles
Bibeau (2007) observe, medical anthropology has been influenced as
much by the vagaries of Italian history as by several key Italian theorists, including Antonio Gramsci (whose analyses of hegemony—see
the Leibing quotation—have had a broad impact on anthropological
thinking about contemporary society), Franco Basalia (a critical psychiatrist whose work has inspired a patient-focused approach), and
Ernest De Marino (a foundational figure, influenced by Gramsci, who
helped to shape the thinking of the first generations of Italian medical
anthropologists). Unfortunately, as Italian medical anthropologists are
well aware, because of language issues, much of Italian anthropology
is not widely read within the broader field. What is more broadly read,
however, has had important impacts. As the two examples discussed
suggest, medical anthropology (or, as some within and beyond Brazil
might urge, the anthropology of health) has been diversely shaped by
national histories, cultural and intellectual traditions, and international
political-economic relations, creating a field that has broadly shared
elements, unique local features and perspectives, and internal tensions
reflective of broader political issues.

## MEDICAL ANTHROPOLOGY THEORIES

As is typical in science generally, medical anthropologists understand the
world in particular ways. One of the influences on how a medical anthropologist approaches issues of health or illness is the particular theoretical
framework or school of understanding employed. There are several such
frameworks in medical anthropology, although many individuals do not
see themselves as adherents of any single perspective but rather take a more
eclectic approach and allow the problem they are working on to shape the
perspectives that they use. Other medical anthropologists consider themselves
adherents or even advocates of particular points of view. Indisputably, however, the perspective they bring to their research will strongly influence the
way a problem is approached, the questions that are asked, and the answers
that are deemed sufficient and adequate. Among the primary perspectives

found in medical anthropology are medical ecology, meaning-centered medical anthropology, and critical medical anthropology.

### Medical Ecology

Rooted in both cultural ecology and evolutionary theory, this approach began with an emphasis on adaptation, defined as behavioral or biological changes at either the individual or the group level that support survival in a given environment, as the core concept in the field. From this perspective, health was seen as a measure of successful (or poor) environmental adaptation. In other words, a central premise of medical ecology initially was that a social group's level of health reflects the nature and quality of the relationships "within the group, with neighboring groups, and with the plants and animals [as well as nonbiotic features] of the habitat" (McElroy and Townsend 2003:12). Beliefs and behaviors that improve health or protect societal members from disease or injury are adaptive. For example, in a volume that has had a significant impact on the field, McElroy and Townsend (1996) point to the indigenous development of snow goggles that shield the eyes of Arctic dwellers from the damaging glare caused by the sun reflecting off of ice and snow as an important health-related cultural adaptation of the Inuit people. Similarly, from the medical ecological perspective, behavioral complexes, such as medical systems, including everything from shamanistic healing of soul loss to biomedicine treatment of heart disease, can be viewed as "sociocultural adaptive strategies" (G. Foster and Anderson 1978:33). In recent years, as a result of dialogue with other perspectives, there has been movement toward "merging medical ecology and the political economy of health into a 'political ecology of health'" (McElroy 2003:33). In the most recent and fifth edition of *Medical Anthropology in Ecological Perspective*, McElroy and Townsend (2009) stress that the ecology of health and disease rests on the following premises:

- There is no single cause of disease. While the "immediate cause" may be a virus, vitamin deficiency, or psychological trauma, disease ultimately is the product of a chain of interacting factors related to ecosystem imbalances including human physical and social vulnerability and resilience.
- Health and disease develop within a context of interaction among physical, biological, and cultural systems.
- The "environment" that people inhabit includes not just the physical ("natural") habitat where they live, but also the culturally constructed

"built" environment (e.g., a city, a village), an acknowledgment that, in health, people impact their environment as much as the environment impacts them.

## Meaning-Centered Medical Anthropology

The approach taken in medical ecology to the understanding of human biology and behavior, as an interactive set of adaptations to ecological and social challenges, makes a lot of sense to many medical anthropologists. Yet others have questioned aspects of this approach. Byron Good (1994:45), for example, argues that in ecological studies, "disease is often taken to be a natural object, more or less accurately represented in folk and scientific thought. Disease is thus an object separate from human consciousness." In turn, medical systems come to be seen in medical ecology as utilitarian social responses to intrusive natural conditions. Good questions both halves of this ecological equation, asserting that in medical ecology "culture is . . . absorbed into nature, and cultural analysis consists of demonstrating its adaptive efficacy" (Good 1994:46). Lost in such understanding, he maintains, is a full appreciation of the human cultural/symbolic construction of the world we inhabit. Humans can experience the external material world only through their cultural frames, Good emphasizes, and thus diseases, as they are known, through body sensations or observations and measurements, by sufferers and healers alike, are containers packed with cultural content. Even medical science and biomedicine do not offer culture-free accounts of the physical world, as these too are cultural constructions. This is because both of these historically intertwined pragmatic ways of knowing the world are cultural products; they emerged within particular cultural systems at particular points in the development of those systems, and they accept without thought or questioning many deep-seated cultural ideas and values derived from their encompassing cultural assemblage. For example, deeply embedded within and strongly supported by the day-to-day activities, theories, and organizational structures of biomedicine and medical science are Western cultural notions of (1) individualism, namely, that each individual is distinct and is responsible for his or her success or failure as well as self-improvement; (2) progress and the belief that history is a process of steady social improvement; and (3) the responsibility of action or a belief in the appropriateness of changing the world to meet human needs. Consequently, from the meaning-centered perspective, a goal of medical anthropology is to "unpack" and analyze everything that makes up the health arena, from the experience of pain to the training and functioning of healers, as a set of systems for creating, experiencing, and communicating meaning in human life.

Some researchers have emphasized that a meaning-centered approach, in addition to its analytic utility, has practical value in addressing health issues. Susan McClement (1998), for example, argues that a meaning-centered approach is needed in children's cancer treatment in that it allows the development of a way for caregivers to understand and respond to children's immediate experience of symptom distress, including the meanings and feelings children attach to particular symptoms throughout their illness trajectory.

### Critical Medical Anthropology

During the early years of medical anthropology's formation, explanations within the discipline tended to be narrowly focused on explaining health-related beliefs and behaviors at the local level in terms of specific ecological conditions, cultural configurations, or psychological factors. While providing insight about the nature and function of folk medical models, the initial perspectives in the field tended to ignore the wider causes and determinants of human decision making and behavior. Explanations that are limited to accounting for health-related issues in terms of the influence of human personalities, culturally constituted motivations and understandings, or even local ecological relationships, some medical anthropologists began to argue, are inadequate because they tend not to include examination of the structures of social relationship that unite (in some, often unequal fashion) and influence far-flung individuals, communities, and even nations. A critical understanding, by contrast, involves paying close attention to what has been called the "vertical links" that connect the social group of interest to the larger regional, national, and global human society and to the configuration of social relationships that contribute to the patterning of human behavior, belief, attitude, and emotion (M. Singer and Baer 1995). Consequently, what came to be called critical medical anthropology (CMA) focused attention on understanding the origins of dominant cultural constructions in health, including which social class, gender, or ethnic group's interests particular health concepts express and under what set of historic conditions they arise. Further, CMA emphasizes structures of power and inequality in health care systems and the contributions of health ideas and practices to reinforcing inequalities in the wider society. Moreover, CMA focuses on the social origins of illness, such as the ways in which poverty, discrimination, stigmatization, violence, and fear of violence contribute to poor health. Both of us, the authors of this book, have been active throughout our careers in the development of the CMA perspective.

From an applied perspective, critical medical anthropologists seek to contribute to critical analyses of issues like the nature of industries and governance structures that facilitate disease by polluting (or allowing the polluting of) the environment and furthering global warming (which constitutes a severe and multidimensional threat to human health) and other ecocrises, an economic system that makes possible the manufacture and release of "killer commodities" (consumer products that cause injury or death) onto the market, and the biocommodifacation of nature including the production of genetically engineered crops and invasive and exploitive biotechnologies (like the global systems that leads to the movement of transplantable organs and tissues from poorer countries to richer countries and poorer donors to richer recipients).

Contrary to what some have asserted, CMA does not take a "top-down approach . . . in which political and economic forces press down upon people represented as having relatively little autonomy or power" over their health and illness (Harper 2002:178). Rather, critical medical anthropologists argue that experience and "agency," that is, individual and group decision making and action, are "constructed and reconstructed in the action arena between socially constituted categories of meaning and the political-economic forces that shape the context [and texture] of daily life" (Baer et al. 2003:44). In other words, people develop their own individual and collective understandings and responses to illness and to other threats to their well-being, but they do so in a world that is not of their own making, a world in which inequality of access to health care, the media, productive resources (e.g., land, water), and valued social statuses play a significant role in their daily options. Conversely—and in interesting contradiction of Harper's reading of CMA theory—Brodwin (1996:197) is not quite correct in asserting that "critical medical anthropologists tend to see all experiences of body/self disorder as a potential register for social critique and resistance." Often, in fact, illness experience and the way it is handled socially serves only to reinforce rather than throw open to question existing structures of power.

Additionally, while recognizing the fundamental importance of physical (including biological) reality in health, such as the nature of particular pathogens, CMA emphasizes the fact that it is not merely the idea of "nature"—the way external reality is conceived and related to by humans—but also the very physical shape of nature, including human biology, that has been deeply influenced by an evolutionary history of social inequality, overt and covert social conflict, and the operation of both physical power and the power to shape dominant ideas and conceptions in society and internationally through processes of globalization (Whiteford and Manderson 2000).

In the following chapters, we return to many of these ideas while emphasizing the ways in which medical anthropology—guided by any of the perspectives described here—actively seeks to understand health, health beliefs and behaviors, and healing systems and practices across time and place and to use this information in addressing health problems, conflicts, and suffering in the world. We begin this process in the next chapter by examining what medical anthropologists do, including the ways they approach problems, the kinds of problems they address, their collaboration with other health-interested disciplines, and their impact on the health arena.

2

# What Medical Anthropologists Do

The distinctive approach of anthropology to research is to go out and see what is actually occurring, and to talk to the people themselves.

—*John Janzen (2001:18)*

In the previous chapter, one of the points that was stressed is that medical anthropologists are involved in a wide variety of issues, places, and kinds of work. This chapter provides a closer examination of just what it is that medical anthropologists actually "do" in these various settings. We begin this process by providing four additional cases of medical anthropologists at work, including an exploration of the kinds of problems they address and how they go about applying medical anthropology. Based on these cases, we then (1) discuss the range of issues medical anthropologists study and the special focus they bring to their work because they are anthropologists; (2) set the distinctive medical anthropological approach to research within the broad, holistic vision of the field of anthropology; (3) examine the specific methods used in medical anthropology research; and (4) examine applied activities in medical anthropology beyond research.

# FOUR SETTINGS, FOUR CASE STUDIES, FOUR MEDICAL ANTHROPOLOGISTS

## Life and Death in Tanala

### Studying Indigenous Healing

Sitting on the doorstep of Ranomafana National Park in the southern part of the island nation of Madagascar is the small Tanala village of Ranotsara (pseudonym). Located in the Indian Ocean off the southeastern shore of Africa, to the east of Mozambique, Madagascar is well known for its shimmering forests and seething mass of biologically unique and richly diverse plant and animal species, such as ancient and exotic baobab trees, exceedingly slow-moving chameleons with strangely rotating eyes, and loud packs of lemurs, including the very rare Golden Bamboo lemur. Sadly, the Republic of Madagascar is also known as a land of aggressive deforestation. Ranomafana National Park, in fact, was established in 1990 with private and public funding from the United States as well as from international entities such as the World Bank. It is administered primarily by U.S. citizens with the expressed goal of preserving biological diversity and ecosystems by linking conservation with improved standards of living for the people who dwell in and near parklands.

When medical anthropologist Janice Harper arrived in the village to begin her research in April 1995, about 180 people, about a third of them children and teens, were living there, divided among thirty thatch-and-tin-roofed homes, most of which were rusted and leaking. Surrounded by irrigated rice fields, the village constituted a manmade island nested on hard-packed reddish dirt. Harper had come to study the indigenous use of medicinal plants and nontraditional medicines, traditional topics of medical anthropology research, but right from the start events on the ground began to challenge and reshape her research plans. As Harper (2002:17) noted in her book based on the study,

> While I set out to do a relatively conventional study in medical anthropology, I was not fully aware of the kinds of relationships that existed between the health status of residents of Ranotsara and the rapidly changing economic circumstance brought about by the [national park] project and other factors.

### The Cultural Construction of Hygiene

Harper initiated her research project with door-to-door introductions with all the villagers, followed by a set of "invasive but excessively polite demographic questions" (Harper 2002:166). Subsequently, she interviewed people about their health problems, understandings of health issues, acquisition and use of forest and Western medicines, and an array of other questions. She observed and participated in daily village activities and filled her notebooks with detailed accounts of what she saw and heard. As she lived among the villagers, witnessing their routines in the fields and around the village, and casually interviewed them about their use of healing plants and other mundane issues of day-to-day village life, Harper realized that the villagers' conceptions of health and cleanliness were different from her own, Western, middle-class ideas. Attempting to be ecologically sound, she tried to bury all her garbage, from crumpled papers (reflecting false starts in her writing efforts) to the tin cans and plastic bags from the used-up Western products she had carried with her to the field. The villagers, who produced little if any garbage, were astonished by the amount she produced—which, very likely, was far less per day than the average middle-class home in the United States—and they believed her to be very rich to be able to make so much garbage. Indeed, many of the things she discarded, such as used-up glass bottles, were coveted by them as useful containers. Everything else that she buried the pigs rooted up and scattered about. Washing was another issue. In a place where a bar of soap costs a full day's wage, water doesn't run from a tap, and the latrine consists of the spaces between the trees in the nearby coffee grove, keeping clean is a constant challenge that is complicated by the fact that daily labor—from sunrise to sunset—in the rice fields means standing in calf-deep mud that is thick with worms and feces, while work on the nearby hillside gardens involves toil in the blazing sun. Most people's clothes were tattered and their bodies scrawny but strong from daily manual labor. As for the children, Harper found that almost all had bloated bellies as a result of worm infestation, their skin was encrusted with lesions caused by scabies (a microscopic burrowing insect), their legs and arms were marked by large boils, their ears were leaking yellow pus from infections, and their bodies were mostly underweight, and yet they were active and playful and filled the village with their laughter.

### In the Company of Death

Harper also was struck by the frequency of sickness and death around her. Indeed, a woman who sought employment from Harper on the anthropologist's first night in the village had died by the following morning. During her fourteen months in the village, 18 people died, a disturbingly high mortality rate of almost 100 per 1,000 population compared with just more than 8 deaths per 1,000 population in the United States. Harper (2002:15) recalled,

In the course of my residency in the village, two social factors critically influenced my research methodology and findings. First, the presence of the
national park project not only affected local lives, it affected nearly every facet
of my research. . . . A second factor shaping my research [was that] many of
[the village] residents were dying. . . . The deaths were variously attributed to
respiratory disorders, seizures, malnutrition, fevers, liver problems and ghost
sickness. [E]very few weeks, or sometimes everyday, another person died,
suddenly or following an illness.

Her fieldwork ultimately ended as it began with the death of a villager. On the
morning of her departure—under pressure from park officials not to express any
criticism of the park or to imply that the park was a factor in village morbidity
and mortality rates—Harper (2002:235) was awakened "not to the eerie cries
of the lemurs," which had enchanted her mornings and nights in Ranotsara, but
to "the ghostly cries of women wailing for the dead. Maily, a young woman in
her twenties, had died during the night."

### Writing Up

On her return to the United States, Harper wrote a book titled *Endangered Species: Health, Illness, and Death among Madagascar's People of
the Forest* to document her findings and to show that while the people she
studied use plants, barks, and roots from the forest to treat (but rarely cure)
debilitating diseases that are readily cured with pharmaceutical medicines,
the latter are usually inaccessible. In her book, Harper (2002:3) argues that
"their continued reliance on the forest's botany for their health care is less
conditioned by their 'culture' than it is by social inequalities that have rendered them cash poor." Even the forest at their doorstep is controlled by
others, turning their social disparities into health disparities, an issue of keen
interest to medical anthropologists that is examined in chapter 6. Rather
than existing in an exotic village with a traditional way of life sheltered by
dense forest from the fast-paced and changing world system around them,
the lives of the people of Ranotsara, Harper found, are shaped, although not
narrowly so, by forces beyond their reach and certainly beyond their control.
Harper seeks to reveal what can happen in contemporary development, including the ecological development movement, when people are not treated
as part of the natural environment that is being protected, issues that are addressed more fully in chapter 7. To make her points, Harper relies not solely
on her own research findings but also on an examination of historic records,
economic reports, and population data.

## Studying Surgeons

### Problems at Meadowbrook

Many miles from Ranotsara and seemingly a world away from its humid green landscape lies Meadowbrook University Hospital (pseudonym) on the outskirts of one of Canada's largest cities. With 800 patient beds, 120 of which are reserved for surgical patients, Meadowbrook doctors perform 15,000 operations each year. As a university hospital, in addition to providing health care to patients, Meadowbrook is a teaching institute and thus is home to a steady and changing flow of medical and other students seeking to become health care professionals, and, further, it is a health care research center oriented to increasing the fund of biomedical knowledge.

Despite its sanitized veneer of orderliness and control, Meadowbrook had a problem. The hospital began to receive urgent complaints from surgical residents in their final stage of training that the staff surgeons who were their teachers and supervisors were not spending enough time training them to be surgeons. In response, as noted in chapter 1, Pearl Katz, a medical anthropologist, was invited by the chief of the Department of Surgery to carry out a study that would help resolve the problem. Katz realized that the study held the potential to be of even greater importance than the immediate needs of the Department of Surgery. Medical anthropology, which views biomedicine as ethnomedicine—if of a special sort, namely, a medical system that has gained global importance and a dominant position in terms of other ethnomedical systems internationally—is keenly interested in understanding how biomedicine works, including its roles in society, its worldviews and underlying cultural models, social structures, and varieties across time and place.

### Expect Rejection

When Katz (1999:16) began her study, she was "warned by friends and colleagues that [she] would have difficulty getting accurate information on what surgeons did." Katz's anthropological colleagues assumed that the surgeons, being privileged and, relative to patients and researchers at least, rather powerful, would limit her access to information, especially to unfettered backstage glimpses of their lives and behaviors. Certainly other researchers have had trouble gaining full access to biomedical practitioners. In her own study of surgeons, for example, medical anthropologist Joan Cassell—a colleague who encouraged Katz to publish her finding—was once sternly asked by a surgeon after an operation that she had been invited to witness by a nurse, "What's an anthropologist doing studying surgeons?" To which she glibly responded, "Well, there were no other primitives left" (Cassell 1998:10). Cassell's experience notwithstanding,

Katz found that the surgeons extended her an extraordinary level of trust and openness; they appeared to her to want to be understood.

By contrast, Katz found herself challenged by her own attitudes toward surgeons. It was much easier for her to identify with patients and she was critical of the disparaging attitude surgeons expressed for the concerns of their patients. She was shocked to find that they referred to an especially frightened patient as the "beast" or the "colon." Only over time, after observing many operations, did Katz realize that she too was depersonalizing patients and why this was a useful mechanism used by surgeons to "protect themselves against the [emotionally burdensome] experience of empathizing with the personal anguish of patients" (Katz 1999:8). Katz also found herself envying the power held by surgeons and came to realize that to some degree such envy fuels diatribes against the status of surgeons found both in the popular mass media and in some social science analyses.

### Following Doctors

In her day-to-day work on the study, Katz focused intensely on six senior surgeons. With each of these key informants she spent approximately three continuous weeks, from the moment they arrived in the hospital early each morning until they left the hospital about twelve hours later, a method known as "shadowing." As one of the doctors she studied noted in introducing her to a colleague, "Look, I've got a girl following me around all the time, taking down everything I say" (Katz 1999:7).

Over time, Katz (1999:91) developed a number of keen insights about "surgeon culture," including the fact that while they act jovial and gregarious in the company of their colleagues, surgeons tend to carefully protect "information about themselves, their patients, their operating loads, operative techniques, referral sources, levels of specific knowledge, specific expertise (particularly deficits in knowledge and expertise), income, and doubts and concerns about medical decisions," in other words, anything that might allow another surgeon to have the upper hand in dealings with them. Feelings of competition with other surgeons, in short, were as strong as or stronger than any sense of collegiality and collaboration. This underlying feature of surgeon culture, Katz found, was a critical component of why residents felt that hospital staff surgeons were not spending adequate time training them for their jobs as surgeons.

## Folk Illness in Haiti

### Illness and Identity

Far to the south of Meadowbrook University Hospital, on the Caribbean island of Haiti, lies the rural village of Jeanty (pseudonym), tucked into the foothills above the Cayes plain, once one of the wealthiest sugar-growing areas of the world. The village itself is hilly and rocky and was probably first populated during the early nineteenth century by freed slaves fleeing plantation labor in the early years of Haitian independence from colonial France. Little more than a cluster of small tin-roofed houses strewn along a grid of unpaved streets, Jeanty is home to three thousand people with a total population of almost twelve thousand in nearby hamlets. With American funding, CARE, a relief agency (one of many in Haiti), had installed a potable water system in the village, and it was with the assistance of CARE that Paul Brodwin, a medical anthropologist, had arrived there in 1987 to study folk conceptions of illness, healing, and mortality. Specifically, Brodwin examined the crisis of illness as a fundamental social experience during which people commonly rework their social identities and confront the contradictions of their life experience, health-related processes addressed in chapter 3.

### The Language of Research

Brodwin's research methods included participant observation of routine health-related activities among village members, semistructured interviews with village residents, attendance at community religious and healing rituals, the collection of life histories of village members, and interviews designed to record detailed narratives of actual illness experiences. He was aided in this effort by being a novelty for the villagers: only a handful of outsiders have ever lived in the village, and thus villagers were interested in talking with him. Initially, Brodwin had an assistant, a young man from the village, but before long his ability to speak Creole—the language born of the merger of French and several languages from West Africa—was sufficient to conduct his own interviews.

### Choosing a Healer

In his study in Haiti, Brodwin addressed an issue that is central to medical anthropology (see chapter 5): in contexts of medical pluralism (i.e., coexistent alternative healing systems), how do people make decisions about which ethnomedical system to go to—for what health issues and why—and what actually happens as patients and healers interact? As he (1996:13) notes, "People who fall ill must choose between multiple and competing systems of healing: this is true both in the small-scale communities where anthropologists usually work and in the urban centers of post-industrial society," where, today, many anthropologists do research as well. To help answer these questions, Brodwin observed more than fifty consultations between patients and herbalist healers and about twenty interactions between patients and *houngans* (male healers in the Vodou folk health care system). In each case, he carefully recorded his observations of what happened, including the nature of the problem brought by the patient, healer questions and actions, patient responses, the context and tone of the interaction, and the issue of payment. For example, about one consultation by a Haitian patient suffering from painful muscle aches and body fatigue, Brodwin (1996:134), who accompanied the patient, named Louis, to the healing session, recorded,

> André [a *houngan* known to the patient] greeted us at the door, and after the necessary introductions, led us into his small consulting room and sat at his table. It was covered with a heavy red cloth, and an assortment of small bottles filled with remedies lined the back. . . . As André settled in his chair, he lit an oil-wick lamp. . . . [After a while] André began to moan and gasp for air between coughs which wracked his entire upper body. . . . He soon began to rock back and forth and softly whistled, a serene smile on his lips. . . . From this moment on until the end of the consultation . . . we communicated only with his lwa [the spirit being named Byenzomal that had possessed André and began to speak through him]. . . . When he had finished the divinations [to determine the source of Louis's symptoms] and given to Louis the names of several [folk] remedies to purchase, Byenzomal rang the bell . . . and announced "We're through."

### Studying Exotica

To his fieldwork project, Brodwin brought a strong curiosity about the exotic, one that was not disappointed by scenes such as the one just described. As Brodwin (1996:129) admits,

> From my very first days in Jeanty, I was eager to begin speaking with houngans and mambos [female healers]; individuals who call up the spirits and explicitly rely on their healing power. Years of graduate training in anthropology had not suppressed my typically American fascination with the exotic side of popular Haitian religion.

To his initial disappointment, however, he was frustrated in this desire at every turn. Several months passed before he was finally able to make contact with and begin interviewing a *houngan*.

In his interviews with village members, Brodwin came to realize that while people may consult *houngans* for their pressing health problems, it is not without a degree of fear of the malign ability of these specialists to "send sickness." Fear—although of a different sort—plays a similar role in the hesitancy many people feel about seeing a dentist or having an operation. As Brodwin learned, ambivalence, uncertainty, and moral struggle are often critical features of illness and healing, lessons learned by medical anthropologists working in diverse social and cultural settings.

## CHALLENGES OF RAPPORT

It is critical that medical anthropologists develop good interpersonal relations and a sense of trust with members of the group they study, relations that facilitate open communication and comfortable social interaction. The importance of skillful use of the indigenous language in developing ethnographic rapport was brought home to the lead author of this book during his own research in Haiti (M. Singer et al. 1988). In that study, Singer was aided during interviews by a Haitian graduate student named Gerdes. Early in the research, which focused on women's reproductive health, Singer had all but given up on an interview with a *houngan* (a spiritual healer) who was evasive and seemed little interested in answering anthropological questions. As he and Gerdes, having grown frustrated and weary of their failed efforts, were about to leave the *houngan's* compound, the other member of the field team, Davison, arrived. Davison was fairly fluent in Creole, which, having watched Singer use an interpreter, the *houngan* did not expect. Quickly surmising that a failure to establish rapport was the reason the interview had gone sour, Davison, using a local idiomatic reference, said to the *houngan* in Creole, "So, is this big potato [i.e., Singer] giving you a hard time?" The *houngan* was so caught off guard by this humorous reference in Creole that he nearly fell from his chair in laughter. Instantly, the atmosphere changed, and the *houngan* became a friendly and talkative informant.

Marsha Quinland (2004:37), who conducted a study of folk medicine in Bwa Mawgo, a village on the Caribbean island of Dominica, found that to sustain rapport with villagers, she had to maintain a careful equilibrium

> between kindness (I was sympathetic and would help out when I could) and professionalism (I was there to do a job, pay research participants for helping me, and remain neutral in some social issues). Fieldwork can be emotionally taxing for anthropologists because they are always at work to some degree. I was always listening and observing and I was constantly being evaluated.

One of the important challenges involves explaining to individuals without prior experience of research what you are doing in their community.

In some settings in which medical anthropologists work, this is not an easy task. Donald Joralemon (2010:24), for example, carried out research on shamanistic healing in Peru, and the entire time in the field he "had the distinct impression that the purpose of my presence was never entirely clear to most of those with whom I spoke." Fortunately, during participant-observation research, involving long periods of time, often one to two years, the people being studied come to be much more interested in the medical anthropologist as a person than they do with him or her as a researcher. It is on the basis of the personal qualities and the conduct of the researcher, rather than the topic of the research project, that rapport is usually established.

## Understanding Urban Nomads

### Hitting the Skids

Working in an environment that economically, socially, geographically, and climatically is radically different from Jeanty, namely, the northwestern coastal city of Seattle, Washington, James Spradley (1970) conducted a study of urban nomads—people mainstream society calls skid-row bums, winos, derelicts, and beggars. Spradley's study is older than the others described previously and, technically, was not carried out in the name of medical anthropology, but because of the rich texture of its written account, the cognitive research methods he employed, and his effort to use his findings to address contemporary health and social problems, it has served as a model for many subsequent medical anthropology studies of the urban poor.

Spradley's research focus grew out of his recognition that while the existence of skid-row alcoholics was well known in the wider society, what was actually known about them was based on outsiders' perspectives, those of the police, the courts, social service providers, and substance abuse counselors. What was the emic, or insider's, point of view? How did urban nomads view themselves, their world, and the people around them? What cultural knowledge did they use to survive on the margins of society and social acceptability? If they, in fact, have a culture, what is the culture of urban nomads? In Spradley's (1970:7) assessment, "If we are successful in discovering the culture of urban nomads, the descriptions should provide an outsider with information and rules to enable him to operate in a manner acceptable to these men, to see the world as they see it, to adapt to that world as they do."

### Listening and Discovering

To achieve these goals, Spradley (1970:7) began his work with "months of listening to men talk about their experiences with law enforcement agencies in order to discover which questions could be appropriately asked of informants, and further, to ascertain the wording of these questions." Thus, Spradley launched his project by conducting participant observation in a criminal court, in an alcoholism treatment center, and on the streets of Seattle's Skid Road, a term that traces to the days when felled trees were skidded down the street on their way to the lumber mill. These efforts were followed up with the administration of a lengthy questionnaire to a sample of one hundred men who had been in jail for public drunkenness and, finally, unstructured interviewing of a smaller sample of key informants. Initially, the work was not easy, and the men did not trust Spradley. They assumed he must be an undercover police officer or FBI agent gathering information that he would use to arrest them. Interestingly, it was the nature of his research method—called ethnosemantic elicitation—that ultimately convinced the men that Spradley was not a cop.

In this type of research, the investigator seeks to uncover the underlying cognitive structure people use to organize information. For example, Spradley would ask the men, What are the kinds of places you can "flop" (a folk term for a place you can sleep for the night)? To this question, he got answers such as boxcars, gondolas, Wheeler's, Bread of Life, the junkyard, and a used-car lot. Further questioning revealed that boxcars and gondolas were related kinds of flops in that both were subtypes of railroad flops. Similarly, Wheeler's and Bread of Life were subtypes of mission flops, while the junkyard and used-car lots were car flops. Ultimately, he elicited more than one hundred different places to flop. The culture of urban nomads, Spradley found, contains numerous taxonomies of this sort (as does every culture). Another cultural category Spradley explored was "ways to beat a drunk charge," which contained numerous types and subtypes of strategies to avoid going to "the drunk tank." Once a domain, such as "places to flop," was known to him, Spradley could then ask a series of questions about how urban nomads differentiate flops in terms of various characteristics said to be important by his informants, such as cost, exposure to the elements, comfort (ability to lie down), drinking restrictions, police interference, availability of food, and demands, such as having to listen to a preacher's sermon first. Interestingly, Spradley (1970:108) found that a "casual comparison of urban nomads with most Americans reveals no other group with such a complex scheme for categorizing sleeping places." Clearly, where to sleep is a central challenge faced by urban nomads, and they have developed an elaborate cultural system for making decisions about it.

### Using Research

Another domain Spradley explored was "the bucket," the name used by urban nomads to refer to jail. Once more, information and folk systems of classification were elaborate, again suggesting their importance because urban nomads wish to avoid arrest and imprisonment or to at least minimize the potentially painful consequences of this common, repetitive experience. Realizing the damaging effects of incarceration and the exploitation of urban nomads by the prison system, Spradley was able to use his research findings to advocate for changes in the handling of men like those he studied. Working with an ad hoc committee of concerned citizens, he wrote a detailed report about the deplorable ways men arrested for public inebriation are treated and delivered it to a local judge, the Seattle mayor's office, the members of the city council, the police department, and various other public policy and health care institutions. Although some people were angered by his indictment of the police, his work began to receive considerable media attention. Over the next few years, the state of Washington (and other states as well) decriminalized public drunkenness and switched instead to a system of detoxification rather than incarceration, a significant achievement of an applied anthropology project.

### Having Impact

As Erickson (2003:3), whose work in medical anthropology addresses reproductive health issues, points out,

> Medical anthropology has a broad mandate—to understand and interpret humans, their diseases and illnesses, and their medical systems. Many medical anthropologists also take on the responsibility of making their research useful for clinical or health educational applications, for influencing public health policy, or for effecting social justice.

Through this brief examination of the fieldwork of four different medical anthropologists in different parts of the world and with very different field sites and populations, as well as different research questions and methods (including, in addition, the three examples provided in chapter 1), we begin to grasp just what it is that medical anthropologists do to fulfill the discipline's broad humanitarian and scientific mandate.

## WHAT MEDICAL ANTHROPOLOGISTS STUDY

### A Diverse Discipline

In the role of applied social scientists, medical anthropologists commonly seek to answer practical questions about the nature of health, illness, healing systems, and related matters across cultural systems, populations, and social contexts. These questions derive from various sources. Some reflect ongoing debates and discussions generated at anthropology (and other health) conferences and in the published literature, primarily books and journals but also government or other reports, policy papers, and other documents of the discipline and related fields. Others are raised by institutions, government bodies, or communities that seek the help of a medical anthropologist in addressing pressing issues. Other questions arise because of changes in the world that impact health. For example, the rapid increase in electronic communication (especially cell phones and computers) has impacted health-related behavior in various ways (e.g. the rapid electronic accessing of health information on the Internet). Increasingly, medical anthropologists, like other researchers, have asked research questions about the intersection of health behavior and electronic communication.

Without doubt, medical anthropologists have diverse points of view and do not by any means fully agree about what the key questions of the discipline are. Some medical anthropologists, those interested in the experience of illness, focus much of their attention on humankind's phenomenological encounter with being sick, asking questions such as the following: What does illness mean to people in particular social roles, sociocultural contexts, and social settings? What is the internal lived experience of illness like for sufferers and what shapes this experience? What impact does illness have on their identities, relationships, and values? Other medical anthropologists are more interested in how people make decisions about what to do when they are ill, including their help-seeking strategies, how they make choices about alternative healing systems, and the role of significant others in shaping these processes. Still other medical anthropologists are especially concerned with the role of environmental, social, political, and economic factors in illness; the nature of the patient-healer relationship; or the relative effectiveness of different approaches to treatment.

Further, as seen in the examples that have been provided, some medical anthropologists work in rural villages in developing nations, others conduct their studies and applied work in modern hospitals, while others carry out their research on the street corners of cities large and small or even on the Internet. Many medical anthropologists work in quite different settings over the course of their careers. A complete compilation of all the topics medical anthropologists have addressed and all the places they have conducted research or implemented programs would be surprisingly long and varied.

### Studying the Life Course

Another reflection of the broad mandate of medical anthropology is the work done by members of the discipline across the various stages of the human life course, from birth (or even before, in terms of reproductive health) to death. In all societies, reproduction and reproductive health are heavily invested with cultural meanings and values. Women's menstruation, likewise, is commonly a focus of cultural elaboration, as menstrual blood often is seen as being especially charged and possibly polluting. The process of giving birth also is culturally shaped and managed in all societies according to group understandings of appropriate birthing behavior. With her classic anthropological study *Birth in Four Cultures*, Brigette Jordan (1993) helped launch the anthropology of birth as a subfield of medical anthropology. Work in this area has shown that cultures develop distinct beliefs and associated practices around pregnancy, delivery, and the treatment of babies during the postpartum period. In biomedicine, for example, the full medicalization of childbirth—characterized by (1) the use of high-tech machinery for monitoring the birthing process that begins early in the pregnancy and continues through delivery, (2) frequent use of surgery to both widen the birth portal and remove the baby, and (3) widespread use of medications to deaden pain or speed up the birthing process—has led Robbie Davis-Floyd (1992) to use the term "technocratic birth" to characterize having a baby in Western society. By contrast, in many societies, traditional birth attendants (i.e., more senior women with considerable personal and apprentice experience in birthing) provide the primary support to a woman in delivery. Low-technology, midwife-assisted birthing systems have resisted the spread of technocratic birth, often with anthropological support. An applied approach to the issue of birthing has led to anthropological work on issues like teen pregnancy as a health and social problem, including showing why teen girls often view pregnancy as a sought-after social status (Erickson 1998). Similarly, medical anthropologists have studied children's health and have been active in applied projects like breast-feeding promotion. Penny Van Esterik (1989), for example, became very involved in the effort to challenge the global promotion of commercial infant formula by Nestlé Corporation and other companies as a replacement for breast milk. In many settings, manufactured formulas, she argued, are detrimental to children's health and sometimes, if clean water for mixing the formula is not available, even life threatening. Breast-feeding, by contrast, not only provides a nutritious food for babies, it also passes important maternal immunities to diseases on to young children.

At the distal end of the life course, anthropologists have also paid considerable attention to aging. Research in this area has shown that old age commonly is marked by a shift in a person's role in society, such as a significant reduction in work responsibility, as well as changes in social status, including, depending on the local setting, coming to be viewed variously as a valued storehouse of important cultural knowledge or as out of touch with the contemporary world. The nature of these transitions varies because the meanings attached to being "old" are culturally constructed in light of other features of a society. In a fast-paced, rapidly changing society, the knowledge and experiences of elders may be devalued; by contrast, in societies that look to tradition as a guide to the present, growing old may be accompanied by a gain in social stature.

Applied work in the anthropology of aging has focused on many issues, including helping to give voice to elders whose needs and capacities have been overlooked in society. Dying and death are also issues of concern in medical anthropology, as they constitute profound arenas of human experience, thought, and emotion. In contemporary medical anthropology studies, dying and death are viewed as "subjects without clear boundaries, and any analytic exploration of those themes now problematizes their definition" (Kaufman 2004:245) rather than viewing them as clear-cut biological states. In other words, death and dying must be understood in sociocultural context because what it means to die in one society may be quite different than what it means to die in another.

### A Peculiarly Anthropological Approach

Whatever the specific issues of immediate concern, medical anthropologists tend to approach health issues in particular ways that reflect the nature of anthropology as a field of study. As seen in the examples provided in this and the previous chapter, medical anthropologists

- often address pressing health problems, and hence there is an applied aspect to medical anthropology research.
- tend to use field methods, immersing themselves into the day-to-day lives and social contexts of the group of concern rather than conducting studies in laboratories or in interview rooms at universities, although these two methods are used by medical anthropologists as well, such as biological

anthropologists who assess the quality of diet through the analysis of teeth or determine ancient diseases by the effects they leave on bones excavated from archaeological sites.

- commonly use qualitative methods, and hence much of their data are words (e.g., tapes of casual interviews or field notes of observations of behavior or social contexts) rather than numbers, although medical anthropologists certainly also use quantitative methods, such as surveys, physical measurements, laboratory tests, or counts of various sorts; indeed, medical anthropology has led the way in the use of quantitative analysis in anthropology.
- are especially concerned with learning the insider's point of view, their understanding of reality, and their values and attitudes and with connecting and comparing this information to actual behaviors that have been observed.
- are inclined to take a holistic, contextual approach, seeing attitudes and behaviors within the natural social settings in which they emerge and function; thus, medical anthropologists tend to develop very detailed, highly contextualized accounts of health issues in terms of multiple interrelated issues.

## CONDUCTING RESEARCH

### Holistic Conception

In conducting research, medical anthropologists tend to assume that the issues of immediate concern to them are embedded in wider sociocultural systems and are intricately interconnected with many other aspects of social life and with complex social environmental contexts. As a result, they tend to cast a wide research net and ask a broad set of research questions. To carry out their research, medical anthropologists usually marshal a number of qualitative and quantitative methods for the collection of health-related data (e.g., see the six-volume set *Ethnographer's Toolkit*, which fully describes the methods used by many medical anthropologists in their research [LeCompte and Schensul 1999]). Moreover, in carrying out their research, they generally seek to move out of the university or other institutional setting in which they are employed to gain direct and intimate access to the daily lives and activities of the people under study. Further, they often spend long periods of time in these field settings observing and participating in the flow of life. This is an approach to research known as ethnography.

### Choosing Risky Behavior

In studying health issues, medical anthropologists often use ethnography to address difficult questions or seek to make sense of puzzling or

## ETHNOGRAPHY

This core research strategy in medical anthropology involves the immersion of the researcher or team of researchers into the social space and lifeways of the people under study. As part of this effort, medical anthropologists seek to participate (to varying degrees) in the normal social life of the group under study. While not all research in medical anthropology is ethnographic, there is a generally shared sense that ethnography offers keen insights about health and behavior that are not easily acquired through other means. Rather than a highly controlled and sharply focused approach to data collection, ethnography focuses on issues of concern within their natural social context and in terms of how they are seen and experienced by group members. Over time, ethnographic researchers are able to glimpse behind the public masks and front-stage performances of social actors to backstage and often hidden arenas of experience and social interaction. In this way, they are often able to develop understandings of behaviors that might otherwise appear irrational, meaningless, or inscrutable or might otherwise go unknown.

In his study of drug addicts in the federal treatment center in Lexington, Kentucky, for example, Michael Agar found that by just "hanging out" and talking with patients, he discovered many things that he was not finding about drug addicts as he browsed through articles and books about them in the center's library. He recalls, "I knew something was wrong the first day I lifted a book off the library shelf. The stories I was hearing from addicts were a lot more complicated, a lot more interesting, and a lot more powerful, than anything I was reading" (Agar 2006:32).While the literature on addiction at the time tended to reflect the interests of psychologists in psychopathology and of sociologists in social deviance, Agar discovered that whether the individual addict was white or black, from the Pacific Northwest or the Deep South, or young or old, involvement in addiction appeared to be shaped by a complex, rich, robust, and socially meaningful cultural system. Something incredibly important about drug addiction was missing from the journal articles and textbooks in the library, and Agar set out to use the ethnographer's tool kit to discover what it was.

misunderstood behaviors. Elisa Sobo, for example, was confronted with the challenge of understanding why people who know about AIDS and routes of infection nonetheless regularly participate in risky behaviors, such as not using condoms during sex. This is an important problem for public health because it is clear that simply teaching people about AIDS as an infectious disease does not eliminate risk; the disease continues to spread. In her study of risky behaviors among impoverished and socially disadvantaged women in Cleveland, Ohio, Sobo (1995) concluded that people who know about AIDS often act as if they are not at risk, a puzzling discovery that needed explanation. AIDS-risk denial, she found, appears to be rooted both in a cultural tradition that values monogamy and personal responsibility and in the actual position of women in society generally and relative to men. Thus, the women whom Sobo studied idealized and desired long-term monogamous romantic relationships and loyal, committed partners. The underlying cultural logic that supported this heartfelt desire is this: good women get good men, and unworthy women get bad men. If you are a good woman, then you should be able to trust your partner. This attitude reflects very basic cultural ideals in American society and leads people to interpret life course and outcomes in terms of how hard people work and how committed they are to achieving their goals. Simply put, those who succeed are seen as having worked hard, and those who do not are seen as slouches. Having an untrustworthy male partner, in short, implied that a woman did not deserve better, putting her very identity and sense of personal self-worth at risk.

Like others in the wider society, the women whom Sobo studied seek good relationships with good men, thereby proving to themselves and their social networks that they are, indeed, women of value. As a result, with their main partners, the women do not use condoms (because as good women they can trust their partners not to have sex with others). One consequence of poverty and social discrimination, however, is that the potential partners whom women like those Sobo studied are likely to meet tend to have comparatively high rates of unemployment and underemployment, lack of health insurance, and limited other resources. As a result of an inability to succeed economically in society and to reap the psychosocial benefits of being successful in one's own eyes and in the eyes of peers, it is a special challenge for poor men to feel good about themselves and about their own worth as human beings. As a psychosocial substitute for economic achievement and hence as a salve for the potential sense of failure in a success-driven society, street culture, in fact, tends to support "sexual achievement"—that is, having multiple partners over time or even at the same time—as a sign of success. Thus, one can still have a sense of achievement in life and the experience of having admirable qualities, even if it is acquired through a nonmainstream method, although one that is not entirely beyond the mainstream, as fantasies of multiple sexual exploits are hardly limited to the poor.

Consequently, poor men and women are pushed by social forces and cultural values to be at cross-purposes, a tension that finds expression in high rates of divorce, failure to marry, and intimate partner violence. In their effort to achieve monogamy and the psychological benefit of feeling that they merit a good man, Sobo argues, poor women are pushed to see their male partners as more loyal and more deeply committed than social circumstances allow them to be. Thus, they may begin prematurely to assume that their partners are not seeing other women. In this context, the decision not to use condoms affirms a woman's desire to feel worthy of a dependable man. Various behaviors reinforce this decision. Sobo (1995:99) notes, "A man who gives his wife or girlfriend gifts, services, or money lives up to—or at least begins to live up to and implies he intends to live up to—the cultural ideal of the male partner as breadwinner or provider and as a woman's protector." Under these conditions, stopping condom use is an act of commitment, an expression of trust, and an investment, through potentially having a child together, in a long-term partnership. The problem, however, is that most women who get AIDS are not infected during one-night stands with poorly known sexual partners because condoms tend to be used in such situations. Rather, they are infected with HIV by longer-term partners, people they trust with whom they are having sex without a condom.

As this account suggests, in explaining health-related behavior, medical anthropologists pay attention to the interplay of a wide range of cultural, social, hierarchical, psychological, environmental, and even biological factors. Only by showing how all these weave together in complex tapestries, something that the ethnographic methods of medical anthropology allow, can we really understand why people do what they do, believe what they believe, and get sick or stay well. One advantage of this perspective is the realization that sexual desire—which is often condemned in moralistic discussions of HIV risk—must be reframed "from an individual to a collective phenomenon" (R. Parker 2009:xiv). Culture provides a frame of reference "though which sexual meanings are organized—and in relationship to which conflicting and contrasting sexual scripts are produced and reproduced" (R. Parker 2009:xiv), and these, in turn, are shaped by other factors like social hierarchies and inequalities.

## THE HEALTH RISKS AND
## BENEFITS OF KISSING

From a public health standpoint, is kissing risky? If so, what are the known health risks of kissing? Conversely, are there health benefits of kissing? These questions have received increasing attention in public health since the early 1950s when, during a speech at Baltimore City College, bacteriologist Arthur Bryan reported that up to 250 colonies of bacteria can be transmitted during a single passionate kiss (fewer if one of the participants is wearing lipstick). To reach this conclusion, Bryan recruited a sample of adults and adolescents to kiss a sterile glass slide or agar plate for various periods of time. Fortunately, Bryan found that the vast majority (95%) of kiss-transferred microbes are not pathogenic. Since then, of course, HIV/AIDS became a global pandemic and concerns about kissing as a route of lethal viral or other microbial transmission have become widespread. In their studies various social scientists have encountered popular uncertainty about kissing as a risk behavior. Burton Cowgil and his colleagues in Los Angeles, for example, conducted semistructured qualitative interviews with 33 HIV-infected parents and their children to investigate fears about HIV transmission. They found that many of these families reported transmission fears, including specific trepidation related to blood contact, contact with bathroom items, food sharing, and kissing/hugging. Many of these fears, including those viewing kissing as an HIV risk, are based on misconceptions about modes of HIV transmission. While kissing is not a very likely route of HIV infection (because HIV cannot survive in saliva), kissing can be a health risk. In fact, an array of infectious diseases can be transmitted through this form of human intimacy, including strep throat, infectious mononucleosis (known colloquially as "kissing disease"), Herpes Simplex Virus-2, Hepatitis B, syphilis, scabies (a contagious skin disease caused by a mite), warts, and meningococcal disease (inflammation of the membranes that cover the brain and spinal cord). College freshmen, for example, especially those who live in dormitories, have been found to be at increased risk for bacterial meningococcal disease compared with age mates who are not attending college or living in a dorm setting. Moreover, research in Britain found that people involved in intimate kissing with multiple concurrent partners face a four times greater risk of developing meningitis than those not engaged in this behavior. Sexually transmitted diseases like syphilis also can be transmitted through kissing if syphilis sores are present in the mouth or lips of one of the participants. In addition to various diseases, several studies have found that food allergens can be transmitted through kissing. Thus Steensma (2003) has reported the case of a severe anaphylactic reaction in a young woman with shellfish allergies after kissing her boyfriend (who had just eaten several shrimp). On the plus side, research shows that there are several notable health benefits linked to kissing, including the fact that kissing

- a partner goodbye in the morning is associated with longer life
- can improve self-esteem and feelings of being appreciated
- burns a small number of calories (two to three calories per minute)
- is a demonstrated reliever of stress (e.g., passionate kissing has been show to lower cortisol levels, an objective sign of stress reduction) and anxiety
- exercises thirty different facial muscles and reduces muscle tension
- especially frequent kissing, helps stabilize cardiovascular activity and reduce blood pressure and cholesterol
- releases natural bodily antibiotic secretions into the saliva and is useful in pain relief

## RESEARCH METHODS

### Multimethod Research

When conducting a study, a medical anthropologist or a team of collaborating researchers generally combines a number of specific methods. This mixed-method approach often includes direct observation and detailed recording of behaviors and events witnessed in the field, as seen earlier in this chapter in Brodwin's (1996) records of folk treatment observations in Haiti. In addition, medical anthropologists commonly conduct casual interviews with people as they are going about their everyday activities, which Katz (1999) did as she followed surgeons around the hospital she studied. Another method frequently used by medical anthropologists is in-depth interviewing, such as the detailed interviews conducted by Bluebond-Langner (1996) in her study of cystic fibrosis. To gain a wider contextual framework for understanding what they find in the field, medical anthropologists routinely review

historic documents or other existing records, such as Harper's (2002) examination of the historical and economic literature on Madagascar.

Medical anthropologists also use ethnosemantic elicitation, a primary approach used by Spradley (1970), as well as a set of specialized systematic cultural assessment techniques, such as free lists, pile sorts, and Q-sorts, that allow
researchers to glimpse how study participants think about and order the components of their world. Pamela Erickson and her colleagues, for example, used
free lists and pile sorts, among other techniques, to study sexual health and
decision making among inner-city African American and Puerto Rican young
adults (M. Singer et al. 2006). In this study, called Project PHRESH, eighteen-
to twenty-four-year-olds were recruited through street outreach in Hartford,
Connecticut, and Philadelphia, Pennsylvania. In small-group settings, they
were first asked to list all the kinds of sexual practices that they knew.

Later, in one-on-one sessions, other participants from the same age and
ethnic groups were asked to sort cards that were printed with descriptions
of sexual behaviors that were listed by at least three of the small groups into
piles ranging from least to most risky for HIV transmission. Participants were
then asked to explain why they put cards together in the same pile. Using a
special set of computer programs called Anthropac developed by anthropologist Stephen Borgatti, the team was able to prepare a scatter plot of the overall
pattern in the sorted cards, based on an assessment of which cards people
tended to put in the same pile or keep apart in different piles, across all the
participants in the study. This approach allowed Erickson and coworkers to
see underlying cultural associations that shape sexual and romantic relations
in their study population. Other techniques commonly used by medical anthropologists include life history interviews, focus groups, consensus analysis,
and diary keeping.

One of the concerns of projects like PHRESH is the recruitment of a sample of individuals who represent a larger population when all of the features
(e.g., overall size, makeup of subgroups) of the larger target population are
not fully known (and hence the recruitment of a statistically representative
sample is not possible). One approach that allows the researcher to combine
location and time factors to obtain a large, diverse, and reasonably representative sample is known as venue-based sampling (VBS). The keys to the
VBS approach are (1) rigorous exploration of possible recruitment sites (i.e.,
venues) where members of the target population can be found (e.g., a study of
street commercial sex workers to assess health risk behavior might attempt—
through interviews with known commercial sex workers and direct street
observation in an given area—to identify "stroll" sites where commercial sex

workers engage customers); (2) focused observation over a period of time at all identified sites to roughly determine the number of individuals from the target group that might be found at each site; (3) random selection of venues at selected intervals from the list of identified venues; (4) recruitment of individuals at randomly selected venues combined with observation of the number of members of the target group present during the time/date of the recruitment; (5) calculation of the relationship of the number of individuals selected from those available at the site during the recruitment episode; and (6) data collect (e.g., through survey, structured interview, in-depth interview) of recruited individuals. As this description suggests, VBS combines qualitative and quantitative strategies to provide researchers with confidence that the individuals they collected data from do not represent a skewed sample that differs in significant ways from the larger population of interest. VBS has been of considerable use in studies of groups at heightened risk for HIV or STD infection. For example, Grant Colfax and colleagues (2001) used VBS to study risk among urban gay and bisexual men in San Francisco and other areas who participate in circuit parties (i.e., large, prolonged dance parties distributed across weekend dates and locations). They found that participants engaged in more frequent risky behaviors (including unprotected sex and drug use) during circuit party weekends compared with weekends when they did not attend a circuit party. They also found that participants engaged in more risk when they attended circuit parties farther from their home than when they attended parties closer to home. These researchers used this information to recommend public health strategies for communities that host circuit parties.

### Examining Lives

The life history interview is used to record the life story of an individual, with a strong emphasis on the meaning of life events for the person being interviewed. James Quesada (1998), for example, used this technique to explore the effects of war, endemic poverty, political instability, and social despair on Daniel, a gangly ten-year-old boy from the central highlands of Nicaragua. Quesada got to know Daniel and his mother while studying health and well-being in the aftermath of war in the Nicaraguan town of Matagalpa. Reflecting the growing interest of medical anthropology in the health and social effects of war, aggression, and interpersonal violence, Quesada analyzed Daniel's life story as an embodiment of the pain and suffering shared by many Nicaraguan children as a result of the U.S.-supported Contra War. Daniel's plight was succinctly and coolly summarized by him one day when he told

Quesada (1998:60) that sometimes he felt like dying: "Look at me, I'm all bones anyway. I'm already dying. I'm too small and I have stopped growing and I am another mouth to feed. My mother can't keep taking care of my brothers and me, and I can't keep taking care of her. I can't do anything." Through this single life history, Quesada gained a far deeper understanding of the embodied experience of war, its profound costs, the jagged social disruption it brings, and the abject poverty it often produces. Because of Quesada's intervention, Daniel did not die, but there are few Jim Quesadas and many Daniels in the world.

In another medical anthropology study using a life history approach, among other methods, João Biehl (2007) interviewed people living with HIV/AIDS in Salvador, Brazil. While Brazil has developed a very advanced and widely hailed program for providing sufferers with AIDS medication and care, in his research Biehl found that the Brazil AIDS program encountered significant problems of implementation with the poor, the unemployed, the homeless, street commercial sex workers, and illicit drug users. Based on life history interviews with a group of impoverished AIDS patients, Biehl (2007:17) explores "how [to] relate large-scale institutions and forces to local politics and personal [life] trajectories." During the interviews, participants told Biehl (2007:17) "about all sorts of financial pressures, battles over discrimination, and the difficulty of obtaining access to quality health care." In so doing, they told Biehl "about their *will to live*" despite numerous social and political economic barriers, obstacles, and challenges.

### Focus Group Interviews

First developed by social scientists, focus groups came to be a favored technique of market researchers concerned with assessing the appeal of new products among consumers. In more recent years, anthropologists and other social scientists have readopted focus groups and used them to study many issues, including health. Marysol Ascensio (2002), for example, used focus groups in a study of sex behaviors among fourteen- to twenty-one-year-old Puerto Rican youth in New York City. Participants were posed questions and allowed time to express their answers and to respond to the answers provided by others in the group. Facilitating such discussion among group members is, in fact, a goal of this method, as it often leads to unexpected findings. Ascensio, for example, found that many youth use "knowing your partner" as a primary means of protecting themselves from HIV and other sexually transmitted diseases. In other words, they made decisions about who it was safe to have sex with on the basis of information they gathered about a potential partner's qualities and reputation. Unfortunately, it is never really possible to fully know partners if they choose not to reveal key information, such as whether they had or are currently having sex with other people, and thus, however widely practiced, "knowing your partner" is not considered an effective disease prevention method. Discovering behavioral practices like this allows medical anthropologists to design health-related interventions that are grounded in actual beliefs and behaviors.

### Considering Consensus

The term "consensus analysis" refers to a quantitative procedure used to determine the modal (i.e., most frequent) answers provided by a group to a set of questions about a particular topic (e.g., "what is a cold?"). Use of consensus analysis allows researchers to determine the degree of cultural agreement in a group or between subgroups of a larger population. For example, asthma beliefs and practices have been found to vary among ethnic groups. One important variation related to ethnicity is the different descriptors used to express an asthma attack. These descriptions can be both physical and psychological in nature. In a multicity cross-cultural comparison of four different Latino groups in the United States, Mexico, and Guatemala, medical anthropology researchers found broad agreement about the major respiratory signs of asthma, including wheezing, cough, chest noise, and fast or difficult breathing (Pachter et al. 2002). Particular to Puerto Ricans in the Hartford, Connecticut, sample, however, was reference to symptoms such as chest pain; decreased activity; increased blood pressure; chest congestion; fast heartbeat; red, tired, or dark eyes; and difficulty breathing or talking to describe asthma attacks. Because these latter symptoms were peculiar to one group, they cannot be considered part of a pan-Latino cultural complex. Rather, they are core elements of only a Puerto Rican cultural conception of asthma. Failure to understand this kind of information can lead to public health efforts that are overly generalized and thus fail to be effective with specific populations, such as Spanish-language prevention materials that assume that the term "asthma" means the same thing to all Latinos.

### Doing Diaries

Diaries commonly are thought of as very personal records of one's thoughts, feelings, experiences, and relationships, but they have been drafted into the study of health as well. Researchers studying issues such as drinking behavior, food intake, and sexual risk have employed diaries as a means of getting insider descriptions of behaviors and experiences as soon after they occur as possible (when memories are at their best). In a study of access to sterile syringes, for example, a team of medical anthropologists, epidemiologists, and other researchers recruited a small sample of active illicit-drug injectors in three cities in New England to record their acquisition, use, and discard of syringes in a daily diary. For example, one of the participants in the study recorded the following information in his diary:

[Thursday] 4-13-00 Went to cop [acquire drugs] last night, nobody was around. So we went all over and found some [drugs] finally. Me and John used that one needle I have. It's really messed up. But after 20 minutes of trying he shot me with 3 bags [injected me with the drugs from three small plastic bags]. He then used my works [syringe]. He didn't clean them or anything. My works are bad. The tip is all bent.

Fri. April 14th. The works wouldn't draw up the dope so we were going to put some cream on the black tip [the syringe plunger] so it wouldn't jam up and [would] slide easier. We continued to have the problem of the works not drawing up. They'd start sucking up the dope then would stop. Finally it sucked everything from the spoon and he hit [injected] me . . . the works are in bad shape. So it takes him longer to get it in the vain [vein]. But he finally did then we shared spoon and cotton [to filter the drug mixture] and works and he did himself next which took a while too because the shape of the needle. It has a burr in it. But we did it.

Through accounts of this sort, the study (Stopka et al. 2004) found that drug users' diaries elucidated useful information on (1) daily patterns of injection drug use, (2) the social contexts of high-risk events, (3) HIV and hepatitis risk related to the street life cycle of a syringe, and (4) emotional correlates of drug use. Furthermore, the study discovered an unexpected intervention effect that keeping a diary may have in the lives of drug users: a number of the individuals who kept diaries approached the researchers seeking help. Being pushed into paying closer attention to the impact of drugs and the frequency of risk in their lives, they decided to get into drug treatment. Assistance into treatment was readily provided. In his work with AIDS prevention among drug users in Miami, Brian Page has found that regular and detailed interviewing about risk behavior can have the same effect. As these examples show, medical anthropology research itself can offer a form of intervention or serve as a model for new intervention approaches in public health.

## Quantitative Methods

In addition to these qualitative research strategies, medical anthropologists use various quantitative techniques, such as the surveys Kendall (1998) used to assess people's beliefs about dengue in Honduras described in chapter 1. Qualitative methods can be used, in fact, to improve the quality of quantitative data. In their research in Brazil, for example, Nations and Amaral (1991) conducted 118 interviews with parents of dead or dying children in three impoverished communities. She learned that official death statistics were faulty because they include only deaths that are recorded at government-authorized sites, which provide people with a material incentive to report deaths. Because reporting a death may require multiple trips to the city and the services of a physician to determine the cause of death and, further, because the death of a child will mean the loss of government milk, food supplements, and other benefits, children's deaths often go unreported. Quantitative approaches add breadth to the number and range of people included in a research sample and allow the use of various analytic techniques to assess both the frequency of a behavior or other items of interest and their association with numerous other factors.

## Broader Collaboration

Medical anthropologists now collaborate with a broad range of other types of researchers. For example, a number of medical anthropologists work with laboratory scientists and collect biological specimens, such as the urine samples described in chapter 1 that were collected by Thomas Arcury and co-workers (2005) among farmworkers to test for pesticide exposure. Similarly, Merrill Singer and his colleagues (2001) in their study of AIDS risk collected the syringes discarded in abandoned buildings or other sites by injection drug users to test for the presence of antibodies for HIV (to demonstrate the risk to drug users of using other's syringes) and, in a different study (M. Singer et al. 2005), used urine testing to determine the content of a popular youth drug of uncertain composition known on the street as "dust" or "wet." In both cases, the medical anthropologists involved teamed up with laboratory scientists who could analyze the sample. As a result, the relative riskiness of discarded syringes and the content of the drug of concern was clarified. Multidisciplinary collaboration of this sort is becoming increasingly common in medical anthropology.

As the global health impacts of climate change have become increasingly clear (Baer and Singer 2009), medical anthropologists have begun to collaborate with climate scientists, health care professionals, community activists, and other concerned individuals. Exemplary is the formation in 2010 of the Northeastern Climate Change Action Research and Education Project (NCARE) at the University of Connecticut. This initiative unites medical anthropologists and other social scientists with a diverse array of climate researchers, scientists, biologists, and other scholars in seeking to increase policy maker, opinion leader, citizen, and student understanding of the habitat, food production, health, and other adverse impacts of climate change.

## MEDICAL ANTHROPOLOGY IN USE

### Mobilizing Research Findings

Beyond research, medical anthropologists commonly are concerned with application, that is, with the practical use of their research-gained knowledge and experience-gained skills. Thus, Bluebond-Langner (1996) not only conducted research on cystic fibrosis but also used her findings to develop a set of guidelines designed to assist physicians in working with families with sufferers of the disease. Similarly, Kendall (1998) used his findings on dengue to help develop programs to prevent people from contracting this painful disease. Spradley's (1970) findings on urban nomads were mobilized in a successful effort to change city policies on the handling of public inebriation, while Katz's (1999) work helped the surgery department of a hospital address a pressing training need of surgery residents. As these examples show (and a very long list of additional examples could be cited), medical anthropology is not isolated in the ivory tower of academia. It is being used daily in numerous places around the world, from the most remote villages to the largest and most technologically advanced megalopolises, to address health-related problems of many kinds, such as community nutrition education (Figure 2.1). Very likely, there is a medical anthropologist working in the city or town where you live (or at least nearby), attempting to use anthropological skills to address real-world health problems.

### Managing Intervention

Not all of applied medical anthropology, however, is a post hoc product of a research project. Medical anthropologists also design and oversee intervention programs, evaluate the effectiveness of programs, and are involved in helping to establish and use ethical standards in health care decision making. For example, working with colleagues within and beyond anthropology, Robert Trotter (1996) designed a program to prevent the spread of AIDS among drug users in Flagstaff, Arizona. In this work, his team faced a number

FIGURE 2.1
Dietician speaking about healthy eating at a community health
education program organized by medical anthropologists and
colleagues. Photo by Merrill Singer.

of challenges. Among these was the fact that there were no obvious locations
where drug users gather to acquire and use drugs. Unlike other cities where
distinct "hot spots" of drug-related activity are detectable on street corners or
other locations—which then can be targeted by public health programs for
intensive outreach and AIDS prevention education—in Flagstaff there is little
or no open drug buying, and drug dealers often deliver their illicit products
to the homes of their customers. Consequently, Trotter and his colleagues focused instead on the social networks of drug users. Research in various places
has shown that drug user networks, possibly containing dozens (or even

hundreds) of people who have somewhat regular contact, share information and resources, including drugs.

Participants for the Flagstaff intervention were recruited through their social networks. For the intervention, identified members of the same network were brought together to conduct group problem solving related to HIV risk, to assist members in developing a clearly articulated set of shared prevention-relevant behavioral norms, and to motivate the group to take action to protect itself (and hence individual group members) from HIV infection. Importantly, these researchers found that their network approach was more effective in lowering HIV risk than was a standard individually oriented model of HIV risk reduction that has been implemented all over the country. In particular, while the standard model of risk reduction with injection drug users has been successful in lowering the frequency of drug-related risk, it has been far less successful in decreasing sexual risks for infection. This is of importance because, although the multiperson use of drug injection equipment is the primary route of infection among drug users, in recent years sexual risk has been shown to be a critical source of infection in drug-using populations. The Flagstaff network model—which actually brought together groups of people that included various kinds of sexual partners (e.g., casual and long term)—succeeded in producing a significant level of sexual risk reduction. Designing, operating, and evaluating disease prevention programs like the one in Flagstaff exemplifies a type of applied work that is common in medical anthropology as a discipline in action.

The value of medical anthropological focus on social networks in the AIDS pandemic (as opposed to one-on-one prevention education models that focus on individuals) is also seen in the work of Robert Thornton (2008) in sub-Saharan Africa. Thornton is particularly focused on sexual networks, which he notes are invisible even to the people who participate in them (in that people know who they have had sex with but not all of the people their partners have had sex with, and certainly not all of the people their partners' partners have had sex with). Thus, he refers to sexual networks as *unimagined communities*. Yet, in sub-Saharan Africa, where sex is the dominant route of HIV transmission, sexual networks are absolutely critical to whom, to where, and to how quickly HIV spreads. Indeed, it is Thornton's view that is precisely because they focus on individuals and not on sexual networks that AIDS education campaigns have little effect in slowing the epidemic in many places. The AIDS prevention effort in Uganda, where Thornton has done research, was comparatively successful, by contrast, because the population is largely rural and dispersed, socially segmented by class, ethnicity, and religion, and not particularly mobile. Moreover, the country was hit early and hard by AIDS. Notes Thorton (2008:231): "All of these factors had the effect of eliminating links between clusters of previously sexually linked people, and the whole [sexual] network collapsed. HIV was no longer transmitted efficiently thoughout the network, and HIV prevalence fell dramatically." Based on his analysis of the AIDS epidemic in Uganda and South Africa, and the behaviors that occur in sexual networks that promote the spread of HIV, Thornton concluded that effective HIV/AIDS prevention should (1) encourage people to limit themselves to one sexual partner at a time (as having concurrent sexual partners with people who also have multiple concurrent sexual partners facilitates the rapid spread of the epidemic), (2) promote the idea that at the end of a sexual relationship people should refrain from having new sexual partners for at least one month (because people are most likely to infect others in the first month or so after they become infected), and (3) uphold the idea that people should avoid sex when traveling away from home (which would slow the ability of the virus to jump to new areas). These recommendations, based on ethnographic research in the frontlines of the pandemic, hold promise for disrupting HIV sexual transmission across sexual social networks and significantly slowing the spread of the disease.

## THE MEDICAL ANTHROPOLOGY CRYSTAL BALL

What is the future of medical anthropology? Where is the field going? How might it change over the coming decades? As jocosely summarized by Danish physicist Niels Bohr: "Prediction is very difficult, especially if it's about the future." One thing, however, is clear: as Nancy Scheper-Hughes and Margaret Lock (1987) have argued, it is a fallacy to believe we will discover a narrow biotechnological salvation to the many health and social problems faced by humankind in light of the critical importance of the social structural and cultural aspects of the human condition, a factor that will likely lead to increasing demand for the input of medical anthropologists. Without question, medical anthropology also will be shaped by the social and physical worlds of the future. That future, as Yogi Berra once quipped, "ain't what it used to be." This is particularly true with reference to health. One of the reasons is because of the impact of *ecobiosocial* changes taking place on planet Earth. A second reason has to do with the configuration of the social worlds we are constructing. As a result of these changes, in addition to many of the current areas of focus, medical anthropologists of tomorrow will be progressively more concerned with issues such as the following:

- The far-reaching and increasingly faster pace of globalism, which facilitates the global spread of diseases around the world (e.g., the SARS epidemic in 2003 and the H1N1 influenza pandemic six years later) and restructures local social contexts and ways of life, creates significant health effects. One critical factor in this regard is what have been termed "killer commodities," that is, products sold for a profit that cause harm to consumers. Linked to killer commodities is the growing rate of dumping in underdeveloped countries of damaged, used-up, and otherwise discarded consumer products by the developed world.

- Anthropogenic climate change has multiple and diverse impacts on the environment. At the same time, the earth is beset by multiple other forms of environmental degradation, including air pollution, depletion of edible ocean fish stocks, acid rain, loss of wetlands, pesticide and other chemical pollution, salinization of agricultural zones, ocean acidification, deforestation, and loss of biodiversity through extinctions. It is likely that over time a growing portion of the toll these changes take on human health will be due to *ecocrises interactions* that multiply adverse effects.

- Growing barriers to access to food or ways to produce it and potable water are already significant sources of disease and death in many parts of the world, and the impact of these factors on human health is likely to grow worse as a result of climate change, other anthropogenic environmental degradations, and displacements and disruptions of human communities.

- The level of threat from infectious disease in the twenty-first century affirms that our world is very different from what health experts in the not very distant past imagined it would be. Globally, infectious diseases today are a leading cause of death, even in highly developed nations. The rapid emergence of new and renewed pathogenic sources of human disease, including growing drug resistance among pathogenic microorganisms, has become a major threat to the future of human health.

- The adverse syndemic interaction of diseases, both acute and chronic, and somatic, emotional, and behavioral in nature, is intensifying the impact of diverse threats to health. While syndemics increasingly have come to be recognized as a significant aspect of the contemporary health profile, especially of impoverished, disadvantaged, marginalized, and oppressed populations, much remains to be learned about the nature of the interactions that occur among comorbid diseases and between adverse social conditions and patterns of disease clustering in affected populations.

- Global health increasingly will be shaped by the urbanization of the human population, including the rapid growth in size and number of megacities with more than ten million residents, including an ever-growing number of highly vulnerable, densely concentrated, underserved, and poorly housed marginalized peoples.
- The development of the "profitable body," associated biotechnologies, and tissue commodification (e.g., organ selling by the poor) are reshaping human health and the social distribution of suffering. At the same time, the global distribution of pharmaceutical drugs has led to the use of these substances in ways that go far beyond their intended or allowable purposes. In addition, the global pharmaceutical industry, in all of its activities, from bioprospecting and the commercialization and patenting of traditional medicines, to clinical trials in developing nations, to the operation in local environments of manufacturing plants, is having increasingly dramatic global health impacts.
- In coming years, mounting global tensions stemming from the growing demands of an expanding global population, unequal distribution of resources, and the dwindling availability of natural resources (e.g., peak oil extraction will occur during this century and then begin to decline), as well as climate change, are expected to intensify the frequency of war and group violence. Consequently, the level of carnage to be produced by future wars—including both the number of battlefield casualties caused by ever-enhanced armaments and the fact that modern warfare increasingly targets civilians through sexual crimes, community destruction, torture, mass displacements, malnutrition, and ethnocide, as well as through the spread of infectious diseases—is likely to set new historic records.

In short, as expressed by João Biehl and Amy Moran-Thomas (2009:282), "Continually adjusting itself to the reality of contemporary lives and worlds, the anthropological venture has the potential of art: to invoke neglected human possibilities and to expand the limits of understanding and imagination." At the same time, it has demonstrated its ability as an applied field to address pressing problems of human suffering in a world in which most of our afflictions involve a complex interface of sociocultural and biological factors, and in which social, economic, and political inequality are the primary forces threatening our species and our planet.

# 3

# Understanding Health, Illness, and Disease

I am interested in physical medicine because my father was. I am interested in medical research because I believe in it. I am interested in arthritis because I have it.

—*Bernard Baruch, New York Post, May 1, 1959*

This chapter addresses some of the core issues and questions of concern to medical anthropology. What does it mean to be healthy or sick and who determines a person's health status? What is the relationship of culture to "health," to "illness," to patterns of mortality? Is there a difference between having an illness and having a "disease"? What does cure mean? What are the varieties of "health care" and "healers" cross-culturally? In this chapter, we define key concepts and attempt to answer questions like those listed here. In this way, we further clarify the way medical anthropologists look at and respond to health problems in the communities they study and work in.

## CONCEPTIONS OF HEALTH AND ILLNESS

### Defining Terms

Medical anthropologists have devoted considerable energy to examining conceptions of health and illness cross-culturally. While "health" and "illness" are everyday terms, what do they actually mean? Like many words in common use, a closer examination shows they are often much more complex and much more loaded with cultural content than is at first evident.

The World Health Organization (WHO) (1978b) defines health as "not merely the absence of disease and infirmity but complete physical, mental and social wellbeing." On further inspection, this definition is somewhat utopian and akin to the notion of wellness associated with the holistic health and New Age movements. It is unlikely that many people in the world would be found healthy in terms of these kinds of definitions. From a neo-Marxian perspective, Sander Kelman (1975) makes a distinction between "experiential health" and "functional health." Whereas the former may be likened to the notion of wellness or the sense that one can achieve great feats and yet experience a sense of tranquility and fulfillment, the latter is what employers expect from their workers to ensure performance levels essential to capitalist production or perhaps what professors expect from their students in showing up for classes and examinations. From this perspective, even though employees or students may not quite feel like going to work or showing up for a 9:00 A.M. lecture, they are functionally healthy if they do so, even if it requires one or more cups of coffee or other stimulants. By contrast to the functional definition of health, critical medical anthropologists define health in terms of access to and control over the basic material and nonmaterial resources that sustain and promote life at a high level of satisfaction. Whatever one's perspective, it is evident that health is an elastic condition that must be considered within an encompassing sociocultural and historical context.

The terms "disease," "illness," "ill health," and "sickness" are often used interchangeably in everyday speech, but much ink has been spilled trying to use them as technical terms with specific meanings. Biomedicine has often depicted "disease" as a maladaptive state, particularly in terms of the environment. For example, long ago, William White, in *The Meaning of Disease* (1926), wrote,

> Disease can only be that state of the organism that for the time being, at least, is fighting a losing game whether the battle be with temperature, water, microorganisms, disappointment or what not. In any instance, it may be visualized as the reaction of the organism to some sort of energy impact, addition, or deprivation. (quoted in Clouser et al. 2004:92)

George Engel, who is often credited as having fathered the biopsychosocial approach in biomedicine, asserted in *Psychological Development in Health and Disease* (1962), "When adaptation or adjustment fail and the preexisting dynamic steady state is disrupted, then a state of disease may be said to exist until a new balance is restored which may again permit the effective interaction with the environment" (quoted in Clouser et al. 2004:92).

## Differentiating Disease and Illness

The meaning-centered perspective in medical anthropology posits a distinction between disease and illness, with the former constituting a natural entity that can be identified through various bodily signs, such as a high temperature, elevated blood pressure (Figure 3.1), or rapid heart rate, and (possibly but not always) a sense of physical and emotional discomfort on the part of a person (Kleinman 1980). The presence of a disease, in other words, is established through a diagnosis by a professional healer, like a physician of biomedicine. As Good (1994:53) emphasizes, a disease label (e.g., diabetes) is a unit for grouping and understanding why people get sick and specifying what condition they are suffering from. The recognized diseases of biomedicine are codified in the International Classification of Diseases (ICD) (World Health Organization 1978a). This catalog includes places for 999 distinct conditions. Influenza in its various forms, for example, occupies codes J10 to J12 (and their associated subcodes). The ICD is designed to be both "exhaustive—to include all conditions—and to ensure that no particular event of sickness will be classified under more than one code number" (Hahn 1995:18). In other words, as reflected in the ICD as well in the *Diagnostic and Statistical Manual of Mental Disorders* (American Psychiatric Association 2000), biomedicine conceptualizes diseases as (1) discrete entities (each disease, be it cholera or paranoia, is assumed to be an objective entity found in nature and not just a product of human attention) and (2) clinically identifiable and hence a boundable item in the world. Normal practice in biomedicine, whether in its diagnostic, research, or treatment capacities, is guided by the conceptualization of diseases as distinct, discrete, and disjunctive entities that exist (in theory) separate from other diseases and from the social groups and social contexts in which they are found at any point in time.

Illness, by contrast, as it is often used in medical anthropology, constitutes a cultural construction that can be identified only through interpretive activities or narratives. Illness is rooted in a culturally constituted explanatory model that seeks to clarify the source of distress and to outline a course of treatment to be pursued by both the healer and the patient. Sociologist David B. Morris (1998:22–23) provides us with a rather colorful definition of illness:

> Illness depends on relatively stable biological features—a cough in every culture uses the same muscles and respiratory organs—but it is also deeply historical, no less changing than the microbes that surround and interpenetrate us. Indeed, the country of the ill assumes the distinctive features of whatever nation or social group inhabits it.

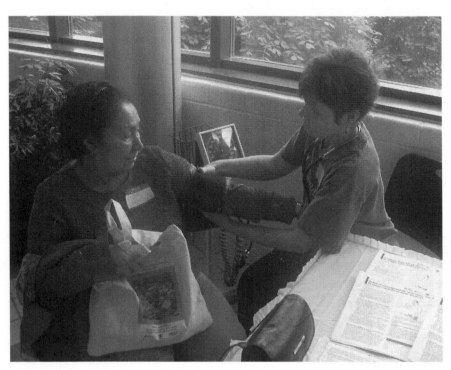

FIGURE 3.1
Screening for high blood pressure. Photo by Merrill Singer.

As Lambek (2003:2) comments, "One way to phrase the distinction between 'illness' and 'disease' [as these terms are used in medical anthropology] . . . would be to suggest that 'disease' refers to a literalization of phenomena whose experience is always culturally, socially, and psychologically mediated and hence open to interpretation ('illness')." By literalization, Lambek means treating the signs and symptoms of disease as direct, natural expressions of a malady (i.e., taking them literally) rather than expressions of a human body and mind that are shaped by culture, social context, and the emotional state of the patient, including such seemingly unambiguous bodily signs and symptoms as blood pressure, cell counts, or pain. From this understanding, diseases are no less cultural constructions than are illnesses, but the former are constructions accomplished by healers (i.e., diagnoses) and the latter by patients and their social support networks.

As a result, as discussed later in this chapter, healers and patients, such as the *curandera* (Hispanic folk healer) and her patient seen in Figure 3.2,

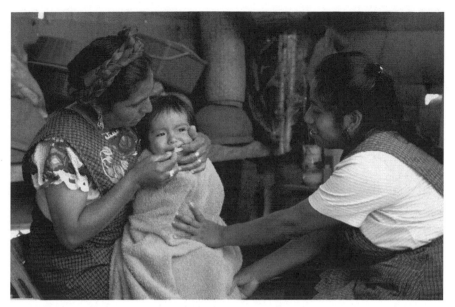

FIGURE 3.2
Maria Ruiz Mendoza, a Zapotec healer (*curandera*) from Teotitlán del Valle, Oaxaca, Mexico, treating a child for "anginas" with a tomatillo coated with salt. Photo by Liz Cartwright.

may reach different conclusions about the nature of a patient's health problem, with varying consequences for healer-patient communication and relationships and patient adherence to healer instructions. While there are always problems with negative definitions (i.e., X is the absence of Y), one way to think about health is that it is the absence of disease (i.e., a doctor finds that the individual is disease-free) and the individual does not feel ill.

### Reconceptualizing Disease and Illness

There has been a tendency in medical anthropology to use the term "disease" for the biomedical diagnosis of sickness and the term "illness" for both the folk healer's and the patient's definition of sickness. However, we suggest that the term "disease" refers to the diagnosis of a sickness made by a biomedical physician or some type of professionalized heterodox medical practitioner, such as an Ayurvedic physician in India or a chiropractor or naturopath in a Western society. Within this scheme, the term "folk disease" refers to the folk healers' label for a sickness, such as *susto*, a label used by *curanderos* in

Latin American cultures for the distress that a person may experience following a frightful experience.

Illness refers to the patient's experience of sickness. In reality, however, the boundaries between disease and illness are fluid, and both conceptions are cultural constructions rooted in both biological and psychosocial processes. Most diseases or illnesses ultimately are self-limiting for reasonably healthy individuals. Conversely, chronic diseases or illnesses exhibit a pattern of regressing to the mean; they wax and wane.

### Understanding Cure

Biomedical practitioners often ascribe "cures" on the part of either professionalized heterodox practitioners or folk healers to the placebo effect. Arthur K. Shapiro (1964:713), a psychiatrist, defines a placebo and the placebo effect as follows:

> A placebo is defined as any therapeutic procedure (or a component of any therapeutic procedure) which is given (1) deliberately to have an effect, or (2) unknowingly and has an effect on a symptom, syndrome, disease, or patient but which is also used as an adequate control in research. The placebo effect is defined as the changes produced by placebos.

In fact, as numerous studies have indicated, the placebo effect occurs within all medical systems, including biomedicine, as randomized double-blind tests on drugs have repeatedly demonstrated. This is something that at least some biomedical physicians recognize as is evidenced by Michael Balint, who recommended in his *The Doctor, the Patient, and Illness* (1957) that "all primary-care physicians in effect became psychotherapists, so to speak commandeering the placebo effect (placebo is Latin for 'I will please')" (quoted in Porter 1996:683).

Daniel Moerman delineates three human responses to injury or sickness: (1) autonomous responses, or "all those processes which the organism can invoke to gain health or equilibrium, including the various immunological and related systems"; (2) specific responses of the body to medical treatment, be it an administration of a medicinal herb or penicillin; and (3) meaning responses, or the "psychological and physiological effects of meaning in the treatment of illness" (Moerman 2001:14). The meaning response tends to encompass most situations that have been generally associated with the placebo effect, whether it is the cure that a patient experiences after taking a sugar pill or the impact of a healing ritual conducted by indigenous practitioners of the kinds that we discuss in the next chapter.

## Folk Understandings

Anthropologists have observed that peoples around the world operate with a wide array of definitions of health and illness, most of which tend to reflect core themes of their underlying culture or contact with other groups (Erickson 2008). The James Bay Cree, for example, a traditionally foraging society in subarctic Canada, view health (*miyupimaatisiun*) as a balanced relationship between individuals and their sociocultural and natural environments. According to Adelson (2003:617), among the Cree, health "implies proper hunting practices and hence a respectful relationship between humans and the animals of the land: a successful hunt means healthy eating and appropriate social relations means that the hunted foods will be apportioned amongst oneself and one's kin." Presumably, gathering activities (of, for instance, berries and other edible plants), conducted primarily by women, also enter into the James Cree conception of health, but Adelson does not address this matter in her account. The James Bay Cree operate with two broad categories of illness: those indigenous to their culture and those that they adopted (and adapted) as a result of their contact with European peoples. Half a world away from James Bay, the !Kung San of the Kalahari Desert in southwestern Africa interpret the ability to sweat as an indicator of good health since sweat is regarded to be a life-giving substance. The Matsigenka, a people in the upper Amazonian rain forest of southeastern Peru, a group with a mixed economy consisting of fishing, hunting, gathering, and horticulture, use the term *shinetagamtsi* to refer to a sense of contentment, productivity, being well fed, and freedom from illness. Jumping to yet another part of the world, the Tongans of Polynesia associate good health with *mana*, or endowment with supernatural power.

To cite one additional example, in their traditional culture, the Han, by far the numerically and politically dominant ethnic group in China, define health as a harmonious relationship between humans and the cosmos and among humans themselves. A healthy body is one in which Qi (a form of energy that permeates the universe), blood, vital essence, body fluid, and nutrients are in careful balance. An imbalance among these elements results in illness and may emanate from a wide array of factors, including wind, cold, heat, damp, dryness, fire, epidemics, emotional turmoil, improper foods, stress, physical injuries, parasites, and blood stagnation.

## Typologies of Ill Health

While numerous anthropologists have devised typologies (or classification systems) of folk categories of disease or illness, probably the most comprehensive of these was created by George Peter Murdock (1980), the inventor of the Human Relations Areas File—a repository of cultural data from around the world that anthropologists use to test cross-cultural hypotheses. Typologies can be based on various factors, such as beliefs about illness causation.

As they vary in their understandings of health, cultures also vary considerably in terms of what they regard to be the agents of disease. The Yanomamo, horticulturalists in the Amazon basin of Venezuela and Brazil, for example, believe that virtually all illnesses are caused by spirits or ghosts of their ancestors. Conversely, in the area where Spradley did his research with urban nomads, the Indians of the northwest coast identify several causes of disease, including soul loss, sorcery, taboo violation, disease-object intrusion into the body, and spirit intrusion. Table 3.1 summarizes many of the diverse theories of the causes of disease or illness (depending on whether a healer or a layperson makes the diagnosis) encountered by medical anthropologists in their research.

Beyond the alternatives listed in the table, many cultures around the world employ a "humoral system" of health and illness of one sort or other. A humoral medical system is organized around the premise that the organs, body systems, and fluids inside the body parallel elements and structures of the natural world outside the body.

For the ancient Greeks, for example, the bodily "humors" of phlegm, yellow bile, black bile, and blood were believed to reflect the natural elements of

**Table 3.1. Theories of Disease or Illness**

**Theories of natural causation**
    Infection
    Stress
    Organic deterioration
    Accident
    Overt human aggression

**Theories of supernatural causation**
    *Theories of mystical causation*
        Fate
        Ominous sensations
        Contagion
        Mystical retribution
    *Theories of animistic causation*
        Soul loss
        Spirit aggression
    *Theories of magical causation*
        Sorcery
        Witchcraft

air, water, earth, and fire, respectively. Maintaining good health, the ancient Greeks believed, depended on preserving a balance of the humors. When a person became ill, Greek healers would drain surplus humors by purging the digestive tract or through bloodletting. These therapies were believed to help restore a balance in the body's humors.

The three major humoral theories found in the world today are traditional Chinese healing, Ayurvedic medicine of South Asia, and the Latin American system, which has its historic roots in ancient Greek and other Mediterranean civilizations. Guatemalan Indians, for example, whose pre-Columbian beliefs were reshaped following colonial contact, generally acknowledge four causes of illness: natural injury such as snakebite, internal bodily imbalance, intrusion of pathogens, and witchcraft. Like other Latin American peoples, they believe that excessive consumption of "hot" foods (e.g., beans, beef, and chicken) or "cold" foods (e.g., corn, eggs, and oranges) can result in chills and coughing. The categories of "hot" and "cold" refer not necessarily to the actual physical temperature of a food or location but rather to its qualities and effects on the body, and the categories often vary from group to group in Latin America (G. Foster 1953).

Humoral systems are not the exclusive domain of peasant populations but also are found in various indigenous societies, such as the Melpa, a horticultural village people in the Mount Hagan area of Papua New Guinea. The Melpa humoral system includes three primary elements: (1) blood, which represents kinship ties through women and is associated with red ocher and red-colored foods; (2) grease, which takes the form of breast milk, semen, fat, the nurturant component of vegetables, and the fertility capacity of the soil and which may become depleted during pregnancy; and (3) a complex hot/cool/cold distinction (Strathern and Stewart 1999). In the last case, blood that becomes "hot" may dry up as a result of sorcery, whereas high altitudes are believed by the Melpa to be too "cold" to maintain life on a permanent basis. Blood and grease exist in finite supply and may become scarce, resulting in illness. The Melpa view blood and grease as analogues to wealth as they know it, including pigs, shells, and money.

Another indigenous people, the Tuareg, a pastoral group that makes its home in the Sahara and Sahel of West and North Africa, also subscribe to a complex distinction between "hot" and "cold," as Rassmussen (2004:1005) points out:

Conditions of "hot/cold" and associated afflictions are sometimes literal, sometimes non-literal or metaphorical in connotations, for example, "hot" illnesses (tuksi) are believed to be caused by too much heat, from "hot" foods (dates, tomatoes), sunlight, or moon-beams (these latter may cause illness from direct [contact or exposure], as in sun-stroke, or, alternately, by sitting on warm mats or from their reflections inside doorways). Tuksi may also result from anger and other strong sentiments. . . . "Cold" illnesses (tessmat) are the counterpart of "hot" illnesses. These include urinary tract problems and STDS.

### Humanizing Biomedicine

In addition to examining conceptions of health, illness, and disease in traditional cultures, medical anthropology examines these conceptions in modern societies. As part of this endeavor, various medical anthropologists have sought to humanize biomedical care by recording patients' illness narratives (their stories of their illness experiences, concerns, and reactions) so as to assist physicians to better understand their patients, their patients' views of illness, and their patients' experiences of being sick. In his 1988 book *The Illness Narrative*, Arthur Kleinman, for example, a prominent physician-anthropologist, seeks to persuade his colleagues within the corridors of biomedicine to listen closely to what their patients have to say, how they say it, and what they are trying to communicate. In other words, research in medical anthropology often has as its goal explication of sufferer experience, especially among those who suffer in silence because their voice is discounted by more powerful social groups or strata.

## SUFFERER EXPERIENCE

### Experience and Cultural Symbols

When Jerry, a gay man living in northeastern Ohio, learned he was infected with HIV, he was twenty-six years old. When he subsequently was interviewed by medical anthropologist Fred Bloom, he had been living with the infection for eleven years. He had remained relatively healthy during this period (diseased but not ill) until just about a year before he was interviewed. By that point, he had developed severe pain in his legs and a general decline in stamina, eventually forcing him to stop working. Still, he told Bloom (2001:43), "I'm a survivor, no matter what, y'know? I can make ends meet. I can get through anything. I guess maybe I get that from the streets, y'know? No matter what happens, you gotta keep going." A very different health-related experience was told to the late medical anthropologist Gay Becker (1994:396) by one of the participants, a thirty-five-year-old woman who was losing hope of ever having a child, in Becker's study of women and infertility:

My chances are getting smaller and smaller. It's like somebody has cancer and you say, "Well, you have a 20 percent chance that you will live"; and then go down to 10, and then to 5, and then you say, "You're not going to live, let's face it. You are going to die any day. Well, you just have to give up," and I guess that's where I am at now. . . . I really equate this with dying.

As these two contrastive "sufferer experiences" suggest, tension between retaining hope, which is often expressed in a militant commitment to struggle for health or to fight against disease, and losing hope, which, in this instance, is expressed by way of a spreading disease metaphor, is a common motif in the accounts of people facing illness in Western culture. In other societies, illness experience is shaped by quite different cultural symbols and metaphors. In parts of Latin America, for example, emotions are seen as powerful forces that not only can cause illnesses but become illnesses themselves. In northeastern Brazil, for example, the experience of having to suppress intense emotions, to avoid interpersonal conflict or social disruption, a behavioral event that is thought to be a common cause of illness, is expressed through the metaphor of swallowing frogs (*engolir sapos*). Thus, speaking of her relationship with a domineering and abusive man, one of the women medical anthropologist Linda Rebhun (1994:367) interviewed in her study of folk illness in Brazil told her,

I always had to swallow frogs, you know, because I was totally dependent on him. . . . Even when I knew I was right and he was unjust, I had to swallow it, I had to obey. I had to apologize, I had to humble myself and submit, and even thank him for mistreating me, in fear of my life.

In short, symptoms, as they are subjectively experienced and as they are talked about to others, are "a necessary condition for us to articulate a relationship to the world and to others" (Biehl and Moran-Thomas 2009:273).

### Cultural Emotions

Anthropologists use the term *subjectivity* as "a synonym for inner life processes and affective states" (Biehl and Moran-Thomas 2009:270). As the examples cited suggest, sickness, trauma, and other incidents of suffering are not narrowly individual experiential events. Rather, illness is experienced by the individual within the frameworks of culturally constructed worlds and commonly is articulated through emotionally charged cultural metaphors and themes. In this sense, culture is not just a cognitive system, something we use to experience, understand, and talk about the world; it is, in addition, an emotional system, something that shapes our feelings and thus motivates our actions. By encapsulating frightening or disruptive illness experiences in familiar and meaningful cultural frameworks, culturally generated metaphors "bind the past and future together . . . and give the appearance of coherence or 'return to the whole' when the metaphor is fulfilled. . . . Metaphors are tools for working with experience, as they embody the situational knowledge that constitutes culture" (G. Becker 1994:385). Use of metaphor, in short, is one of the ways pain, uncertainty, fear, and other physical and emotional challenges of illness are culturally managed and, to greater or lesser degree, tamed or even routed, as the case of Bloom's informant with HIV infection suggests. Indeed, as Singer and his colleagues found in their study of the experiences of illicit-drug users living with HIV infection, illness can even be experienced as salvation. As one of the participants in this study, a man who had lived with HIV disease for seven years, explained,

> The way I'm starting to look at it is that God got a plan to make you wake up and see things sometimes from this virus, to make you stop doing what you're doing [e.g., using drugs], killing yourself. . . . I guess He wanted me to stop suffering and start looking inside myself and He presented this virus to me and said, "Hey, this is it! You want to keep doing this and die, or do you want to live and look at life on life's terms?" And it worked. (Mosack et al. 2005:595)

Coming to view having HIV/AIDS as a "wake-up call" from God suggests the importance of cultural themes in individual sufferer experience. In this instance, the cultural themes mobilized by the sufferer are probably derived from Christian beliefs about individual agency and salvation through God's generosity. In this light, sufferer experience can be seen as a social product, even though individuals from the same complex society may experience the same disease in somewhat different ways. From the perspective of critical medical anthropology, sufferer experience emerges from the action arena situated between socially constituted categories of meaning. This includes finding culturally meaningful reasons why a person gets sick, such as "I failed to exercise enough," "I was exposed to a virus when she sneezed on me," "I could not stay away from drugs" (Figure 3.3), and the political-economic forces that shape daily life and thereby place individuals in harm's way, such as black lung disease among miners, malnutrition among children of the poor, or drug use among socially marginalized individuals.

In her highly acclaimed and controversial 1992 book *Death without Weeping: The Violence of Everyday Life in Brazil,* Nancy Scheper-Hughes presents a

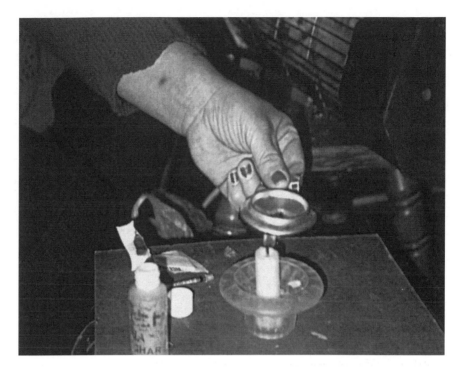

FIGURE 3.3
Drug user preparing drugs for injection. Photo by Robert Booth.

vivid and moving portrayal of human suffering in Bom Jesus, a dismally poor favela, or shantytown, in northeastern Brazil. She contends that the desperate and constant struggle for basic necessities in the community contributes to an indifference among mothers toward the weakest of their offspring. Scheper-Hughes recognizes that what mothers of deceased children in Bom Jesus have in common is intricately related to the collapse of the sugar plantation economy, which left many people in the region without even a subsistence income. While there has been local development, most of the residents of Bom Jesus have not benefited from the growth of agribusiness and the industrialization sponsored by both transnational corporations and the Brazilian state, resulting in inadequate diet and a high level of infant death. Maternal indifference to infant death, rather than the mournful response we expect of mothers who have lost a small child—much like the laughter over tragic events reported among the shantytown dwellers elsewhere in Brazil (Goldstein 2003)—can be understood only in a social context. Goldstein (2003:39), in recounting the death of a poor man named Zeca, who died a prolonged, painful death and whose corpse initially was put in a refrigerator in a butcher shop while awaiting burial, notes,

> After Zeca died, the family had to pull itself together to dress him for the burial, but it was difficult to do so because his body was so stiff. The final, even more grotesque aspect of the story was that Zeca had a little "hard-on," a detail that during each telling of the story [of his death] brought laughter to those who listened and remembered one more time the details of this tragic story. For Soneca [his sister] and the others who witnessed his death, there was nothing left to do but laugh. The laughter was mad and absurd, similar to the conditions under which they lived.

### Social Suffering

Suffering, in other words, is far from a narrow individual experience, and indeed much suffering in the world today is intimately connected to changes in the global capitalist economic system as these are played out and leave their effects on local physical and social settings and the people who inhabit them, including sparking rebellions against subjugation, some of which inflict considerable suffering of their own. Medical anthropologists use the term "social suffering" (Kleinman et al. 1997) to link individual experience of pain and distress to the wider social events and structural conditions that often are the ultimate sources of human misery. Social suffering, in other words, refers to the immediate personal experience of broad human problems caused by the cruel exercise of political and economic power, such as forced abortion, coerced sterilization, terror warfare (i.e., the use of physical brutality to break the will of the opposition in war), political rape (often used as a form of ethnic oppression), exploitation, and abject poverty, topics that have gained attention in medical anthropology in recent years. As Fassin and Rechtman (2009:25) point out, "The discovery of the painful memory is a major anthropological phenomenon of contemporary societies"; painful memories include *cultural trauma*, which are "wounds in the collective memory that contribute to the construction of identity in different social groups" (e.g., the trauma of slavery and the formation of African American identity, the trauma of the Holocaust and the construction of Jewish identity). In the analysis of the death of a Puerto Rican man in New York from the ravages of alcoholism, for example, we, together with our colleagues (M. Singer et al. 1992) sought to show the lines of connection between individual distress and disease and the colonial transformation of life and society on the island of Puerto Rico following the U.S. takeover in 1898; the subsequent dispossession of thousands of Puerto Rican farmers of their land as a result of federal taxation and the thirst of giant U.S. agricultural companies for choice farmlands on the island; the resulting survival migration of thousands of Puerto Ricans to the U.S. mainland, where they had citizenship imposed on them during World War I so that they might be drafted; the dashing of their hopes for a better life as the migrants encountered intense discrimination in housing, jobs, education, and everyday activities in their new home; the ensuing massive layoffs from factory jobs—one type of employment that, for a while, had been open to the migrants because of industry's ravenous need for labor—as owners moved production south or out of the country in search of ever-cheaper, more exploitable labor; and the consequent experience of hopelessness, worthlessness, and failure among the unemployed, including the Puerto Rican man whose life we studied.

The scale and depth of social suffering in the world can at times overwhelm our ability to fully comprehend it. As Chopp (1986:2) comments,

> Knowledge of suffering cannot be conveyed in pure facts and figures, reportings that objectify the suffering of countless persons. The horror of suffering is not only in its immensity but in the faces of the anonymous victims who have little voice, let alone rights, in history.

### Beyond Social Suffering

Yet sometimes, under the bleakest of conditions, there are lessons to learn about the nature of our species, insights that go beyond recognition of our capacity for rampant brutality. Carolyn Nordstrom (1998), for example, has studied resistance to terror warfare and the crafting of identities based on an embrace of such resistance among the people of Mozambique during the war of 1976 to 1992. Nordstrom (1998:108) captures the startling brutality of that war in the following description by Adriaan van Dis: "Thousands of children have seen their parents die before their eyes, hundreds of children have been boiled in the presence of their parents. Heads of old people have been used as stools by the bandits, unwilling farmers are nailed to trees." Despite this inhumanity, Nordstrom's (1998:113) field notes "show that the majority of conversations I had with Mozambicans during the war in one way or another reflected their preoccupation with both healing the wounds of war—physical, emotional, and social—and defusing the cultures of violence that war had wrought." These accounts and the heroic efforts they describe stand "as reminders that under the most extreme circumstances, the majority of people work to re-create a viable society, not to demolish it" (Nordstrom 1998:113). This too is a mission of medical anthropology.

### Disability and Chronic Illness

At the opening of this chapter, there is a quote from statesman and financier Bernard Baruch indicating that he became interested in arthritis when he became an arthritis patient. Similarly, the anthropologist Robert Murphy began his research on the issue of disability and being wheelchair-bound when cancer of the spine caused his legs to be paralyzed. On the basis of his experience and work in this area, he wrote a book titled *The Body Silent* (1987), which has become an important piece in the disability and chronic disease literatures.

### The Patient in the Body

Murphy focuses his book on the insider's experience: what it is like to be unable to walk, what it is like to be dependent on a wheelchair, and how this kind of loss is far more than a painful physical transition. In addition to the loss of the use of his legs, Murphy realized that he had lost an essential part of his sense of self. Despite strong social support from loved ones, he felt alone and isolated, a diminution of everything he used to be. At times, Murphy reported, he had a strong wish to withdraw from the world, to crawl in a hole and disappear, and to angrily mourn his loss of self. Additionally, he realized he felt embarrassment and a lowered sense of self-worth.

Before he was paralyzed, Murphy realized that he really did not see disabled people; he, like many people, had been practicing a kind of selective blindness when in the presence of a disabled person. This radically changed when he was the disabled one, as he became hypersensitive to the social position and social treatment of the disabled, including the common tension and awkwardness of personal interactions between the disabled and the able-bodied. Social scenes of this sort often lack clear-cut cultural guidelines about how to act, leaving people quite uncomfortable or in open distress. Murphy realized that people were giving him a wide berth and avoiding directly looking at him. He had begun to socially vanish. He also retreated from his own body; like many paralytics, he felt less and less attached to his own body, less that he was his body. He suffered, in short, not just a disease of the body but a disease of selfhood and a disease of social relationships.

As Murphy's poignant account makes vividly clear, disability is far more than a physical problem; rather, examination of disability, an issue that has engaged a number of medical anthropologists, raises important questions about the basis of selfhood as a culturally constructed yet often taken-for-granted attribute. Additionally, it raises difficult questions about the ways in which cultural expectations shape social interactions and social relationships while challenging conventional ideas about what being normal means.

## The Cultural Construction of Disability

An especially important figure in the anthropology of disability is Joan Ablon. In her various studies of disabled groups, Ablon (1992:10) has focused on "the daily insults which endanger their personal identity and self-image, their social life, their economic opportunities." In other words, she has been especially concerned with social exclusion associated with being disabled and how to overcome these barriers, including both those internalized by disabled people and those imposed by the able-bodied. In her well-known research with dwarfs, for example, Ablon (1984) has emphasized that the dwarf body is different but not disabled and that dwarfs experience themselves and their bodies as normal. In interactions with the wider society, however, they are subject to discrimination and frequent messages about abnormality. Increasingly in recent years, medical anthropologists have studied a growing range of disabilities and chronic health problems, including blindness (Ainlay 1989), deafness (G. Becker 1980), postpolio syndrome (Scheer and Luborsky 1991), and impairments of mobility (Luborsky 1995). In their work at the Philadelphia Geriatric Center, for example, Scheer and Luborsky found that the decisions people make about disability-related issues are infused with broader concerns about their identity and the fulfillment of personal and cultural expectations. People who survived polio, for example, often learned from their health care providers that they should forget about having had a bout with polio, put the past behind them, and move on with their lives. This attitude reflected a wider cultural orientation during the era that polio was prevalent. Veterans returning from World War II similarly were told to put their war experiences behind them and get on with their lives. Only in more recent years, both for people who survive polio, many of whom suffer disabling consequences of the disease later in life, and for many war veterans or others exposed to traumatic experiences, it has become clear that the past cannot always be left so easily behind. For polio survivors who suffer polio-related disabilities later in life, the early polio cultural expectations they learned and embraced can come back to haunt them as they encounter a new wave of functional losses many years after their initial bout with the disease.

**Stigmatization**

Another and related topic of concern to medical anthropologists is the process of health-related social stigmatization and the creation of what have been called socially "discredited selves" in which disease sufferers are blamed for their health problems. People with AIDS, for example, often are accused of being responsible for their illness through immoral or illegal behaviors. What medical anthropologists have found is that the experience of illness is far more than the exposure to physical symptoms. Fear of discrimination and stigmatization may prevent people from being tested or treated for HIV/AIDS infection. Rubel and Garro (1992), for example, found that fear of being diagnosed with a stigmatizing disease was a primary factor in why Mexican laborers in California waited an average of eight and a half months before going to see a doctor for symptoms that turned out to be tuberculosis. Similarly, in his study of breast cancer beliefs among Latina women in southern California, Chavez and coworkers (1999) found that about one-third of women who had immigrated from Mexico (but only about 10 percent of those from El Salvador) believed that God gives people breast cancer because they lived a "bad" life, such as using illegal drugs. Notably, various studies have shown that Latinas have comparatively lower rates of self-screening or mammogram screening for breast cancer and as a result tend to be diagnosed at a later and more life-threatening stage of disease development.

A major contribution of medical anthropology to the study of stigma has been in the examination of its local social construction cross-culturally and over time. As part of this work, medical anthropologists have examined the interface between local cultural beliefs and practices and stigmatization for a variety of diseases, such as leprosy and AIDS. Additionally, medical anthropologists have challenged approaches that limit the analysis of stigma to narrow cognitive explanations without regard to larger structural forces, such as the exercise of power, the existence of social conflicts, and the use of structural violence.

Additionally, by seeking to know sufferers directly, by striving to understand their experience and point of view, and by bridging the barriers that divide the well from the sick, the able-bodied from the disabled, and credible from discredited selfhoods, medical anthropologists are able to use this otherwise unobtainable information in developing needed recommendations or programs designed to minimize the many social harms attached to physical illness, including the damage done by stigmatization. In the case of the study of beliefs about breast cancer among Latinas, Chavez and his colleagues used the information they gathered to design a culturally appropriate intervention aimed at improving Latinas' knowledge about and attitudes toward breast cancer as a means of increasing their use of breast self-examination and mammography. In developing their program, these applied researchers "felt that it was imperative to incorporate the Latinas' beliefs into the intervention rather than dismissing them as silly or folkloric" (Chavez et al. 1999:133). Consequently, as part of the intervention, a cancer educator led a guided, nonjudgmental discussion of intervention participants about their beliefs and attitudes concerning breast cancer that in turn led to a discussion of possible steps to improve screening for the disease as well as other subsequent intervention components. Outcomes with a sample of eighty-eight Latina women, in which fifty-one were assigned to the culturally appropriate intervention and thirty-seven to a control group, found that the culturally based intervention was associated with greater increases in knowledge about breast cancer and a significant lowering of stigmatizing beliefs about the disease compared to the control group.

### Nonstigmatization

Disability is not always stigmatized; sometimes it is culturally rewarded. In rural Korea, for example, some blind men are accorded special status. They are believed to have the power of *pongsa*, a special ability to tell the future, select optimal building and grave sites, bring rain through prayer, and place damaging curses on one's enemies. These men are believed to have their physical ability to see replaced by an "eyesight of the mind" that transcends material limitations, time, and space. Parallels to *pongsa* can be found in other societies as well, such as the tendency of blind people in some cultural settings to become religious scholars, storytellers, or other kinds of public entertainers. In other words, whatever the physical or other impairment, there is tremendous variability in the cultural construction of disability.

### Human Rights and Health

The issue of suffering—and medical anthropological approaches to it—raises an important issue of urgent concern within contemporary anthropology, namely, the discipline's approach to human rights, including its stance toward the notion of health as a human right. Since just after World War II, anthropology has struggled with this issue. This chapter in the history of the discipline opened with the "Statement on Human Rights" written by Melville Herskovits and thereafter adopted by the American Anthropological Association's Executive Board (American Anthropological Association 1947) as a reflection of the discipline's initial perspective on this issue of global concern.

The statement was drafted as part of an international effort led by the United Nations to craft what would eventually be called the Universal Declaration of Human Rights. The latter was intended to serve, in the grisly shadow of Nazi atrocities, as a collective affirmation of global respect for human dignity and inalienable liberties. Specifically, Herskovits, as an internationally known anthropologist, was asked by the UN Educational, Scientific, and Cultural Organization to bring cross-cultural anthropological insight to the task of establishing an agreed-on bedrock of universal moral imperatives concerning human rights and justice. Instead, reflecting an important theme within the discipline, Herskovits rebuffed the idea that anthropology could contribute to this effort on three grounds: (1) the conception of rights and morality varies considerably cross-culturally; (2) as a science of culture, anthropology does not make normative judgments about particular cultural practices, an approach the discipline deems ethnocentric; and (3) in use, a universal declaration can be used to justify sanctions against a society acting within the boundaries of its own culturally constructed moral system.

While this approach was formally adopted by the American Anthropological Association, it never won universal agreement even among American anthropologists, especially in terms of the application of anthropology in addressing social issues. As Micaela di Leonardo (1998) and others (Rylko-Bauer et al. 2006) have pointed out, anthropologists long have been active in various social justice and human rights movements, including the fight against McCarthyism, the civil rights movement, the debunking of racism, the environmental movement, the women's movement, and the struggle to gain acceptance of health as a human right. These efforts ultimately challenge the finality of Herskovits's stance while, for the most part, recognizing the importance of being alert to his cautions and accepting anthropology as an objective, scientific discipline. The foundation of this challenge is that (rigorous scientific) anthropology can make important contributions to lessening human suffering and that moral detachment in the face of suffering is not neutral; rather, it helps sustain suffering in the world. Silence, as they say, can speak louder than words.

In recent years, as Goodale (2006:2) points out, the moral compass has swung away from Herskovits's position to the point that at least some anthropologists now believe that in a world of exploitation and suffering, "only anthropological knowledge that is politically instrumental is worth pursuing." More broadly, at the turn of the twenty-first century, the American Anthropological Association (1999), in accepting that anthropology in use involves the application of scientific skills and knowledge to the solution of immediate human problems, adopted its Declaration on Anthropology and Human Rights, which unambiguously rejected Herskovits's position. According to this document,

> Anthropology as a profession is committed to the promotion and protection of the right of people and peoples everywhere to the full realization of their humanity, which is to say their capacity for culture. When any culture or society denies or permits the denial of such opportunity to any of its own members or others, the American Anthropological Association has an ethical responsibility to protest and oppose such deprivation. This implies starting from the base line of the Universal Declaration of Human Rights and associated implementing international legislation, but also expanding the definition of human rights to include areas not necessarily addressed by international law. These areas include collective as well as individual rights, cultural, social, and economic development, and a clean and safe environment.

This statement well reflects a broadly held view within contemporary applied medical anthropology that it is possible to "create knowledge that is at once empirically grounded, theoretically valuable, and contributes to the ongoing struggle for greater justice" (Speed 2006:75).

The issue of social suffering stemming from structural inequalities or human conflict and the problem of hindered and unequal access to quality health care are natural entry points for medical anthropology into the issue of human rights. Today, a struggle is being waged by health and human rights activists to gain global acceptance of health/health care as a human right. Medical anthropologists have a wealth of data corroborating the suffering associated with lack of health and health care internationally. In the view of many people within the discipline, medical anthropologists have a moral responsibility to use medical anthropology knowledge to promote health as a human right in order to reduce suffering in the world and improve access and availability of quality health care for everyone.

Among the infamous "human wrongs" for which the twentieth century will forever be marked is that of *genocide/ethnocide.* The link that some have described between globalism and genocide raises it as a critical human rights issue for the twenty-first century. In response to such calamity, medical anthropologists are in a position to contribute to the establishment of universal health care, safe and sustainable living environments, freedom from poverty, access to adequate diets and clean water, and protection from physical and structural violence as inalienable human rights with significant health implications. As Paul Farmer (2004:245–46) asserts:

Utopian ideals are the bedrock of human rights. By arguing that we must set standards high, we must also argue for redistribution of some of the world's vast wealth. . . . Claims that we live in a world of limited resources fail to mention that these resources happen to be less limited now than ever before in human history. . . . [I]t is time to take health rights as seriously as other human rights, and . . . stand side by the side of those who suffer most from an increasingly harsh "new world order."

## ILLNESS NARRATIVES

Personal accounts of illness experience, like the "swallowing the frog" example cited previously, are called illness narratives, and they have become an important subject of research in medical anthropology. Telling stories about life is a central human social activity around the world (and often a prized one), with good storytellers being socially rewarded. Narrative has been defined as "a discourse featuring human adventures and sufferings connecting motives, acts, and consequences in causal chains" (Mattingly 1998:275). In other words, as contrasted with other kinds of talking, a narrative is a story about a specific event or a set of linked events in which the actors perform specific behaviors with socially meaningful outcomes. Narratives need not be full, elaborate stories with a moral, and they may be embedded in the course of other kinds of talk. In the case of illness narratives, expressing feelings and recalling actions around a particular illness form the core elements.

### The Social Uses of Narration

Illness narratives have been interpreted by medical anthropologists and others in several different ways, including as a common way "by which people organize, display and work through experiences" (Rubinstein 1995:259). Notes Gee (1985:11), "Probably the primary way human beings make sense of their experience is by casting it in narrative form." This form, in addition, often "affixes blame and assigns responsibility" (Mattingly 1998:286), thereby setting moral boundaries around what is acceptable and what is unacceptable behavior from the perspective of societal members and pointing to a course of action. In this, narratives may be future oriented. In medical anthropologist Laurie Price's (1987:315) apt phrase, based on her field work in Ecuador, hearing a narrative augments a listener's "fund of cultural knowledge" with which to confront future life challenges, including key cultural knowledge about symptoms of various illness, their course and causes, and beneficial responses. At the rise of the AIDS epidemic in Haiti, for example, narratives about individual cases helped Haitians come to grips with understanding this new threat to life by "providing the matrix within which nascent representations were anchored" (Farmer 1994:801). Moreover, writing about illness narratives in Turkey, medical anthropologist Byron Good (1994) asserts that narratives often point to the future to imagined ends our lives are intended to fulfill. In addition, as Cain (1991) showed in her study of the personal stories told at Alcoholics Anonymous meetings, narratives are a cultural mechanism people use to acquire or assert particular social identities and self-understandings.

**Analyzing Narrative**

Frank (1995) maintains that people who are suffering from significant illness tend to tell three kinds of stories. The first of these he calls "restitution narratives," a term he uses to refer to linear stories that begin with a serious illness and end with the restoration of health, often through medical intervention. Such stories affirm to listeners that illness need not be an end point: people recover. Such stories often are told to people when they are ill to help them maintain hope and good spirits. The second type of illness narrative Frank calls "chaos stories." These are filled with uncertainty, confusion, and a sense of powerlessness in the face of overwhelming forces, as seen in the spreading cancer and dropping survival chances mentioned by Gay Becker's informant or the statement made by the Nicaraguan boy Daniel, interviewed by James Quesada, that was presented in chapter 2. In yet another example of this narrative type, in the study of drug users living with HIV by Singer and colleagues, one of the participants stated,

> I can [tell] . . . my body is getting smaller, like something sucking me at like the neck, and everything is getting stringier and weaker, and I know this. And everything's showing, like my ribs and stuff, and the flab outside my face is gonna sink and I know this. (Mosak et al. 2005:597)

The final story type in Frank's typology is called the "quest narrative." Rather than return to health, as in the restitution narrative, in quest narratives a metamorphosis occurs. Rather than recover, the person advances to a higher or superior state of being. While the person may not always return to physical health, spiritually or morally illness delivers them to an elevated plane. New religions, in fact, often are started by individuals who have been sick but during their illness undergo a transformation, believe they have communicated with the supernatural, and never resume their prior identity but instead become missionaries for their new faith. Typical is Handsome Lake, a

Seneca Indian and alcoholic who lived at the turn of the eighteenth century. Lying in bed, deathly ill, Handsome Lake had a series of three transformative visions involving the receipt of messages from the Creator. These events led to the development of the Code of Handsome Lake, a religious doctrine for healing the Seneca people of the social and individual devastation wrought by colonial contact.

From an applied standpoint, M. Singer and coworkers (2001) use the narratives of street drug users to gain lessons for culturally appropriate AIDS prevention. They argue that analysis of the corpus of narratives they collected from street drug users holds three important lessons for confronting the AIDS epidemic in this highly vulnerable group. First, it is evident in the stories that acts of generosity and caring on the street are unexpected and that when they occur they are seen as especially welcomed surprises. As a result, these applied researchers maintain, programs that work with drug users should go out of their way to treat them with dignity, respect, and authentic concern. Second, drug user stories emphasize the survival value of always remaining wary of betrayal. Avoiding actions that can be construed (rightly or wrongly) as duplicity should be avoided to the degree possible. Finally, the narratives stress the skills and abilities of drug users, attributes that fly in the face of the usual way they are depicted in society, namely, as "losers," unproductive burdens, and threats to social tranquility and safety. Reversing the social message of denigration and worthlessness, by treating drug users as socially resourceful, knowledgeable, and goal-oriented individuals, offers promise of engaging them in health programs.

## EMBODIED HEALTH EXPERIENCE

Over the course of the past three decades or so, anthropologists, sociologists, and other scholars have turned their attention increasingly to historical and cross-cultural studies of conceptions of the human body and of embodied human experience (i.e., experiencing the world from within the confines of our bodies). The anthropology of the body, however, harkens back to French anthropologist Marcel Mauss's assertion that bodily sensations are mediated by culture and Maurice Merlau-Ponty's concept of "embodiment," which draws attention to how the body internalizes cultural meanings. Today, the body is a central focus of work being done under the banner of medical anthropology, and that focus includes embodied experience, such as the folk illnesses in which people "feel" invasive forces or beings in their body, representations of the body, and the actual cultural shaping of the body through decoration or tattoo or as a result of unintentional factors such as culturally constituted or structurally imposed diets that impact body size, shape, appearance, or health. Although the body is generally viewed as a biological entity, particularly within biomedical circles, it also in large part is a sociocultural construction. Further, the body functions as a vehicle for learning about our environment. In the view of many societies, perhaps particularly indigenous ones or peasant communities, it is an open system that links the self, society, nature, and spiritual world.

### Why Bodies?

In part, interest in the body is driven by recognition of its increasing fragmentation and commodification within the contexts of biomedicine and global economics. With reference to the former, Hahn and Kleinman (1983) argue that in diagnosing and treating sickness, biomedicine focuses on human biology, more specifically human physiology and even more specifically human pathophysiology. Hospital physicians often refer to patients as body parts based on the primary site of the patient's disease (e.g., the liver in room 327 or the kidney in room 783). Biomedicine tends to radically separate the body from the nonbody, although critiques of biomedicine in recent decades have prompted some biomedical physicians to turn to a biopsychosocial orientation and/or to embrace complementary and alternative therapies as well as to improve on their bedside manner by more actively touching patients.

Various social factors also have contributed to a growing interest in the body in the social sciences. Modern art, particularly as exemplified in the work of Picasso with his Cubist paintings depicting rectangular-shaped body parts, stimulated an awareness of the way the body has become fragmented in modern societies. The growth of a consumer culture with its emphasis on the cult of the body exemplified by cosmetics, fashion, and advertisements (as well as tattooing and piercing) also played an important role in enhanced focus on the body. At the same time, the feminist movement, particularly with respect to its emphasis on reproduction and sexual violence and the harmful effects of the objectification and manipulation of the female body, technological innovations associated with reproduction, and the replacement of bodily organs, as well as cosmetic surgeries like face-lifts and breast implants, all contributed increased focus on the body as the site of immediate human experience. Last but not least, the emergence of AIDS, a disease that can leave its cruel mark on the body (e.g., skin lesions and severe loss of weight), has contributed to a profound scholarly interest in the body.

## Body Theory

Michel Foucault, Pierre Bourdieu, and Bryan Turner are perhaps the three most important social theorists in recent times whose work has contributed to an enhanced appreciation of the role of the body in societal processes and the role of society in bodily attitudes and practices. Foucault argued that the transition from premodern to modern society entailed a shift from sovereign power to disciplinary power. Whereas in premodern society power, at least in the European context, resided in the body of the monarch, in modern society it resides in the bodies of diverse populations. Disciplinary power, which refers to the ways in which bodies are regulated, trained, maintained, and understood, is exerted particularly in schools, prisons, hospitals, and asylums. According to Foucault, disciplinary power is expressed by various instruments. One of these is an elaborate system of hierarchical observation and tracking designed in the form of a Panopticon in which officials can observe all "prisoners," normalizing judgments made particularly by teachers, physicians, social workers, psychologists, and health promoters and allowing a detailed comparison of the actions or attributes of individuals. An instrument of particular interest to the medical anthropologist is the physical examination or "clinical gaze" of biomedicine. Within the context of the clinic, the biomedical examination facilitates the categorization of diseases in terms of various symptoms, such as the patient's expressed experience of pain, and signs, such as pulse rate. Knowledge of the body translates into power over the body, or what Foucault called biopower, on the part of not only the physician but also the state he or she serves. For Foucault, biomedical knowledge is one of the several discourses by which modern populations are disciplined and controlled.

Pierre Bourdieu argued that the body as manifested through its shape, speech, and gait translates into physical capital, which, along with economic capital (e.g., money, wealth, and property), cultural capital (e.g., education and knowledge of arts and high culture), and symbolic capital (e.g., presentation of self), serves to influence an individual's position in the social hierarchy of a particular society. In other words, from Bourdieu's perspective, people experience the bodies of others and, in turn, may attempt to have their own bodies experienced by others in terms of various qualities, such as (1) being trim and fit as signs of having high self-esteem; (2) speaking "properly," such as what is termed "the King's English"; and (3) having good upright posture as an expression of confidence that conveys meaning about the character and social standing of the person being observed. This kind of body language, in fact, can speak louder than words in establishing a person's rights and entitlements, as seen in plays and movies such as *My Fair Lady* and *Pretty Woman*, in which a sweeping change in body qualities to what are deemed upper-class attributes allows access to social places and groups that had previously barred entrée.

Bryan Turner, in books such as *The Body and Society* (1984) and *Regulating Bodies* (1992), argues that modern communities have been moving toward a new "somatic society"—a social system in which the body constitutes a central field of political and cultural activity as exemplified by an emphasis on safe sex, sex education, free condoms, clean needles, pollution, healthy eating, proper amounts of exercise, and other physical concerns expressed by various social movements, particularly those focusing on feminist, abortion, fertility, and environmental issues.

### Bodies in the Age of Immunology

In his pioneering book *The Age of Immunology: Conceiving a Future in an Alienating World*, David Napier (2003) examines one of the important ways in which culture shapes the sufferer conception and experience of disease in bodily terms. It is Napier's thesis (2003:3) that "immunology as a cultural paradigm . . . has found its way into our lives, and the power of that way of seeing may be evidenced in various personal and professional domains, including—because they focus on 'well-being and its absence'—the medical sciences." Immunology, Napier argues, offers a paradigm (i.e., a particular way of understanding and experiencing "reality") that shapes how patients, doctors, and many others in and far beyond the health/healing domain think about their bodies but also about the world as well. Central to this paradigm is the notion that the world exists as two opposed categories: *self* (at the individual level: one's identity, body, internal organs, and at the social level: us, members of one family or social group, friends) and *not-self* (at the individual level: things that may intrude into my body and cause illness like infections, toxins, bad influences, drugs, and at the social level: them, outsiders, foreigners, enemies, terrorists). As Paul Stoller (2008:30) observes: "In the immunological age, the self/not-self opposition is fundamental. In this fundamental confrontation, selves become immune—safe—if and only if the dangerous not-self—bacteria, viruses, tumors, or radically different others—is either destroyed or neutralized." As a result, to take the example of cancer, doctors and patients (depicted as allies in the language of modern biomedicine) fight a internal war on cancer (which is portrayed as an invading not-self entity), complete with reconnaissance missions (X-rays and other technological weapons for internal imagining), incendiary bombing (radiation), search and

destroy missions (surgical removal of tumors), and use of biochemical warfare (chemotherapy), all of which are expected to produce a certain amount
of damage from friendly fire (i.e., killing cells that are part of self, not other).
As a result of exposure to this culturally constructed metaphoric world, "it is
not uncommon for . . . people . . . to think of malignant cells as alien invad-
ers that are completely separate from . . . [their] bodies" (Stoller 2008:34).
Stoller, himself a cancer patient, notes the statement of Ronald Reagan who
as president was diagnosed with cancer and after surgery commented, "I don't
have cancer. I have something inside of me that had cancer in it, and it was removed [namely a segment of his colon]" (quoted in Stoller 2008:34). Notably,
however, it is in fact the case that malignant cells are self; they are something
the patient's own body produces (although possibly upon exposure to pollutants or other toxins). But cancer sufferers tend to deny this fact because of the
pervasiveness of the cultural division of self and not-self, a theme that extends
far beyond the health of the individual body to debates about the health of the
social body (e.g., debates about immigration).

### Cyborg Bodies

   In modern societies, the boundaries between bodies and machines have
become increasingly blurred, as anyone knows who has watched people
engaged in nonstop video gaming, Internet chatting, cell-phone calling, or
listening to music through a headset. This is particularly exemplified in the
contemporary incarnation of cyborgs, mythical creatures that were half human and half animal or machine. Modern-day cyborgs include test-tube babies (assisted conception), people with organ transplants from other people
or animals, and people using artificial body parts as well as those who have
undergone plastic surgery or taken steroids. Various social forces, including
sports, dance, yoga, military training, construction work, computer work, social class, ethnicity, nationality, and gender, shape bodies. Within the context
of late capitalism, the commodified body functions as a site of production,
a source of labor power, a "baby machine," an object of sexual pleasure in
the form of prostitution or sex work, a supplier of transplanted body parts, a
source of beautification in the form of cosmetic surgery (e.g., nose jobs, face-
lifts, body tucks, liposuction, and the removal of the epicanthic fold in Asian
women), and a source of profit.

### Mindful Bodies

   Within anthropology and more specifically medical anthropology, Nancy
Scheper-Hughes, Margaret Lock, and Emily Martin in particular have made

major contributions to the scholarly study of the body. Lock and Scheper-Hughes point out that in addition to its array of anatomical features, such as a set of interrelated biological systems, the human body is mindful in that it is the site of individual experience, social expression, and the inscription of structural relations. On this basis, these researchers delineate what they refer to as the three bodies of concern to medical anthropology.

The first of these is the "individual body," which comprises the "lived experience of the body-self" (Lock and Scheper-Hughes 1996:45). While the notion of the individual body, conceived of as a separate and unique entity, driven by intention and will, is quite compatible with Western ideas about individualism, the Gahuku-Gama of Papua New Guinea conflate individual and social identity (Read 1955:276). In other words, they do not conceive of themselves as fully distinct individuals; rather, their identities are embedded in their roles and responsibilities as members of a social group. In such cases, the good of the group overwhelms personal interest or intention, and thoughts of oneself separate from the group are unsettling.

With reference to the individual body, an area of growing interest among medical anthropologists is the topic of organ transplantation. This operation, which often is seen as a pinnacle of biomedical skill and achievement, a "medical miracle," is of keen interest to medical anthropologists in part because it involves the crossing of traditional cultural and physical boundaries (e.g., the notion that body and self are intertwined and integral to each other) and the corporal mixing of "self" and "other" in ways that challenge cultural notions of personhood, personal property, the distinction between life and death, and what medical anthropologist Donald Joralemon (1995:347) has called "the intuitively unambiguous connection we feel to our bodies." Sharp (1995), for example, has written that undergoing such an operation, as a recipient, can be a personally transformative experience. Afterward, the individual's sense of self and self-worth often is changed. At the same time, Sharp documents a case of the family members of a deceased organ donor seeking out the recipients of their relative's transplanted organs, people they had come to think of as new kinsmen, a phenomenon that has begun to occur, as well, among the children of diverse mothers with a common sperm donor biological father. On the other side of the transplant operation, in the arena of organ procurement, especially in low-resource countries, the poor often are subject to exploitation and may be pressed to literally sell their body parts to survive, while large numbers of citizens in wealthy countries refuse to donate organs even at death. In her study in India, for example, medical anthropologist Patricia Marshall found that kidney donors were paid approximately $1,500 and that most used the money "to pay off debts incurred for wedding dowries and other types of loans," among other uses (Marshall and Daar 2000:213). In addition, at times, criminal elements in the procurement business have kidnapped individuals to steal transplantable organs such as kidneys for sale on the organ market. Indeed, a worldwide system that has been called "organ tourism" has emerged in which individuals from wealthier countries gain life by acquiring organs from the people of poor countries, a practice that some have interpreted as a veiled form of structural violence.

In a grisly turn of events in the world of organ transplant, over the past several decades more than fifteen thousand families in the United States have brought suit against funeral home employees, crematorium operators, and morgue workers claiming that body parts, from knees to skin, were harvested without consent from their deceased relatives and sold for profit. Police have found that entire bodies have been sold for tens of thousands of dollars, with elbows and hands fetching $850 each (Amour 2006). While the sale of body parts is illegal in the United States, the sheer demand has motivated the creation of a black market in transplantable organs and other body parts. From an anthropological perspective, this turn of events represents a further commoditization of human life and experience, namely, the transformation of objects, nature, emotions, relationships, indeed, ultimately everything, into salable products in the capitalist marketplace.

In their focus on individual bodies, medical anthropologists are especially concerned with sufferer experience, including what it feels like to be sick, how individuals invest and derive meaning from illness, and how illness impacts identity. In medical anthropology, sufferer experience is understood as a social product rather than a completely unique and individual occurrence. We get sick, so to speak, socially, and this is why we can identify cultural patterns in the symptoms people have and the ways they think about and act on those symptoms. Additionally, illness shapes and is shaped by social patterns.

The "social body," the second component of Lock and Scheper-Hughes's tripartite body, refers to representations of the body as a "natural symbol with which to think about nature, society, and culture" (Lock and Scheper-Hughes 1996:45). Indeed, one often hears expressions such as a "healthy society" or a "sick society" to refer to either societies with a high degree of social cohesion or societies with a high degree of fragmentation, as if societies could get illnesses the way bodies do. To a large degree, Lock and Scheper-Hughes note, talk about the body and sexuality tends to be talk about the nature of society and about socially acceptable standards of moral behavior. This assertion reflects a broader point made by Mary Douglas (1973:98) that "the human body is always treated as an image of society [and therefore] . . . there can be no natural way of considering the body that does not involve at the same time a social dimension." This point is well captured in a statement made by Richard Carmona, surgeon general of the United States, about the problem of obesity in the United States. Speaking at the University of South Carolina, he stated, "Obesity is the terror within. Unless we do something about it, the magnitude of the dilemma will dwarf 9-11 or any other terrorist attempt" (quoted in J. Harris 2006). Terrorism, by intent, is targeted at societies, not individuals per se. In likening obesity, a problem of individual bodies, to terrorism, a social threat, the surgeon general affirms our tendency to use the body as a symbol of society and vice versa, a pattern found around the world.

Finally, there is the "body politic," a concept that draws from the work of Foucault and that refers to the "regulation, surveillance, and control of bodies (individual and collective) in reproduction and sexuality, work, leisure, and sickness" (Lock and Scheper-Hughes 1996:45). With respect to biomedicine, Lock and Scheper-Hughes (1996:68) assert that a medicalized body is a "manifestation of potent, never settled, partially disguised political contests about how aging and rebellious bodies should be managed." In this regard, we are reminded of Rudolf Virchow's often-quoted statement that "politics is medicine on a grand scale." In looking at the body from the standpoint of political relations in society, health is a reflection of the hierarchy of relations in society, and medical anthropologists are mindful of the ways in which inequality, exploitation, and structural violence are recorded "under the skin" in the social distribution of health and in the patterning of biology across social classes and other lines of social difference. A nutrient-deficient diet, for example, is more likely to be found among the poor than among the wealthy in a society, and this difference is reflected in the actual formation of the teeth and bones of societal members.

Gender is another important arena of bodily social control. As contrasted with societies characterized by limitations on food availability, in which a plump figure often is seen as a sign of beauty, in modern America a slender, androgynous body has become a valued female physique. Expectations of thinness are reinforced heavily by the advertisement industry. Studies of magazine content have found high numbers of ads and articles about food, including recipes and accounts of the newest chic dishes. At the same time, magazines frequently give voice to social angst about obesity while exhibiting images of perfectly sculpted bodies attained through the use of exercise machines, workout routines, and an endless array of miracle diets. The cultural celebration of thinness and stigmatization of obesity are critical factors in the emergence of epidemic levels of food-related disorders, such as anorexia and bulimia, in U.S. society. Although eating pathologies have been a peculiarly Western and middle-class phenomena, in recent years they also have begun appearing in non-Western countries, as well as across socioeconomic classes, ethnicities, age-groups (including among the elderly), and even genders. Recent analysis has focused on the role of globalization and the diffusion of American or other Western images of the "ideal" body type as critical elements in the changing international face of eating disorders.

## Medicalization

The term "medicalization," mentioned in chapter 2, was introduced into anthropology from sociology and refers to the role of medicine in social control. Within medical anthropology, an issue of concern is the ever-creeping boundaries of problems defined as appropriate for medical intervention and hence medical social control. Lock (2003:117), with reference to the medical management of everyday life, notes:

> First, . . . emotions and sexuality become targets of medical technology, with the result that reproduction of populations and even of the species are medicalized. Similarly, other activities, including breastfeeding, hygiene, exercise, deportment, and numerous other aspects of daily life are medicalized—largely by means of public health initiatives and with the assistance of the popular media.

With some issues, such as substance abuse, medicalization may be less repressive than the alternatives, such a criminalization. Ironically, in the United States, during the very period that the National Institute on Drug Abuse, an arm of the National Institutes of Health, began declaring chemical addiction and dependence to be diseases of brain chemistry, involving a restructuring of neural pathways in response to exposure to drugs, the country continues to build many new prisons each year so that it can house the large number of individuals arrested for the possession of these substances. Alcoholism and alcohol dependence, by contrast, have been much more fully medicalized, and skid-row alcoholics, for example, are no longer arrested and incarcerated for public inebriation.

## Engendered Bodies

Much of the work on the anthropology of the body focuses on gender issues, including the cultural construction of gendered bodies, that is, bodies that are not just different biologically (e.g., sexual organs, roles in reproduction,

## UNDERSTANDING MEDICALIZATION

At the simplest level, medicalization means giving a condition or behavior a medical label, defining the problem in medical terms, and using a medical intervention to treat it. While many medical anthropologists now use the term, medicalization was coined by the influential sociologist Irving Zola. He pointed out that when a problem, such as overeating, is medicalized, there tends to be a reduction in the degree to which the disorder is stigmatized because other causes besides individual moral failings are ascribed, be they the consequence of pathogens or the effects of genetics. Conrad and Schneider (1980) called this process the transformation from "badness to sickness." At the same time, as conditions are medicalized, there is an ever-growing expansion of the jurisdiction of medicine over arenas of social life and experience. In that medicine is now highly commodified, medicalization also involves the medical marketing of profit-making commodities, such as menopause treatments, clinical weight-loss programs, sleep deprivation interventions, and smoking cessation initiatives. Theorists such as Ivan Illich (1975) have warned about the ways physicians are expanding their power over the public through what he calls "the medicalization of life." In recent times, there have emerged "demedicalization movements," such as the largely successful struggle to have homosexuality removed from the list of medically recognized psychopathologies. At the same time, as Lock (2003:123) points out, with "molecularization, geneticization, digitization, computerization, and globalization . . . the potential exists to make the body increasingly the site of control and modification, much of it carried out, in the West at least, in the name of individual rights or desires."

capacity to nurse infants) but are constructed as different within cultural frames and conceptions. In *The Woman in the Body*, for example, Martin (1989) asserts that the body in the United States is viewed through the cultural lens of a machine metaphor that emerged during the industrial era. Biomedicine, she maintains, treats women's reproduction of the social group by giving birth as a cultural form of factory production in which "uterus machines" produce babies with the physician managing this process. It also regards menstruation as a failed production process. Biomedicine also has treated the body as a passive object over which particularly women came to lose control, although the women's movement eventually challenged this trend.

In another case, in contrast to the anorexic-like female body that has become idealized in Western societies, Fijians, a Melanesian people in the South Pacific, value a well-proportioned, robust body (A. Becker 1994). They believe that such a body indicates that a person is capable of arduous labor and that he or she has been well nurtured.

A third example comes from the Mediterranean area, where, as Maria Olujic (1998:34) observes, women "represent the code of *honor* of the family and the code of shame via the blood revenge for nonfamily member's transgressions. . . . The honor/shame dichotomy is evident in the highly guarded aspects of women's virginity, chastity, marital virtue, and especially fertility."

As these examples indicate, cultures ensnare and diversely elaborate biological differences, with significant but different social and health implications for women and men.

## HEALER VERSUS SUFFERER CONCEPTION OF DISEASE

### The Two Sides of Compliance

As documented in many studies, patients do not always follow doctors' orders, a behavior that often is labeled "noncompliance" in biomedicine. But this finding is not peculiar to patients in biomedicine and has been documented for folk medical systems as well. In fact, studies have shown that doctors themselves often are out of compliance with existing standards of care. As Atul Gawande (2002:236), a physician, comments, "Physician compliance with various evidence-based guidelines ranges from over 80 percent of [cases] in some parts of the country to less than 20 percent in others." Supporting Gawande's assertion, a twelve-city U.S. study of medical care by Elizabeth McGlynn and coworkers (2003) found that patients received recommended care for their diagnosed health problem only 54.9 percent of the time, ranging from a high of 78.7 percent for senile cataract treatment to a low of 10.5 percent for the treatment of alcohol dependence, findings that led the researchers to conclude that the failures of clinical adherence pose significant threats to the health of the American public. Further, research by Jack Wennberg (1999) shows that how doctors handle the same diagnosis varies considerably; the likelihood, for example, that a patient with a gallbladder problem will be sent for surgical removal varies by 270 percent by city, and for a hip replacement the variance is 450 percent. Not only are physician decisions highly variable, but in a series of articles in the *Journal of the American Medical Association* by David Eddy (1990), a physician who studies clinical decision making, they have been described as often being arbitrary.

While medical anthropologists have not focused much of their attention on physician compliance with established medical procedures, they have been quite interested in patient behavior. In this, they have been quick to point out that an important component of illness behavior stems from the fact that patients are not blank slates waiting to be inscribed by their healers; rather, they have beliefs and ideas of their own. Illness, especially one with familiar symptoms, does not elicit an empty response; rather, sufferers and their significant others, including those in one's social network who are thought to have greater experience in handling health problems (e.g., grandmothers), commonly engage in folk diagnosis, and it is on the basis of such reflection that specific kinds of professional, folk, or popular treatment are sought. As medical anthropologist Susan Schrimshaw (2001:53) observes, "Health programs that fail to recognize and work with indigenous beliefs and practices also fail to reach their goals." A case in point is reported by Anne Sigfrid Grønseth of Tamil refugees living in Norway but from Sri Lanka, where they were used to being treated in the Ayurvedic medical tradition. Suffering from diffuse aches and pains in their body, the Tamil seek therapy from the local biomedical health care system. The experience, however, is often disappointing. As one of Grønseth's (2006:152) informants told her, "The problem is that Norwegian doctors only see my body and organs. They don't see my person. Very often doctors do nothing. We feel very uncertain." The problem in this instance is that Tamil think of their health problems in term of a humoral system of hot/cold balance. The failure of Norwegian physicians to address the imbalance, Tamil patients feel, makes them appear unconcerned and useless. As another of Grønseth's (2006:153) informants stated,

> I don't know how to explain. I only know that sometimes a sickness makes you too hot or too cold. So, you need to make food and use mixtures that will bring you back in balance. . . . When you visit a Tamil doctor you always get some pills, maybe herb mixtures and prescriptions for a diet. Sometimes the doctor give you advice for meditation and oils to used in massage. Here, the doctor doesn't want to know our problems and give no advice and no pills. They can't cure our difficulties.

### Insider and Outsider Assessments of Health Status

What do sufferers know, subjectively, about their health status, and how does sufferer knowledge compare to that of the healers who are treating them?

Several studies on this topic have produced interesting results. In a study in Denmark, Geest and coworkers (2004) asked 456 middle-aged individuals who subsequently had a health screening performed by their general practitioners to rate their health status on a five-item scale ranging from "very poor" to "excellent." In 68 percent of cases, doctors and their patients agreed about the patients' health status. In a U.S. study of noninstitutionalized elderly individuals, Ellen Idler and coworkers (1990) found that self-assessments of health were a better predictor of mortality than objective biomedical assessments. Similarly, Yelin et al. (1980) found that self-assessment is a superior predictor of return to work among individuals suffering from chronic pain than objective clinical or radiological test results, while Shadbolt and coworkers (2002:2514), based on a study among cancer patients, concluded that self-assessment "is valid, reliable, and responsive to change as a predictor of survival of advanced cancer." These findings are striking because traditionally biomedical physicians have tended to discount patient self-assessment as a source of information about patient health.

### One Word, Two Meanings

Another aspect of the sufferer versus healer conception of disease involves the existence of various disease names that mean one thing to sufferers and another to healers. For example, medical anthropologist Susan McCombie has studied a phenomenon she refers to as "folk flu." In her study in the American Southwest, she found that the word "flu" "does not mean the same thing to the epidemiologist that it does to the public, who include illnesses with a number of clinical presentations" (McCombie 1999:31). Importantly, McCombie found that the discrepancy between the health care system and lay sufferers in the meaning of the term "flu" is more than a matter of semantics because people think they have the flu when, from a biomedical perspective, they are suffering from a different disease, including giardiasis, viral hepatitis, and salmonella infection. Similarly, in a study in Washington, D.C., Merrill Singer and coworkers (1984) found that the folk illness "hypoglycemia" (low blood sugar) was fairly common, especially among middle-class women, who reported a range of symptoms. However, many physicians would agree and would find that the majority of those who believe they are sufferers of this affliction do not meet diagnostic requirements for the disease. While some physicians have suggested that underlying emotional problems are the real cause of widespread folk beliefs about hypoglycemia, those who believe themselves to suffer from the disease are critical of biomedicine's failure to understand this affliction and its victims. In this sense, hypoglycemia functions as an idiom of distress among middle-class women who think that their lived experience of suffering is not taken seriously by biomedicine.

As these examples show, even when patients and healers use the same disease labels, they may be, in effect, speaking different languages or, more precisely, marshaling different bodies of information and different understandings. The potential for provider-patient miscommunication in such cases is enormous. By exploring diagnostic labels and their meanings to the parties involved in a clinical encounter, medical anthropologists are in a position to help minimize this problem.

### Diseased but Not Ill

Given the definitions that have been offered for illness (as subjective experience) and disease (as objectively measured phenomenon), it is possible to have a disease but not feel ill. This disjuncture is quite common with diseases such as hypertension, which has been called "the silent killer"; the early stages of various cancers; and infectious diseases such as HIV/AIDS that generally do not produce many symptoms, although very early symptoms are often misinterpreted as the flu until sufferers have been infected for a number of years. In such cases, adherence to medical instructions is complicated by the fact that the patient feels fine and has difficulty believing they are suffering from a life-threatening disease. Conversely, it is possible for sufferers to feel quite ill but be told by their physicians that nothing is wrong (e.g., folk hypoglycemia) or that their problem is psychosomatic. In some cases, however, the real problem is that disease exists but is unknown to biomedicine. Chronic fatigue syndrome, for example, was producing misery among sufferers long before it was recognized as a bona fide disease by biomedicine. It was not until 1988 that the disease was recognized by the Centers for Disease Control and Prevention, although the term "myalgic encephalomyelitis" began appearing in the medical literature in 1938 and is still used today in some parts of the world, particularly in the United Kingdom, to label this disease. Even still, controversies about the disease, which was once derided as the "yuppie flu" and its sufferers mocked as "rich, whiny white women," continued until 1994 when an international panel of researchers was convened and a clearer definition of the disease developed to assist clinicians in making a diagnosis. Accepted signs of the disease, which afflicts about a million people in the United States, most of whom are neither rich nor white, include having a significant level of fatigue that has lasted for over six months and having four or more of the following motley array of symptoms: substantial impairment in short-term memory or concentration; sore throat; tender lymph nodes; muscle pain; multijoint pain without swelling or redness; headaches of a new type, pattern, or severity; unrefreshing sleep; and malaise lasting more than twenty-four hours following exercise. Like the definition for AIDS, there is no clear-cut indicator but rather a set of factors occurring together that definitively signals the presence of the disease. Complex diagnostic criteria such as these often are the source of communication problems between patients and physicians.

### Mismessaging

Another type of miscommunication that can occur is exemplified by findings in a study of HIV testing among drug users carried out by several medical anthropologists and in collaboration with researchers from other disciplines. In this project, the researchers offered oral HIV testing because it was far easier for participants and less risky for research staff in terms of accidental "sticks" with a syringe that had been used to draw blood from a participant who was HIV positive. In oral HIV testing, a small antibody collector that looks like a short-handle toothbrush is inserted for a short time between the inside cheek and gum of the participant. The collector does not capture the HIV virus (which does not tend to survive in the mouth) but rather draws out antibodies (if they are present) that the body produces to fight off infection. While HIV is not frequently transmitted orally (e.g., through kissing), it occurred to the researchers that being tested orally might convince participants that HIV could, in fact, be transmitted through oral contact. Subsequent interviews with individuals who had and had not been tested orally affirmed the researchers' suspicion. Those who had been tested orally were significantly more likely to believe that HIV could be transmitted through kissing, sharing a cup, or other types of oral contact (Clair et al. 2003). Why is this finding important? Does it matter if people think HIV can be transmitted in ways that are not in fact common routes of infection? If people believe that no matter what they do they are likely to get HIV, then they are less likely to follow any prevention strategy (e.g., using condoms). Consequently, it is critical that false beliefs about transmission be understood and corrected to increase the likelihood of adopting effective behaviors for preventing disease. Here again, medical anthropology, which generally sees understanding the insider's point of view as a topic of concern, can make a contribution to community health.

### Analyzing Health Discourse

This discussion of communication in the health domain suggests the growing importance of discourse analysis in medical anthropology. This type of study focuses on the communication (be it verbal or involving gestures, written texts, or electronic media) that takes place between people in the health domain, such as clinical conversations between doctors or other healers and their patients. In part, this work has focused on the ways health care providers and patients construct shared cultural worlds through conversation or other communication. Additionally, this kind of analysis has emphasized the ways that inequalities in access to knowledge shape health-related communication and help to undergird medical authority (Briggs 2005). Similarly, a keen interest to medical anthropologists involved in medical discourse analysis is the social origin and structural functions of the messages exchanged in clinical encounters. Thus, medical discourse may have as its effect "the creation and maintenance of the interests of certain hegemonic groups" (MacDonald 2002:464). Silences are also of importance. Consider the implications in a biomedical encounter in Australia as a provider attempts to record a patient's medical history and the patient happens to be a member of an Aboriginal community that culturally bans talking about one's past serious illnesses. Exploration of change is also essential, especially in the kind of fast-paced globalizing world that we all now inhabit. As Wilce (2009:209) reports, "Rooted in close analysis of dyadic clinical encounters and other forms of medical discourse, recent studies trace interactions between globally circulating discourse forms and local traditions that have constituted medical relationships, broadly construed."

# Ethnomedicine

## *The Worlds of Treatment and Healing*

Ch 4

Formerly, when religion was strong and science weak, men mistook magic for medicine; now, when science is strong and religion weak, men mistake medicine for magic.

—*Thomas Szasz, The Second Sin (1973)*

In the previous chapter, we examined conceptions and explanations of health, disease, and illness with which people around the world operate. In this chapter, we introduce the notion of ethnomedicine in order to demonstrate that all medical systems, be they national guises of biomedicine or indigenous medical systems or folk medical systems in complex societies, either preindustrial or postindustrial, are part and parcel of culture and society. We also discuss how various anthropologists have attempted to categorize medical systems. Finally, we introduce an evolutionary model of disease and healing systems drawing on the work of others that examines how various types of societies ranging from nomadic foraging to postmodern societies seek to explain the causes of illness as well as the categories healers use in order to identify and treat sickness.

## APPROACHING ETHNOMEDICINE

Historically, medical anthropologists have devoted considerable attention to the study of medical systems in indigenous or tribal societies, in peasant communities, and among subgroups of urbanites in developing nations. Even before the emergence of medical anthropology as a named area of specialization within anthropology, ethnographers recorded data about health beliefs and practices, including healing techniques, in indigenous societies. Medical systems in indigenous societies and peasant communities and among other ordinary peoples have often been defined within anthropology as "ethnomedicines." Charles Hughes (1978:151), a renowned medical anthropologist, defined ethnomedicine as "those beliefs and practices relating to disease which are the products of indigenous cultural development and are not explicitly derived from the conceptual system of modern medicine." However, many medical anthropologists since Hughes did his seminal work have noted that biomedicine also constitutes an ethnomedical system, one that has diffused from Western societies to many other societies around the world. Indeed, some medical anthropologists regarded "ethnomedicine" (Rubel and Hass 1996), along with "ethnopsychiatry" (Hughes 1996), "ethnobotany," or "ethnopharmacology" (Etkin 1996), as distinct subfields of medical anthropology.

Ethnographers, including those working in the anthropology of religion, have long been fascinated by the shaman, a part-time religious healer who makes contact with the supernatural realm, often by going into a trance, in order to alleviate the distresses and diseases of his or her patients. Others have been struck by the role of the modern biomedical physician, a healer with unparalleled technological resources for measuring, visualizing, and treating disease who still must deal face-to-face with a nervous patient in need of as much care as cure, such as the patient interacting with a podiatrist in Figure 4.1

In reality, all medical systems constitute ethnomedicines in that they developed from and are embedded in particular sociocultural systems, regardless of whether they are small-scale or state societies. In this sense, all healers, from shamans to cardiovascular surgeons, are ethnohealers, even though the latter have far transcended the boundaries of any single ethnic group or population because their orientation to healing is rooted in Western culture (Erickson 2008).

Moreover, as Lynn Payer (1988) notes in her highly entertaining and readable book *Medicine and Culture*, biomedicine is shaped by its specific cultural or national setting, as she found to be the case in France, Britain, Germany, and the United States. American biomedicine relies much more on invasive forms of therapy, including cesarean sections, hysterectomies, breast cancer screenings, bypass heart operations, and high dosages of psychotropic drugs, than does biomedicine in the other three countries. British physicians are less concerned about moderately elevated blood pressure and cholesterol counts

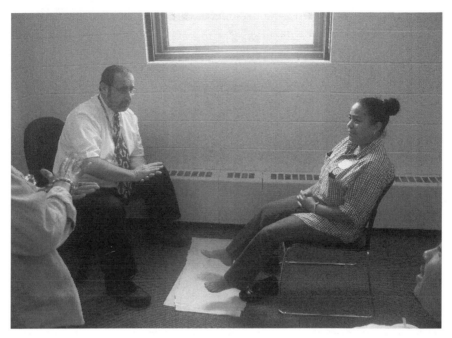

FIGURE 4.1
Podiatrist examining a diabetic patient's feet at health program organized by medical anthropologists and public health activists. Photo by Merrill Singer.

than are their U.S. counterparts, and German physicians are much less likely to prescribe antibiotics than U.S. physicians. In large part, the latter pattern is due to the fact that German biomedicine emphasizes the self-recuperative aspects of the body and has long been open to natural healing techniques. German biomedicine, in fact, consists of two varieties: (1) *Schulmedizin,* or "school medicine," which is taught in major medical institutions, such as Humboldt University and the Charite, and (2) *Naturheilkunde* (nature cure), which biomedical physicians may acquire training in through special workshops and apprenticeships. In contrast to Americans and the British, French biomedical practitioners generally take rectal rather than oral temperatures because of the greater accuracy of the former despite the fact that this method can result in rectal bleeding. Finally, whereas American women tend to prefer breast enlargements, French women tend to prefer breast reductions.

While this chapter focuses on the ethnomedical practices of indigenous peoples around the world, it also discusses biomedicine as both a "global medical system" (i.e., an ethnomedicine that has transcended multiple cultural boundaries) and a structured array of somewhat interconnected ethnomedical subsystems. As Mark Nichter (1991:138) observes, "Ethnomedical [research] entails the study of how well-being and suffering are experienced bodily as well as socially; the multivocality [i.e., having many voices or, more precisely in this context, having multiple means of expressing different kinds of information] of somatic [bodily] communication; and processes of healing (their relative success and limitations) as they are contextualized and directed toward the person, household, community and state, land and cosmos."

## WHAT TO CALL IT?

Whereas biomedical physicians generally simply refer to their healing practice as "medicine," anthropologists, because they recognize a wide array of other medical systems, have over time referred to it by a wide array of terms, including Western medicine, scientific medicine, and cosmopolitan medicine, because of its global scope. It has also been referred to as bourgeois medicine because of its strong ideological underpinnings in global capitalism. Over the past two decades, however, the term "biomedicine" has become common in medical anthropology and has even been adopted by some biomedical physicians and biomedical research scientists. Ironically, some biomedical physicians refer to their form of practice as traditional medicine, a term that medical anthropologists have generally reserved for medical systems in indigenous societies and peasant communities. In this book, as has become fairly standard in medical anthropology, we use the term biomedicine.

## INDIGENOUS AND FOLK MEDICINE SYSTEMS

While the term "primitive medicine" was in use in the early days of anthropological interest in health and healing, the term is problematic for several reasons. In addition to implying a priori (before it is empirically tested) that indigenous or folk medicine is not effective, it also lumps all nonbiomedical systems into one box, but in fact there is considerable diversity in such healing systems.

## Ways of Healing

One thing that many indigenous and folk medical systems or traditional ethnomedical systems do have in common is that they tend to place a strong emphasis on magico-religious rituals as well as to seek to reestablish harmony between humans and/or between humans and the supernatural and natural realms. They also often incorporate members of the community who function as a *therapeutic management group*. All of these dimensions are exemplified among the Navajo where the singer (as healers are known in the Navajo or Dine tradition) constructs an elaborate sand painting depicting the Holy People and chants over the patient in order to reestablish harmony, the loss of which is believed to cause illness. As the singer destroys sections of the sand painting, it is believed that various aspects of the patient's sickness are eradicated. Traditional medicine, like Navajo healing, often stresses emotional catharsis for the patient and draws the supportive attention of fellow members of the community to the patient's illness. At the same time, Navajo healing has a naturalistic orientation, as is evidenced by its broad pharmacopoeia consisting of herbs, powders, teas, and animal substances (e.g., powdered insects, cow dung, and so on). The Incas of the Andean region practiced trephination, which entailed the removal of part of the skull in treating fractures or removing brain tumors, purportedly in order to release a malevolent spirit.

An estimated 25 to 50 percent of the substances in the traditional nonbiomedical pharmacopoeia of indigenous healers have been shown empirically to be effective as measured by conventional scientific and biomedical standards. Other naturalistic techniques found in traditional medicine include herbs, powders, bone setting, massages, sweat baths, and mineral baths, as well as the suturing of wounds with various items, such as sinews among Native American groups, thorns among the Masai, and biting mandibles from the heads of termites among both Somalis and Brazilian Indians. The Aleut and Inuit people are adept surgeons as a result of a pool of anatomical knowledge that they have developed from their hunting of sea mammals. The Masai, in turn, operate on abscesses of the liver and spleen.

People sometimes view healers from other cultures or societies as more powerful and efficacious than their own healers. For example, the Iraqw of northern Tanzania often seek healers from other ethnic groups, such as the Sukuma, the Ihanzu, the coastal Swahili, and ones from Somalia, even if these healers do not speak the Iraqw language. The Iraqw often state that "we believe the medicine of other's peoples to be stronger than our own" (quoted in Rekdal 1999:460). Cross-cultural healing may serve as a means of fostering social connections that prevent or reduce interethnic conflict and avoiding local healers who may be viewed as capable of malevolent or exploitative acts. Ironically, in developed societies, including the United States and Australia, large numbers of people have come to embrace non-Western medical systems, such as traditional Chinese medicine, Tibetan medicine, and Ayurveda.

### Typologies of Healing Systems

In their efforts to summarize the broad diversity and range of health beliefs and practices found in a wide diversity of sociocultural systems around the world, medical anthropologists have created various typologies of conceptions of disease etiology within medical systems. Erickson (2008), for example, has developed a matrix of the geographic distribution of various ethnomedical theories of disease causation. This chart shows that three types of causation beliefs are worldwide: biomedical understandings, theories of illness due to loss of internal balance within body systems, and acceptance that illness can be caused by exposure to someone with an "evil eye." We present three alternative ethnomedical typologies here, although these by no means exhaust the range of schemes that have been developed. In one of the earliest of these, George M. Foster and Barbara Gallatin Anderson (1978) suggested that every medical system embraces both a "disease theory system" and a "health care system" and, further, that medical systems include both an ideological component and a social structural component. The disease theory system includes ideas about the nature of health and ideas about the causes of disease or illness. Foster and Anderson make a distinction between personalistic systems and naturalistic systems. The former view disease as resulting from the action of a "sensate who may be a supernatural being (a deity or god), a nonhuman being (such as a ghost, ancestor, or evil spirit), or a human being (a witch or sorcerer)" (G. Foster and Anderson 1978:53). Naturalistic systems, by contrast, view disease as emanating from the imbalance of certain inanimate elements in the body, such as the male and female principles of yin and yang in Chinese medicine. Personalistic and naturalistic explanations are not mutually exclusive. The health care system, according to Foster and Anderson, refers to the social relationships and interactions between the healers and their patients. The healer may be assisted by various assistants and in the case of complex societies may work in an elaborate bureaucratic structure, such as a clinic, health maintenance organization, or hospital.

Using a different approach, one based on types of healers within an ethnomedical system, Loustanunau and Sobo (1997) categorize shamans, mediums, sorcerers, and priests as examples of personalistic practitioners, while they group herbalists, chemists, bodyworkers, and lay midwives into the category of naturalistic practitioners. Herbalists are found in the great majority of societies and prescribe or treat patients using medicinal plants but also minerals, as is the case in the Madagascar village studied by Harper described in chapter 2. Chemists or pharmacists dispense both over-the-counter and prescription drugs and in developing countries often give injections. Indeed, in developing countries, chemists, without a prescription from a biomedical physician, often dispense both brand name and generic drugs, including what are generally legally defined as controlled substances in developed countries. While surgery is a highly prestigious specialty within biomedicine, various individuals in indigenous and archaic state societies practice or did practice surgery. One common surgical technique of traditional surgery is trephination. The Incas have already been mentioned as practitioners of this surgical art, but many other types of surgery have been described in indigenous societies around the world. Bodyworkers are musculoskeletal specialists who massage or manipulate the body in order to alleviate muscular tensions or skeletal misalignments. Finally, lay, or "direct-entry," midwifery around the world has been the focus of much medical anthropological research (Davis-Floyd et al. 1992). Midwives have generally delivered infants in indigenous societies and continue to do so, particularly in developing countries but increasingly so in developed societies as well. In reality, specific healers may be a blend of the various types delineated by Loustanunau and Sobo, such as when humoral doctors act as both chemists and herbalists or healers mix naturalistic and personalistic techniques.

Individuals follow various paths in becoming traditional healers. One is by "divine selection," in which the prospective healer has a dream involving the visitation of a spiritual guide who reveals that the dreamer has been chosen to serve the people in this manner. Individuals who themselves have been healed from a serious disease commonly are chosen to become traditional healers, thus the term "wounded healer," which has even been applied as well to many professional psychologists and psychiatrists in modern and postmodern societies. In addition, individuals who desire to become healers may undergo an apprenticeship with an established healer, often a member of one's kinship group.

Finally, Alan Young (1976a), a medical anthropologist with a strong interest in medical knowledge, has developed two separate models that focus on the manner in which medical systems organize knowledge about diseases. In the first of these, he distinguishes between (1) internalizing systems, which focus on physiological explanations and biophysical signs that the healer can detect, indicating the nature of disease episodes (such is the case in bio-medicine), and (2) externalizing systems, which stress events outside the sick body. In the latter, the disease-causing agents are generally animate and even human or at least humanlike, such as a witch or a sorcerer. It is the healer's job to determine what events prompted the disease-causing agent to attack the patient, as is the case in Navajo medicine where the singer attempts to restore a balance between the patient and social group, natural environment, or the wider cosmos. Young argues that externalizing medical systems tend to develop into internalizing medical systems with growing social complexity.

In his second model, Young (1976b, 1977) posits two types of systems: (1) accumulating medical systems, which consist of accumulated, formalized teachings, generally in written form, that are shared with prospective practi-tioners in training institutions or with colleagues at conferences or in profes-sional associations (e.g., biomedicine, Ayurveda and Unani in South Asia, and Chinese medicine), and (2) diffusing medical systems, in which practitioners generally do not share medical knowledge (thus making it rather diffuse or unsystematic) with one another and regard it to be secret (e.g., shamans and magical healers).

Finally, using a biocultural or medical ecological perspective, Horacio Fabrega (1997) has developed an elaborate scheme of medical systems on which we draw in this chapter and elaborate on in our discussion of medi-cal pluralism in the next chapter. Fabrega proposes the abbreviation "SH" to refer to a hypothesized biological adaptation for sickness and healing (i.e., like the biological adaptations that have been made among desert-dwelling animals to allow them to live in great heat with limited moisture, species have also adapted to the survival challenge of sickness with healing behaviors). For example, he maintains that chimpanzees exhibit some basic behaviors, such as the use of leaves to wipe themselves and the use of leaf napkins to dab at bleeding wounds, suggesting a prehuman SH adaptation, but also observes that chimps exhibit some non-SH responses as well, such as aversion to and exploitation of sick group members. More recently, it has been discovered that certain species of caterpillars when infected with various diseases will eat plants that have chemicals that are effective against the specific attacking disease agent. Fabrega suggests that many of the SH characteristics of chim-panzees existed in early hominid societies and that SH became more refined during prehominid stages of human evolution, as is implied by the presence of healed fractures in some Neanderthal remains. He maintains that patterns of food sharing and reciprocity between the sexes provided a social context for the SH adaptation because the latter also entails cooperative behavior.

Asserting that "SH constitutes the foundational material for the elaboration of medicine as a social institution," Fabrega (1997:70) argues that the providers of SH (i.e., healers) in early foraging societies were highly insightful individuals who possessed an elaborate knowledge of the social organization of their society.

## AN EVOLUTIONARY MODEL OF DISEASE THEORIES
## AND HEALING SYSTEMS

Drawing on the work of Fabrega (1997), Winkelman (2000), and others, we propose an evolutionary model of disease theories and healing systems, shown in Table 4.1.

### Health, Illness, and Medicine in Family-Level Foraging Societies

Family-level foraging societies, such as Australian Aborigines and the Inuit of the Arctic region, tend to have shamanic healers who often employ idiosyncratic techniques that they try to conceal from other practitioners. The juncture of medicine and religion is particularly exemplified in the role of the shaman, who has been depicted by anthropologists, scholars of comparative religion, transpersonal psychologists, and New Agers as the prototypical traditional healer. The word "shaman" is a term associated with the Tungus, a reindeer-herding group in Siberia who use it to label a part-time religious healer who is in direct contact with the supernatural realm. Other terms used to refer to this practitioner include "magician," "medicine person," and "witch doctor." The shaman has one or more spirit guides at his or her command, may be male or female, and is often "called" by spirit familiars through dreams or visions. Shamans often are considered eccentric and have been described by various ethnographers as moody, highly introverted, highly perceptive and intelligent, and intimately aware of their sociocultural system. Shamans among the Chuckee people of Siberia often are homosexuals, and those in some societies may be transvestites. There are several ways by which individuals become shamans, including inheriting the position from a parent, receiving a "call" from a spirit, recovering from a serious illness, or possessing outstanding abilities, such as being an excellent hunter, having psychic abilities, or being insightful.

In essence, the shaman is a complex figure with multiplicity of roles. As a religious intermediary, the shaman visits the supernatural realm to petition favors, including the curing of diseases; as a diviner, the shaman locates wild game for hunting or lost objects or diagnoses illness; as a judge, the shaman determines when people have violated rules, such as having eaten taboo food

**Table 4.1. An Evolutionary View of Illness Theories and Healing Systems**

| Type of Society | Purported Causes of Illness | Types of Healers |
|---|---|---|
| Nomadic foraging | Self, ancestors, gods, outsiders | Shamans, diviners |
| Village level—simple horticulturalists | Same as foragers plus group members as possible agents, simple ethnopathologies | Shamans, magico-healers, mediums, herbalists |
| Nomadic pastoralists | Same as simple horticulturalists and in some cases imbalances between hot and cold foods | Healers, mediums, exorcists, and sometimes religious healers associated with world religions |
| Chiefdoms—sedentary foragers and intensive horticulturalists | Same as simple horticulturalists | Healers, mediums, herbalists, shamans among sedentary foragers |
| Early state societies | Same as above | Same as above plus priests |
| Early empires/civilizations | Individual behaviors, moral failings, elaborate ethnopathologies, imbalances in body humors | Priests, professional physicians, folk and religious healers |
| Modern industrial societies | Germs, genes, lifestyles, highly elaborate ethnopathologies | Orthodox and heterodox professional physicians, religious and folk healers, diversity of additional healers |
| Postmodern societies | Same as above plus emotions interacting with body, return to humor theories in some medical subsystems | Same as above plus movement to integrate orthodox and heterodox modalities |

or expressed anger inappropriately; and as an entertainer, the shaman carries out elaborate performances, including dance, sleight of hand, ventriloquism, shaking the ceremonial tent by pulling a series of strings and thus simulating the entrance of the spirits, and wearing colorful costumes. As a healer and psychotherapist, the shaman uses both naturalistic and supernaturalistic techniques. Ritual healing techniques include soul retrieval, removal of disease-causing objects, exorcism, confession, and sacrifice.

Michael Winkelman (2000) argues that shamanistic practices induce extraordinary experiences and healing by producing integrative processes in the limbic system or paleomammalian brain. He further asserts that shamanism evolved during the course of human history as a practice for symbolically and psychophysiologically enhancing well-being, both in the shaman and in patients. In entering into an altered state of consciousness, the shaman—unlike the Haitian *houngan* described in chapter 2—is not possessed by the spirit guides but rather controls them in order to achieve many tasks, including healing, dream interpretation, divination, clairvoyance, handling of fire, communications with spirits of the dead, recovery of lost souls, mediation between the gods and mortals, and protection against spirits and malevolent practitioners. The shaman's curing ceremony functions as an important social event that provides a means of integrating the patient into the immediate social group but also contributes to the social and psychic unity of the larger collectivity.

Winkleman (2000:276) asserts that shamanistic practices serve as a "set of sophisticated traditions for managing self, emotions, and consciousness." He views shamanism primarily as a phenomenon of foraging or hunting-and-gathering societies but maintains that aspects of classical shamanism persist in later or more complex societies. McClennon (1997) argues that shamanic/ hypnotic rituals and their associated altered states of consciousness induced by mimetic rituals, such as chanting, singing, drumming, dancing, and other repetitive behaviors, activated the human relaxation response that provided early human societies with a survival advantage. Weston LaBarre (1980) argues that shamanism constituted the earliest form of religion, which, like later variants of religion, constituted an adaptation to inner anxieties and a culturally constituted defense mechanism for society in confusing and crisis-torn times.

Shamans are found in societies such as the !Kung or San of the Kalahari Desert, the Semang of the Malay Peninsula, and the Jivaro of Bolivia. Winkelman argues that shamanistic practitioners and somewhat similar magico-religious healers are found in technologically more complex socio-cultural systems. He maintains that sociocultural processes have contributed to the disappearance of shamans and other shamanistic healers. For example, in state societies, these practitioners are in competition with the monopolistic claims of institutional religions over which priests preside. The shaman does not completely disappear in modern state societies but goes underground in the form of spiritualists, faith healers, and New Age psychics and neoshamans.

Most adult males and some adult females among the !Kung of the Kalahari Desert of Namibia and Botswana function as shamans and perform community healing rituals about four times a month. Several men, who are sometimes joined by women, dance around a fire and a group of singers, thus inducing a trancelike state of "boiling" energy, or *num*. The healers may also ingest plant substances that contain *num*. While in trance, !Kung healers treat sick spectators by imploring the ancestral spirits to restore them to health. Among the !Kung and other foraging societies, shamanic healing techniques tend to be public because they are utilized by numerous individuals in the group. Healing techniques tend to be focused on immediate restoration of well-being or accommodation to death through ritual activities and social practices.

In her classic work on health-related issues among the Yirrakala or Yolngu, who were traditionally foragers, of northeastern Arnhem in the Northern Territories of Australia, Janice Reid (1983) identifies two types of healers: the *marrnggitj*, or traditional healer, and the *raglak*, or sorcerer. Some individuals become a *marrnggitj* in the wake of a frightening supernatural experience in which a spirit confers healing powers on them. Ultimately, of course, the prospective traditional healer must have the ability to counteract sorcery or the work of the *raglak* to consistently attract patients. Reid found only two men, a boy, and a woman who still practice Aboriginal medicine in the Yirrakala vicinity.

Not all foraging societies have shamanic healers per se. A case in point is the Penan, a group in Brunei Darussalm on the island of Borneo in Indonesia who were traditionally hunters and gatherers but who are in the process of being transformed into village horticulturalists. Voeks and Sercombe (2000) argue that the rudimentary medical belief system associated with their foraging lifestyle is a consequence of the fact that they did not suffer from many debilitating diseases, as was the case with surrounding village peoples. Nevertheless, the Penan do recognize the existence of numerous unnamed spirits that can inflict harm on humans for violating various taboos and rely on "dream readers" to divine the sources of illness episodes, but they often disregard the advice of these medical practitioners. The Hadza, a foraging people in Tanzania, do not have any medical specialists other than women who perform clitoridectomies. Every adult has knowledge about medicinal plants and can treat anyone with an illness. In addition to shamans, the Toba, a traditionally foraging society that engaged in some horticulture, have herbalists (some of whom today are called *curanderos* and act as healers in Christian evangelical sects) and other specialists who treat specific illnesses, such as those found among infants and children.

## SHAMANISM AND NEOSHAMANISM

Shamanism is associated generally with foraging societies, but shamans are found in other indigenous societies as well, such as village-level societies like the Yanomamo of South America or the Fore of New Guinea. Indigenous cultures in central and northern Mexico exhibit two types of shamans in the modern context: traditional shamans, who serve as intermediaries between their people and the supernatural realm, and *curandero* shamans, who are not community religious healers and "draw on a wide range of folk belief including colonial Spanish and modern rural beliefs" (Dow 2001:69). In recent times, adherents of the counterculture and the New Age movement have embraced a phenomenon referred to by scholars as neoshamanism, which incorporates beliefs and rituals drawn from knowledge about traditional shamanic healing systems from around the world, particularly from those found among North and South American Indian groups and Aboriginal Australians. Michael Harner, a former anthropology professor at the New School for Social Research in New York who studied shamanism among the Jivaro and Conibo Indians of South America, has become the most prominent purveyor of neoshamanism in the world and is the director of the Foundation for Shamanic Studies. Many indigenous people, however, believe that neoshamanism is yet one more instance of the appropriation of their cultures by dominant cultural groups for monetary purposes.

## Health, Illness, and Medicine in Village-Level Societies

Village-level societies, such as the Ainu of Hokaido in northern Japan and the Yanomamo in the Amazon basin of northern Brazil and southern Venezuela, are characterized by the appearance of specialized healers, elaborate healing ceremonies attended by community members, and an expansion of the sick role manifested, for example, in growing attention to the psychosocial needs of sick individuals. The healer role in these societies confers social power on "individuals selected in part because of their psychological, social and political as well as strictly medical talents" and who are in a position to "profit from positive and favorable outcomes of healing" (Fabrega 1997:99).

As is the case in foraging societies, shamans are also often found in village-level societies. For example, among the Yanomamo, shamans call the spirits, who take the form of tiny humanoids, to implore them to release their victims from disease. Conversely, women are the primary repositories of herbal lore that is derived primarily from wild plants but also from some cultivated ones. The Fore, a New Guinea highlands horticultural people who, like the Yanomamo, had a village-level society at the moment of contact with European expansion, depend on what they call Dream Men or Smoke Men, healers who rely on dreams and hallucinations induced by inhaling tobacco smoke in order to identify offending sorcerers.

The Dani, a horticultural village people who also inhabit the New Guinea highlands, have two types of magico-religious healers. One type is the *hathale*, who tend to be women who carry out a variety of medico-religious functions, ranging from serving as midwives, carrying out abortions, administering medicinal herbs, and performing simple curing ceremonies or even allegedly casting spells. The other type includes political leaders who seek to appease the ancestral spirits by sacrificing pigs in order to ensure fertility both among women and in garden plots as well as general health and prosperity.

Robert Desjarlais, a medical anthropologist, participated in some twenty healing rituals as a shamanic apprentice to a sixty-five-year-old healer called Meme during his fieldwork among the Yolmo Sherpa, an ethnically Tibetan horticultural people residing in the Helambu region of north-central Nepal. Desjarlais (1992:241) notes that while Yolmo shamans often are not successful in their efforts to cure primarily physical ailments, such as arthritis or tuberculosis, "they are adept at healing illnesses related to personal distress or social conflicts (especially when compared with biomedical treatments)."

Recovered patients in various horticultural village societies became members of curer societies or sodalities. The Ndembu, who reside on a wooded plateau in the Mwininlungu District in the North-Western Province of Zambia, are a case in point. According to Victor Turner, a diviner who diagnoses the source of patients' afflictions resulting from an offended spirit, directs his clients to a senior practitioner who propitiates the spirit, and assigns a "band of adepts, consisting of persons who have themselves undergone as patients or novices" portions of curative ritual. He observes, "If the patient is deemed to be cured, he or she may then assist at later performances as an adept" (V. Turner 1968:16). Whereas Mircea Eliade (1964) coined the term "wounded healer" to refer to shamans, the concept may also be applied to other types of healers, including diviners or *ngoma* practitioners in Swaziland of southern Africa. In Swazi traditional healing the person possessed by an evil spirit can be healed while undergoing training as a diviner. Furthermore, as Reis (2000:73) observes, "suffering certainly is a lived reality for diviners, but as a sign of a calling it is also an ideology."

### Health, Illness, and Medicine in Pastoralist Societies

The Datoga, a pastoral people in Tanzania, make a distinction between an "illness of God" and an "illness of human beings," although many illnesses may be ascribed to both agents. Human-caused illnesses include witchcraft (generally believed to emanate from neighboring indigenous groups), the evil eye, and the administration of poisons. Male healers belong to one of two healing clans and treat patients by spitting on their bodies as a type of blessing ritual that may be combined with the application on patients' bodies of mixtures of herbs and animal fat. Women healers, who are far fewer in number, function as mediums through which patients can petition the spirits for advice or a cure. The Tuareg, a traditional pastoral people found in the Saharan and Sahelian areas of West and North Africa who have been heavily influenced by Islam, believe that disease may be a result of imbalances of hot and cold in the body, malicious gossip, or sorcery. The Tuareg have a wide array of healers to which they can turn, including herbalists, bonesetters, Islamic religious healers, diviners, and exorcists. Like many pastoral peoples around the world, the Tuareg have been influenced by the medical practices of other peoples, particularly the Hausa, another Islamic group. The Mongols, the most renowned and feared pastoral nomads in human history, blended their naturalistic practices, including massage, bone setting, midwifery, and shamanistic practices that called on spirits to alleviate disease or misfortune, with medical beliefs and practices from first Tibetan Buddhism and later Russian biomedicine.

## Health, Illness, and Medicine in Chiefdom Societies

According to Fabrega (1997), chiefdom (or prestate) societies, such as those of Hawaii and the Maori of Polynesia; the sedentary foraging societies of the Pacific Northwest Coast; and early state societies, such as Sumer, a city-state in Mesopotamia, exhibit the beginnings of the "institution," or "system," of medicine, which includes (1) an elaborate corpus of medical knowledge that embraces aspects of cosmology, religion, and morality and (2) the beginnings of medical pluralism (a topic on which we elaborate in chapter 5), manifested by the presence of a wide variety of healers, including general practitioners, priests, diviners, herbalists, bonesetters, and midwives who undergo systematic training or apprenticeships. Traditional Maori recognize two categories of disease: *matetangata* (those caused by human mishaps) and *mate atua* (those caused by supernatural forces). As in other parts of Polynesia, both types of diseases emanated from a violation of a *tapu*, or social norm, that invoked the wrath of the gods. *Tohunga*, or traditional healers, either recited chants to induce religious healing or prescribed medicinal plants.

Some male healers, or *fojo*, in Samoa, another Polynesian chiefdom society, are also chiefs, and some women healers are the wives of chiefs. The former tend to restrict their practices to kinfolk whereas the latter do not. Some *fojo* are general practitioners who treat a wide range of ailments and others are specialists who treat either natural illnesses or supernatural illness, or employ certain medical procedures, such as massage or administration of herbs. Healers also vary in their range and depth of knowledge of the disease etiology and diagnostic and treatment techniques (MacPherson and MacPherson 1990: 102, 117–18,140).

## BIOMEDICINE AS THE PREDOMINANT ETHNOMEDICINE IN MODERN SOCIETIES

Various scholars have debated the time of the emergence of biomedicine and its branching off from the traditional allopathic medicine that was practiced, for example, during the colonial era in the United States. Michel Foucault argued in *The Birth of the Clinic* (1975) that biomedicine emerged around 1800 in Europe as it systematically began to classify diseases into families and species and focused more on the body, thus the term the "clinical gaze," than on the ill person. According to Foucault (1975:169), "Clinical experience sees a new space opening up before it; the tangible space of the body . . . the medicine of organs, sites, causes, a clinic wholly ordered in accordance with pathological anatomy." He went on in subsequent writings to portray medicine as one of a series of forms of social control, along with the state and prisons. Chrystal Jaye and her colleagues apply Foucault's social construction-ist analysis of bio-power to biomedical education at the University of Otago on the South Island of New Zealand (Jaye et al. 2006). Based upon interviews with preclinical medical students, clinical instructors, and medical educators, they observed that the new crop of biomedical students are expected to be more humane, compassionate, and culturally sensitive than their mentors, in essence internalizing new forms of subjectivity:

> These new subjectivities are subject to scrutiny through surveillance techniques that assess behaviours and attributes such as reflectivity, self-awareness, pa-tient-centredness, humanitarian values, ethics and maintenance of professional boundaries. Mechanisms of formative and summative feedback constitute regimes of normalizing judgment from teachers—but these normalizing judg-ments are also exercised through subtle positive and negative reinforcements from within the learning environment as successive generations of doctors teach the new generation what it needs to know (Jaye et al. 2006:150–51).

In contrast to the social constructionist perspective adopted by Jaye and her colleagues in their analysis of biomedical education, Brian McKenna (2010) applies a critical medical anthropological perspective in his analysis of biomedical education at Michigan State University. He examined a six-year project called the Community/University Health Partnership, which aimed to produce more community-oriented primary care practitioners. Because the project challenged biomedicine's orientation toward curative care, profes-sional rivalry, overspecialization, and hospital-based education, it met with stiff resistance and ultimately collapsed, despite support from a dean who ultimately resigned from his position.

Biomedicine is often depicted as an example of a profession par excellence because its physicians generally enjoy prestige, high incomes, relative au-tonomy over work, and a monopoly over the prescribing of dangerous drugs, declaring people mentally incompetent, signing birth and death certificates, and referring patients to other health practitioners. Freidson (1970) likens the position of biomedicine in modern societies to that of state religions in preindustrial civilizations. But state religions as instruments of social control were always subordinate to the wishes of ruling elites of their societies. Thus, the professional dominance of biomedical physicians is *delegated* rather than *absolute*. The corporate class and its political allies in advanced developed and many developing societies delegate power to biomedicine in the form of financial support and licensure or statutory registration (Baer 2001:46–47). Biomedical physicians also often are highly represented on the registration boards of other biomedical health practitioners, such as nurses and allied health professionals. They also tend to be overrepresented on hospital boards, government health departments, health advisory boards, the National Institutes of Health, and the World Health Organization. Nurses and allied health workers often embark upon drives for professionalization that emulate the training and organizational structures of their biomedical superiors.

In recent decades, biomedical physicians have encountered challenges to their professional dominance from several quarters, including new models of health focused on prevention, the social determinants of health, and community; the rise of corporate medicine with its strong emphasis on managed care; the changing nature of state involvement and regulation, which includes cost-cutting measures and performance indicators; the lessening public status of biomedicine due to media exposés of medical fraud and negligence; the recognition of patient rights; and the increasing popularity of complementary and alternative medical systems. Beginning in the early 1970s, particularly in the United States, an increasing number of biomedical physicians became salaried employees rather than independent entrepreneurs. Scholars began to see biomedicine as a "big business" manifested in an array of large health care corporations and proprietary hospitals that were part and parcel of a medical-industrial complex (Wohl 1984). While biomedical physicians tend to enjoy considerable prestige in most societies, in some developing societies their status is relatively low or declining. For example, in Mexico, biomedical physicians constitute the least prestigious profession out of the ten most popular professions and earn less than engineers, lawyers, and architects (Harrison 2000:301–2). In 1993 about a quarter of Mexican biomedical physicians were unemployed or underemployed, despite the fact that many rural areas lacked biomedical physicians.

The hospital is the primary biomedical health care setting in the provision of not only acute care but also outpatient services, such as lab work, X-rays, physical therapy, and programs addressing alcohol and drug addiction, weight reduction, and fitness. The hospital started out as a charitable institution that served as a last resort for the critically ill poor. In the nineteenth century, affluent patients received health care at home administered by either a house-calling physician or a full-time private-duty nurse. Hospitals come in different forms, such as voluntary community hospitals, or religiously supported hospitals, proprietary hospitals, and public hospitals. Hospitals may be general in scope or specialized, such as in the case of mental or heart hospitals.

The hospital has evolved into an elaborate social system with subsystems and a wide array of occupational subcultures, including those of administrators, physicians, nurses, medical technologists, and even patients. The hospital is a highly authoritarian (some would even say quasi-militaristic) organization where orders are to be executed without question. It manifests a dual pattern of authority consisting of (1) administration, which includes a board of trustees, administrators, and paid staff, and (2) medical staff, some of whom are paid employees but others who are visitors, and an elaborate occupational support structure that includes nurses, nurse aides, medical technologists, therapists, social workers, orderlies, and (in teaching hospitals like the one studied by Katz as described in chapter 2) medical students as well as, sometimes, medical anthropologists. Registered nurses function in two worlds in that they are responsible for carrying out administrative policy and regulations and serve as the physicians' representative on the floor by carrying out orders for patients. At the same time, nurses have struggled to define their own arena of expertise, emphasizing the "care" aspects of healing as opposed to the "cure" activities undertaken by physicians. Increasingly, however, with the rise of the nurse-practitioner and related roles (e.g., nurse-anesthesiologists), nurses have penetrated the curer role as well.

Patients often experience "culture shock," a term used by anthropologists adjusting to the challenges of life in a culture that is foreign to them, on being admitted to the hospital because they undergo an ordeal of depersonalization, loss of self-identity, exposure to unfamiliar jargon, and a "stripping" process in which they must check their personal belongings and forgo many preferences. They find themselves in a state of total or near-total dependency in which they are fed meals not of their own choosing, may be bathed by strangers, receive medications at all times of the day and night, and must wear standardized, ill-fitting, and, for many people, far too revealing clothing. Poked, prodded, questioned, and awakened for testing at odd hours, they often respond by trying to personalize their immediate space by decorating their room or section of a room with gifts from friends and relatives or pictures from home, sometimes getting cranky or resistant, and, for many people, asking frequently when they can "go home." Hospitalization, in short, is often experienced as a kind of sacrifice that is endured in exchange for the hope of returning from the world of the sick to the land of the well.

An increasing number of medical anthropologists conduct both teaching and research activities in hospitals. Some of this work is carried out by physician-anthropologists, but even more of it is carried out by nurse-anthropologists, many of whom belong to the Council of Nursing and Anthropology, a constituent unit of the Society for Medical Anthropology. Within this context, some medical anthropologists are involved in what is termed clinical anthropology or clinically applied medical anthropology. Much of this work occurs in hospitals or other clinical settings and often involves the anthropologist serving as a cultural translator who facilitates the physician-patient relationship. The range of issues addressed in clinical anthropology can be glimpsed by reviewing the topics covered in a 2006 conference session on hospital ethnography. Papers presented at this gathering addressed topics such as clinical cartography (i.e., the ethnographic mapping of hospital spaces), peer support among hospital-based health care professions, the negotiation of space in the operating theater, migrant doctors in Australian hospitals, and the social nature of the hospital mortuary, where the most unfortunate patients end up (see Long et al. 2008; Wind 2008). In contrast to sociologists Gail Henderson and M. Cohen, who produced a book-length ethnography of the Second Attachment Hospital complex on the outskirts of Wuhan, the fifth-largest city in China, no anthropologists to date have conducted an ethnography of an entire hospital. In the case of the United States, Elisa J. Sobo, who worked for several years in a San Diego hospital but now teaches at San Diego State University, reports,

> Much of my work has to do with improving the quality of hospital care. For example, I am presently leading a project that asks why implementing evidence-based health care practices can be so difficult, and aims to propose ways to facilitate change and improvement. I also am involved in HIV medication adherence research and several child services projects. All of these projects concern, among other things, patient-provider (or, in the case of pediatrics, patient-parent-provider) communication. (Society for Medical Anthropology 2006)

Nevertheless, in keeping with a growing interest in hospital ethnography, Anna Harris (2009), a biomedical physician, conducted an in-depth study of how overseas biomedical physicians, particularly ones from developing countries, in two outer suburban hospitals in a large Australian city have adjusted to the larger national health care system as well as the larger society. In addition to learning about a different hospital system and its biomedical routines and procedures, they spent much of their time "improving their English language fluency, sorting out their visas, making sure their families were settled and they had a decent salary to support them." In addition to occupying the less prestigious positions in urban hospitals, overseas biomedical physicians in Australia increasingly find themselves practicing in "country towns" or rural areas, places that domestic Australian general practitioners and specialists have in many instances abandoned.

Beyond the hospital is the clinic or health station, often set up in more isolated, lower population density, and rural areas to serve the health needs of dispersed communities. The health station, like the one studied by Leslie

FIGURE 4.2
Government health post in
highlands Western Papua,
Indonesia. Photo by Leslie
Butt.

Butt (Figure 4.2), is especially important in areas with limited health budgets and comparatively fewer medical professionals.

As medical anthropology has evolved, it has taken on new topical interests, including ones intimately related to biomedicine. Two of these new topic interests are pharmaceuticals and biotechnology, both of which touch on the anthropology of the body.

### Medical Anthropology and the Pharmaceutical Industry

Medical anthropologists have become increasingly aware of the importance of studying the enormous pharmaceutical industry, as pharmaceutical drugs are dispensed around the globe with tremendous impact on health and health behavior and are used in ways that are culturally meaningful, whether

## NURSE-ANTHROPOLOGISTS AND PHYSICIAN-ANTHROPOLOGISTS

Many nurses have found anthropology and specifically medical anthropology to be of great utility in their work. Consequently, numerous undergraduate nursing programs require their students to take a course in cultural anthropology, and many nursing schools now teach courses in medical anthropology and related subjects. Indeed, many of the people teaching these courses are nurses who have obtained graduate degrees in medical anthropology. Some anthropologists have argued that, in contrast to biomedical physicians, who tend to be "disease oriented," nurses are inclined to be more "person oriented." Conversely, while many biomedical students regard medical anthropology and related fields to be intrusions in their demanding studies, medical anthropology includes some prominent physician-anthropologists, including Arthur Kleinman and Paul Farmer, both of whom are based at Harvard University and have had significant productive influence on medical anthropology.

or not they are in line with or reflect medically approved patterns of use. Etkin (1988), for example, has examined the cultural construction of the efficacy of pharmaceutical drugs in light of varying cultural understandings of what efficacy means. While pharmaceutical drugs are intended to have specific physical, emotional, or behavioral effects, their effectiveness may be judged by quite different standards in local cultural settings.

Moreover, as Bodenheimer (1985:190) explains, to understand the impact of the pharmaceutical industry we must recognize its global character: "a pharmaceutical company might have its corporate headquarters in the United States, [test its drugs in Uganda], produce its drugs in Ireland, assemble its capsules in Brazil, and sell the products in Bolivia." Adds Mehrabadi (2005:1),

Pharmaceutical/biotechnology companies cannot be pinpointed to one location as they function as any transnational corporation would; globally. As with any corporation that is transnational in scope, operations are carried out depending on where labor is cheapest, raw materials are the least expensive, where taxes can be most easily evaded, as well as where market regulations are the least strict.

As a result of the pharmaceutical industry's global reach, its products appear in societies that lack a developed health care infrastructure, sometimes with dramatic effect. In the case of El Salvador, for example, Ferguson (1981) found that the arrival of pharmaceutical drugs pushed out locally produced indigenous medicines and the healers who produced and dispensed them. Local community structures then began to break down. Nichter (1989) has described a similar case in South India, where the traditional use of herbal remedies has been overwhelmed by the widespread sale of pharmaceutical drugs. Nichter analyzes the appeal of pharmaceuticals in this setting as reflecting their association by local populations with modernity and progress. By using Western medicines, in effect, people are attempting to reap the benefits of development, including the standard of living and concentration of wealth found in Western countries. In this sense, pharmaceuticals sometimes acquire culturally constructed fetishized qualities in the same sense that possessing a lucky charm will bring personal fortune. The popularity of pharmaceuticals internationally has led to the formation of an informal sector for the distribution of commercial drugs, such as folk injectors who give single shots of antibiotics in community markets in various countries. Given the need for receiving a course of antibiotic treatment, not only is this emergent folk practice ineffectual from a medical standpoint, but it can also contribute to the development of strains of bacteria that are drug resistant. In Cameroon, for example, Van der Geest and Whyte (1988) show not only how self-medication with pharmaceutical drugs can be detrimental to health but also that the available resources of low-income households are wasted on useless medication.

Moving from the micro level to the macro level, we can see that because pharmaceutical corporations are profit driven, their actions are not necessarily shaped by a health agenda, sometimes with significant health consequences. For example, in 2005 the pharmaceutical company Eli Lilly agreed to plead guilty to a single misdemeanor count and to pay a fine of $36 million for its violation of the Food, Drug, and Cosmetic Act in its promotional campaign for the anti-osteoporosis drug Evista (Corporate Crime Reporter 2005). According to this law, pharmaceutical companies must specify the medical purpose(s) of new drugs in their applications to receive marketing approval from the Food and Drug Administration (FDA). Once a drug is approved by the FDA, it can be legally promoted and sold only for the purposes for which it has been approved. Promotion for what is called "off label" uses is outlawed. In the case of Evista, Lilly executives were disappointed with sales levels during the first year that the drug was on the market, as it brought in only about a fourth of the projected annual sales of $400 million. To make up for this loss in expected income, Lilly decided to widen the market for its drug by promoting it for several unapproved uses. Although application by Lilly to the FDA to include these new uses was rejected, the company began pushing use of the drug in the prevention of breast cancer and cardiovascular disease. The consequences of such action are not trivial in that doctors, assuming that the drug is effective in cancer and heart disease prevention, may prescribe it instead of drugs that have proven in clinical trials to be effective in treating these diseases. In its expanded promotion efforts, Lilly used a variety of strategies, including training sales representatives how to get physicians to ask about other uses of Evista, sending unsolicited medical letters to physicians promoting unapproved uses of the drug, distributing an "Evista Best Practices" videotape that states that "Evista truly is the best drug for the prevention of all these diseases" (referring to osteoporosis, breast cancer, and cardiovascular disease), and distributing a medical reprint highlighting findings about the various benefits of Evista that was written by company employees and paid consultants while hiding a line in the reprint that acknowledged that the effectiveness of the drug in reducing cancer risk or cardiovascular disease had not been established, among other legerdemain strategies to promote and sell Evista (M. Singer 2007).

In another case involving the painkiller Vioxx in which it appears that improper procedures were followed in clinical trials, it is estimated that at least 25,000 heart attacks and strokes occurred after taking the drug (Bazerman and Chugh 2006). In the estimation of one pharmaceutical drug expert, David Graham, associate director for science in the Office of Drug Safety at the FDA, Vioxx may have contributed to the deaths of 88,000 to 138,000 people, putting it at the top of the list of known deadly pharmaceuticals to be released to the public (M. Singer and Baer 2007).

## Biotechnology

In addition to pharmaceuticals, biotechnology is a topical interest that medical anthropology and other medical social sciences share with science studies. Anthropologists have conducted studies of new reproductive technologies, organ transplants, and the new genetics arising from the mapping of the human genome. The primary beneficiaries of biotechnological developments are people in developed societies, but people in developing societies are forced by impoverishment to provide the body parts that make organ transplants possible. Margaret Lock and Vinh-Kim Nguyen (2010:22) describe biomedicine as technology, in that much of biomedicine consists of a wide array of technological devices, ranging from the highly sophisticated and complex such as mechanical ventilators, X-ray machines, magnetic resonance imagers, prosthetic limbs, and heart pacemakers, to relatively simples devices such as over-the-counter drugs, Band-Aids, and cotton balls. In fact, biomedical technologies have become so pervasive and commonplace in at least developed societies that some individuals "apparently concerned more about personal enhancement than civic virtue, lobby government for unhampered access to technologies such as genetic testing, genetic engineering, reproductive technologies, organ transplants, and even cosmetic surgery" (Lock and Nyugen 2010:23). Even in a remote but highly affluent developed society such Iceland, the Human Genome Project, an endeavor to unravel the genetic code of each individual with the goal of purportedly improving human reproductive patterns and early detection of disease, constitutes an example of how the "new genetics" has become part and parcel of everyday life (Palsson 2007).

At a more concrete level, the ventilator and other life-support technologies have facilitated the procurement of solid organs from brain-dead patients, such as those who incurred a fatal injury in the form of a motor vehicle accident, a drowning, or a stroke. Although the notion of "brain death" is universally recognized, its significance can be mediated by culture, as Margaret Lock (2002) has demonstrated to be the case in Japan, which constitutes the leading user and exporter of biotechnology in the world. Whereas North Americans and many Europeans generally accept both legally and culturally the practice of organ transplantation as long as the deceased had granted written permission for the use of their body parts for this purpose, in Japan the family is the final arbiter as to whether an individual's organs can be donated. Moreover, the Japanese mass media have tended to be staunch critics of the notion of brain death, a concept that attained legal recognition only in 1997. Most Japanese view death as a communal event to be controlled by the family and view and regard the concept of brain death as a "clumsy creation of technological medicine, devised to hasten the end of life" (Lock 2002:369). Organs for transplant had been obtained from only nine brain-dead individuals in Japan through 2000.

In contrast to Japan, the notion of brain death has gained wide acceptance in Germany but with significant controls on the processes of organ and tissue transplantation that have not developed in North America or even other European countries. Linda Hogle (1999) ascribes the German ambivalence about organ transplantation in large part to the Nazi practice of using Holocaust victims for forced medical experimentation and organ procurement. During the Nazi era, German anthropologists, along with biomedical physicians, acted as accomplices in a national program of racial classification, experimentation, and annihilation of categories of people regarded to be inferior and defective on the basis of ethnicity, mental status, sexual orientation, and political leanings. As a result of practices during the Nazi regime, including the use of skin from concentration camp victims in the manufacture of lamp shades, book covers, and other decorative items, the German organ and tissue procurement industry never obtained skin and bone from within Germany but rather from other countries.

Given the growing demand for organ transplants especially in the developed world, biotechnology has played a crucial role in the commodification of body parts, particularly those obtained from developing nations, not only from brain-dead individuals but from living ones as well. For example, poor working-class people in many developing countries have come to view certain of their bodily organs, such as one of their kidneys, as dispensable appendages that may be sold for sorely needed cash. An even more tragic scenario is one in which people are killed in order to procure body parts in high demand. As Nancy Scheper-Hughes (1998:5) aptly observes,

> Organ transplantation now takes place in a trans-national space with both donors and recipients following the paths of capital and technology in the global economy. In general, the movement of donor organs follow modern routes of capital: from South to North, from third world to first world, from poor to rich bodies, from black and brown to white bodies, productive to less productive, and female to male bodies.

As a result of biotechnology, many humans, particularly in developed countries, as Donna Haraway (1991) has argued in much of her work, are modern-day cyborgs who blur the boundaries between human bodies and machines. In contrast to classical cyborgs, the mythical creatures that were half-human, half animal, such as the Centaur, modern-day cyborgs include test-tube babies, people with organ transplants from animals or other humans, and those with artificial body parts, as well as individuals who have undergone plastic surgery or athletes who take steroids so they can perform seemingly superhuman physical feats.

# Medical Pluralism in the Contemporary World

Throughout this century and even before, there has been a general assumption—even a conviction . . . that folk and popular systems of health beliefs and practices would inevitably decline in modern and industrialized societies. . . . Yet this has not been the case.

*—Bonnie Blair O'Connor (1995:1)*

In the previous chapter, we examined the concept of ethnomedicine and conceptions of health, illness, and medicine in family-level foraging, village-level pastoral, and chiefdom societies. We move on in this chapter to consider the phenomenon of medical pluralism in complex societies by examining it in two locales in developing societies, namely, a village in the Bolivian Andes and a city in Java, Indonesia, and then in a technologically developed society, namely, Australia. We then examine various typologies of plural medical systems but particularly stress the concept of a dominative medical system, which points to the fact that medical systems do not exist in a vacuum but rather reflect the class, racial, ethnic, and gender relations and inequalities of the wider society. In a dominative medical system, several different healing traditions coexist in the same society, but one tends to be more closely aligned with the dominant social groups in that society and to be the dominant healing tradition as well.

Indigenous or tribal societies exhibit a diversity of healing beliefs and practices as well as an array of different kinds of healers, but these tend to be rather loosely organized and often reflect idiosyncratic patterns resulting in part from the fact that healers commonly are secretive about their medical knowledge. In contrast, state societies manifest the coexistence of a highly elaborate array of medical traditions at both the conceptual and the practice level, a pattern medical anthropologists call medical pluralism. In other words, the medical system of state-level societies tends to be made up of various medical subsystems that coexist in a social environment that ranges between extensive cooperation and open conflict.

Before we discuss various general dimensions of plural medical systems, we present three case studies of medical pluralism in three distinct sociocultural settings. The first is a small village in the Bolivian high plain (altiplano) based on ethnographic research done by Libbet Crandon-Malamud, the second is an administrative/university city in Java based on ethnographic research done by Steve Ferzacca, and the last is Australia based on social historical and ethnographic research conducted by Hans Baer.

## A CASE STUDY OF MEDICAL PLURALISM IN A RURAL AREA
## IN A DEVELOPING SOCIETY: THE ALTIPLANO OF BOLIVIA

Libbet Crandon-Malamud (1991) conducted fieldwork between 1976 and 1978 on medical pluralism in Kachitu (pseudonym), a rural town on the Bolivian altiplano. Kachitu is the center for a canton consisting of some sixteen thousand Aymara Indians living in thirty-six *communidades*. The town proper has some one thousand residents consisting of three ethnoreligious groups: Aymara peasants, Methodist Aymara, and Catholic mestizos (those of mixed European and indigenous blood). Before the Revolution of 1952, the mestizos, which constitute about half the population of Kachitu, supervised the labor of the Aymara on behalf of the national elites, who generally resided in La Paz and other cities. Since the revolution, the mestizos have been seeking to avoid poverty and are a socially fragmented ethnic category that includes teachers, small shopkeepers, and poor occasional agricultural laborers. Before 1952, the Aymara, which make up another third of the village, lived in Indian communities that were heavily taxed or on haciendas (plantations).

Some Aymara were miners and performed personal services, such as domestic work, for mestizos. Many Aymara peasants migrated to Kachitu from the haciendas upon acquiring land through fictive kinship ties with mestizos. Following the revolution and land reform, others moved to town and claimed land on the outskirts that had been confiscated from the mestizos. The Methodist

Aymara are converts or descendants of converts to the Methodist church, which established a mission in Kachitu in the early 1930s. The Methodist Aymara attended mission schools and became entrepreneurs who took over local administrative and political offices when the revolutionary government threw the mestizos out of these positions. They function as the economic and political backbone of Kachitu. Crandon-Malamud (1991) argues that the people of Kachitu tend to conflate ethnicity and social class, noting that Aymaraness, mestizoness, and even Methodism constitute "masks for social class."

## Themes

Crandon-Malamud identifies four themes that permeate the dialogue about medical etiology and diagnosis in Kachitu—pervasive hunger, subordination, victimization, and exploitation—within the context of the Bolivian political economy. Pervasive hunger is a by-product of race and differentiates the purportedly white elites from mestizos and Indians as a means to justify unequal access to the political process and economic resources. The second theme entails an economic system that exploits Indian labor, the third one consists of caudillo (strong authoritarian leadership) political structures that suppress dissent on the part of rural mestizos and Indians, and the fourth one is conflict that exists between mestizos and Indians.

## Medical Subsystems

Five different medical subsystems are used by those in Kachitu, depending on the diagnosis: Aymara home care, shamanistic or *yatiri* care, mestizo folk home care, biomedical clinical care, and hospital care in La Paz. Crandon-Malamud examines the intricate ways that the residents of Kachitu utilize the local plural medical system for purposes of establishing their sense of cultural identity and obtaining the few resources available to them. Contrary to the wishes of biomedical practitioners and indigenous healers, decisions concerning illness etiology and diagnosis tend to be made primarily by patients themselves, their families, and other interested parties. Biomedical physicians who practice in Kachitu must abandon many of their preconceptions and adjust themselves to the local belief systems if they expect to establish rapport with their patients. The various medical ideologies in Kachitu function as options that address different types of ailments. As Crandon-Malamud (1991:202–3) observes, "All things being equal, if one has tuberculosis, one goes to the physician in the Methodist clinic; if one suffers from khan achachi, one goes to yatiri; if one has a stomach upset, one resorts to medicinas casera [home care]." (*Khan achachi* refers to a sickness stemming from a phantom, *khan achachi*, who consumes meat, alcohol, and other gifts that it demands from people.)

Kachitunos, regardless of their social standing, tend to be pragmatic when it comes to seeking medical treatment. Medical dialogue serves as an idiom by which a person identifies his or her ethnic identity within the larger context of Bolivian society—one that is characterized by frequent economic crises, unstable governments, and military coups. Mestizos in Kachitu who find themselves downwardly mobile may, in essence, gain access to greater health care by turning to Indian indigenous medicine. Crandon-Malamud argues that they use medical dialogue, namely, debate about the most appropriate explanations of disease etiology and therapies to eradicate disease, as a mechanism of empowerment in the face of overwhelming external oppressive political-economic forces at both the national and the international level. Unfortunately, this medical dialogue has served as a rather limited form of empowerment and in reality serves more as a coping mechanism rather than an oppositional fulcrum within the larger Bolivian political economy and the global economy.

## Status of Health Care

Health services in Bolivia underwent a serious decline during the 1980s. According to Morales (1992:135),

> The infant mortality rate was now the highest in all of Latin America, given the national average of more than 200 per 1,000 live births in 1985 and as many as 650 per 1,000 in some rural areas, compared to 150 per 1,000 live births in 1975: 50 percent of children between one and six years of age were malnourished; and 60 percent of school-aged children suffered from goiter and 45 percent from anemia as a result of iodine and iron deficiencies, respectively.

Cuts in government spending contributed to a lack of potable water in 65 percent of urban households. Elsewhere, Klein (1992:280) reports that "life expectancy at birth over the past three decades has only risen some five years, or from the mid-forties to fifty years of age. But this is still some twenty years from that of the more advanced Latin American societies."

To no small degree, Bolivia's health problems and other socioeconomic problems emanate from a national social structure in which "the wealthiest 5 percent control 39 percent of the national income and the poorest 20 percent, only 2 percent" (Morales 1992:203) and its peripheral status within the global economy. Bolivia, along with Haiti, is one of the poorest countries in the Western Hemisphere. According to Klein (1992:279), despite heavy state investment in health care and education, the "continuing poor performance of the economy has meant that the indices of health and welfare remain among the lowest in the Americas." The ruined Bolivian economy has forced many Bolivian peasants either to revert to barter as the only means of economic exchange or to turn to coca production for the international cocaine market. Indeed, Bolivian peasants account for approximately one-third of the world's illicit drug production. It is difficult to convince Bolivian peasants to stop growing plants that are the source of illegal drugs when such production is all that stands between them and starvation, a fact that has largely been ignored in the U.S. war on drugs.

## A CASE STUDY OF MEDICAL PLURALISM IN AN URBAN SETTING OF A DEVELOPING SOCIETY: A VIEW FROM CENTRAL JAVA

Steve Ferzacca, an anthropologist based at Lethridge University in Canada, adopts a meaning-centered perspective, described in chapter 1, in seeking to unravel "phenomenological meanings of plurality of health care and perception in lives" (2001:5) among residents of Yogyakarta in the Republic of Indonesia. This city is the site of Gadjah Mada University (the country's first postindependence university) as well as many other colleges, institutes, and vocational schools, and it is a mecca of the classical arts, dance, music, and literature. In addition to visiting various biomedical clinics in Yogyakarta, Ferzacca conducted ethnographic research in Rumah Putri, a neighborhood within a subdistrict of the city consisting primarily of working-class people and lower-middle-class clerks, teachers, and public servants. Like various other countries in Southeast Asia, Indonesia, particularly under President Suharto's New Order, has promoted an authoritarian program of modernization, or *pembangunan* (development), and westernization in the form of elaborate Five Year Plans. Ferzacca (2001:210) views medical pluralism in Yogyakarta generally and among the residents of Rumah Putri specifically as a "social practice that produces hybrid forms of medicine," that is, a mixture of traditional and modern medicine, utilized by people who lead "hybrid lives." Medical pluralism in Yogyakarta is manifested largely in two broad forms: biomedicine and *pengobatan tradisional*, or traditional medicine. Biomedicine is practiced in clinics and hospitals that serve as "entry sites into modernity where exposures to the hegemony of scientific medicine takes place" (Ferzacca 2001:68). It is more or less universally available to everyone on the Indonesian island of Java, particularly in urban areas, and is situated in various settings, including private biomedical clinics, public health centers, mobile units, integrated health posts, and numerous government health programs. It is provided not only by biomedical physicians but also by nurse practitioners and health cadres. Many Javanese view biomedicine as a system that is useful in treating diseases (such as adult-onset type 2 diabetes, hypertension, and heart disease) associated with development or modernization, and hence they see it as complementing traditional indigenous and newly emerging medical subsystems.

## Medical Subsystems

Traditional medicine itself consists of a wide array of medical subsystems, therapies, and practitioners, including herbalism, massage, the use of amulets and talismans, patent medicines, Chinese herbalists and acupuncturists, Ayurvedic and Unani doctors, and indigenous Javanese healers and psychics. *Dukuns*, or traditional Javanese healers, practice various forms of shamanism, divination, exorcism, magic, midwifery, pediatrics, massage, spinal manipulation or bone setting, herbalism, and counseling and, rather than being valued as culturally familiar, are often regarded with suspicion because they may seek to exploit patients or place curses on unsuspecting victims. Conversely, psychics, or paranormals, are generally held in high esteem as paragons of modernity and development. These individuals find missing persons, perform astrology, tell fortunes, foretell the future, heal the sick, and perform rituals at various public events and rites of passage. The paranormals in particular have found a devoted clientele among politicians, businesspeople, and professional people, including members of the Javanese intelligentsia, such as professors, film and music stars, and even Catholic priests. In essence, while associated with *pengobatan tradisional*, paranormals practice a hybrid medicine that blends traditional practices with modern ones associated with Western and Eastern psychic traditions. In summary, Ferzacca (2001) argues that medical pluralism in urban Java provides a public sphere where both practitioners and patients can try to cope with everyday hardships of living under the domination of an oppressive regime intent on forcing them into modern life and the global economy.

## A CASE STUDY OF MEDICAL PLURALISM IN A DEVELOPED SOCIETY: THE AUSTRALIAN DOMINATIVE MEDICAL SYSTEM

While many Americans or Canadians would find many similarities between their societies and Australia, there are numerous subtle and not-so-subtle differences that underline the importance of culture in health care. Like Canada, Australia has a nationalized health care system that is also called Medicare, but the Australian health care system lies somewhere between the Canadian and the U.S. systems in that it is more privatized than the former and less privatized than the latter. Australia, which has slightly more than twenty million people in an area slightly smaller than the lower forty-eight U.S. states, is unique in that it has gone further than perhaps any other developed country in providing public support for the training of practitioners of complementary and alternative medicine (CAM), both in terms of degree-granting programs in chiropractic, os-teopathy, Chinese medicine, and naturopathy in public universities and in terms of partnerships that have developed between private CAM colleges and public universities that allow students in the former to upgrade an advanced diploma into a bachelor's degree. In contrast, aside from public colleges of osteopathic medicine, which in the United States have evolved into a parallel medical system to biomedicine with an emphasis on family medicine and reliance on manipulative therapy as an adjunct treatment approach, all training programs in chiropractic, Chinese medicine, and naturopathy are embedded in private insti-tutions in both the United States and Canada. As the Australian case indicates, the manner in which medical pluralism is expressed in a particular society is significantly shaped by political, economic, and social structural forces specific to that society, a point that was made in the case of Bolivia described previously (Baer et al. 2009).

## COMPLEMENTARY AND ALTERNATIVE MEDICINE

Historically, various terms have been bandied around to refer to alterna-tive medical systems. One term that has been used in the past to refer to conventional or allopathic medicine was "regular" medicine, which was contrasted to "irregular" medical systems (obviously a derogatory designation), such as homeopathy and chiropractic. Biomedicine also has been referred to by some writers as "orthodox" medicine, which was differentiated from "unorthodox" medicine (another derogatory designation). When referring to medical subsystems, such as natu-ropathy and herbalism, as examples of heterodox medicine, we prefer a designation that is more neutral and illustrates medical diversity. The term "complementary and alternative medicine" (CAM) appears to have emerged in the early 1990s as a biomedical construction in which the latter refers to medical subsystems that function as distinct alternatives to biomedicine, whereas the former refers to those that function along-side biomedicine. Despite its origin, CAM has quickly been adopted by both medical social scientists and health policymakers alike. Conversely, Australians tend merely to refer to a wide array of heterodox medical subsystems as complementary medicine.

## Biomedical Dominance

Whereas the Australian medical system with its various medical subsystems was relatively pluralistic in the nineteenth century, early in the twentieth century, with the transformation of regular or allopathic medicine into biomedicine, the latter adopted a scientific guise to distinguish itself from heterodox or alternative competitors. The Australian medical system evolved into a plural system in which biomedicine achieved dominance over other medical subsystems, a configuration medical anthropologists call a "dominative medical system." In his book *Biomedicine and Alternative Healing Systems in America*, Baer (2001) argues that the U.S. dominative medical system reflects class, racial and ethnic, and gender relations in the larger society inasmuch as practitioners of more prestigious medical systems, such as biomedicine and osteopathic medicine, tend to be white males of higher socioeconomic categories, and practitioners of religious and folk medical systems tend to be females, often belonging to lower socioeconomic categories and commonly being people of color. Table 5.1 depicts a model of the Australian dominative medical system.

Biomedicine began to dominate rival medical systems in Australia during the late nineteenth and early twentieth centuries. It formed associations of members to challenge competition, lobby the state to ban or at least restrict heterodox practitioners (who were called "quacks"), build alliances with conservative forces in government, and monopolize state funding for education and research on health-related issues. The cost of regular medical education tended to serve as an important factor in the transformation of regular medicine into a high-status occupation. According to Willis (1989:60),

> Entry to [regular] medicine . . . required substantial family backing involving the purchase of both a private school and university education. Once qualified there were further costs which heightened this class restrictiveness, such as the cost of setting up in practice. As a result, three quarters of native born doctors who commenced practice during the 1880s were sons of professional men.

As regular medicine assumed the guise of being scientific, it evolved into biomedicine in the early part of the twentieth century and increasingly achieved dominance over heterodox practitioners. Like in the United States, Britain, and other capitalist industrial societies, the germ theory, which downplayed the role of political, economic, and social structural determinants of diseases by focusing narrowly on only biological factors, appealed to the Australian corporate class and its political allies situated in the national government and the various state governments. As Willis (1989:89) notes, various "business interests, both national and international, were involved in promoting the paradigm of scientific

**Table 5.1 The Australian Dominative Medical System**

**Biomedicine**
**Fully legitimized professionalized heterodox medical systems**
    Osteopathy
    Chinese medicine in Victoria
**Semilegitimized professionalized heterodox medical systems**
    Chinese medicine outside of Victoria
    Naturopathy or natural therapies
    Direct-entry midwifery
    Homeopathy
**Limited or marginal heterodox medical systems**
    Homeopathy
    Massage therapy
    Reflexology
    Reiki
    Kinesiology
**Religious healing systems**
    Spiritualism
    Pentecostalism
    Liberal Catholic Church
    Scientology
    New Age healing
**Folk and ethnic medical systems**
    Anglo-Australian folk medicine
    European immigrant groups' folk medical systems
    Asian folk medical systems
    Aboriginal medical systems

medicine in Victoria," presumably because a focus on individual biology and behavior as the causes of illness avoids focus on the role of corporations in illness. The 1908 Medical Act not only ended the registration of foreign practitioners but also closely restricted the scope of practice of homeopaths and herbalists. While biomedicine achieved dominance over alternative systems, it by no means became a monolithic entity in Australian society. During the early decades of the twentieth century, tensions existed between graduates of British medical schools and Australian ones. Today, there are tensions between highly paid hospital specialists and overworked general practitioners and between physicians who are strong advocates of nationalized health care and those who want to see more privatization in the system.

## Avenues to Dominance

Evan Willis (1989), a prominent Australian health sociologist, asserts that Australian biomedicine employed four methods in its efforts to exert dominance over its competitors: (1) subordination that ensured that some health workers, such as nurses and midwives, were placed under direct authority of biomedical physicians; (2) limitations that legally restricted the occupational domain of certain health workers, particularly dentists, optometrists, podiatrists, and physiotherapists, through biomedical representation on registration boards; (3) exclusion by denying legitimacy to heterodox practitioners, such as chiropractors, osteopaths, naturopaths, herbalists, homeopaths, and acupuncturists, and excluding them from registration, state-supported education and research, and nationalized health coverage (which was first implemented in 1974); and (4) incorporation of certain medical procedures, such as child delivery, spinal manipulation, and, more recently, acupuncture, into the scope of biomedical practice, thereby absorbing techniques that had become the hallmarks of other medical traditions.

When individuals from lower social strata are denied entrée into the dominant medical profession, they sometimes turn to alternative healing groups as a vehicle for pursuing upward social mobility. Historically, professionalized heterodox systems have held out the promise of improved social mobility to numerous lower-middle-class and working-class individuals as well as members of other social categories. In attempting to enter the medical marketplace, as Larkin (1983:5) observes, "innovatory groups in medical science often commence with low status, particularly through their involvement in activities previously regarded as outside of a physician's or surgeon's role."

## Alternatives to Biomedicine

Beginning in the late nineteenth century, Australia as a relatively open society conducive to maverick individuals and social experiments served as what historian Phillippa Martyr (2002) aptly terms a "paradise of quacks"—a veritable haven for homeopaths, herbalists, phrenologists, hydropaths, lay midwives, spiritual healers, and purveyors of home remedies and patent medicines. While the 1921 census listed 3,959 "regular" medical practitioners, it also listed 412 "irregular" practitioners, showing that early on the Australian medical system was plural in nature. The nature of some of the medical subsystems in Australia is examined next.

### Osteopathy

Although initially developed in the United States, osteopathy diffused to various countries, particularly Anglophone countries, such as Canada, the United Kingdom, Australia, and New Zealand, where, unlike in the United States, it has remained primarily a manual medical system. In contrast to various other countries, the development of Australian osteopathy has been intertwined with that of chiropractic. Some Australian practitioners attempted to institutionalize a merger of chiropractic and osteopathy as was evidenced by names of various professional bodies and training institutions (e.g., the Chiropractic and Osteopathy College of Australia). Several osteopathic colleges reportedly transformed themselves into chiropractic colleges in the mid- and late 1960s.

### Chiropractic

Willis (1989) delineates four periods in the development of Australian chiropractic: (1) the establishment period (1918–1953), in which various groupings of chiropractors emerged in Victoria, including ones drawn from the ranks of British-trained osteopaths and others who obtained chiropractic training in the United States; (2) the period of expansion (1954–1961), which witnessed a considerable increase in the number of chiropractors trained in Australia (as well as many trained overseas); (3) the period of agitation (1961–1973), resulting in 1964 in the passage of the Western Australian Chiropractors' Act, which provided statutory registration for chiropractors in that state and included them under private health insurance plans; and (4) the period of legitimation, which began with a federal parliamentary committee report in 1977 that recommended registration for both chiropractors and homeopaths although not naturopaths. Chiropractic and osteopathy constitute fully legitimized professionalized heterodox medical systems in the sense that their training programs are embedded in public universities and one private university, namely, the chiropractic program at Murdoch University. The Australian Bureau of Statistics (1999:5–7) cited the following information for the number and gender composition of the chiropractic and osteopathic professions in Australia for 1997–1998: chiropractors, 1,555 males and 498 females, and osteopaths, 284 males and 111 females. O'Neill (1994:11) describes Australian chiropractic as a "small, well-paid, predominantly male, private practice occupation."

### Chinese Medicine in Australia

Although traditional Chinese medicine was first introduced in Australia in the mid-1850s in places like the gold fields of Victoria, where Chinese migrants first settled, it did not attain widespread popularity until the development of the holistic health movement. Chinese medicine also grew in popularity during the 1980s because of the influx of traditional Chinese medicine practitioners from Taiwan, Hong Kong, China, and Vietnam and the development of easier access to raw Chinese herbs. Chinese medicine has been and continues to be a fractionated profession as is evidenced by its wide array of associations and private training programs, some of which are situated in Chinese medicine colleges and others in colleges of natural therapies. Four public universities, namely, the Royal Melbourne Institute of Technology, the University of Western Sydney, the University of Technology–Sydney, and Victoria University, offer degree programs in Chinese medicine.

Despite the opposition of organized biomedicine, the Victoria Parliament passed the Chinese Registration Act in May 2000, making Victoria the only Australian jurisdiction to formally recognize regular Chinese medicine practitioners. However, Chinese medicine is slated for federal statutory registration under the Allied Health Professions Act in the very near future. In essence, depending on jurisdiction, Chinese medicine finds itself situated on the border between fully legitimized and partially legitimatized status as a heterodox medical system.

Bensoussan and Myers (1996) conducted a survey that provided a social profile of Australian Chinese Acupuncture and Chinese Medicine Association members: 55 percent were male and 45 percent female, and 30 percent of the respondents were of ethnic Chinese background. Traditional Chinese medicine practitioners find themselves in competition with many other practitioners, including chiropractors, osteopaths, natural therapists, physiotherapists, and biomedical physicians who utilize acupuncture in their practices.

### Naturopathy

The historic development of Australian naturopathy can be divided into three periods: its emergence between the 1920s and 1940s, a holding pattern between the 1950s and early 1970s, and its explosion from the late 1970s to the present under the umbrella of the holistic health movement. Early naturopaths in Australia obtained their training through apprenticeships, self-education, or overseas training (Evans 2000).

The overlap between naturopathy, osteopathy, and chiropractic was exemplified by the creation in 1936 of the Australian Chiropractors, Osteopaths, and Naturopathic Physicians Association. Many private naturopathic colleges and new naturopathic or natural therapies associations were established during the 1960s and 1970s and added to the list of those that had been created earlier.

While the terms "naturopath" and "naturopathy" continue to be used in a variety of contexts in Australia, including academic programs and professional associations, the terms "natural therapies" and "natural medicine" have become commonplace and are applied to a wide array of therapeutic subsystems, including Western herbalism, acupuncture, massage therapy, homeopathy, reflexology, and aromatherapy (Wiesner 1989). Naturopathy (or the natural therapies), acupuncture, and traditional Chinese medicine all constitute semi-legitimized professionalized heterodox medical systems in that, with the single exception of Chinese medicine in the state of Victoria, they have not achieved statutory registration in the various political jurisdictions. They have achieved, however, some degree of legitimation inasmuch as an increasing number of their training programs are situated in public institutions of higher education or in partnerships with private colleges and public universities. Furthermore, the federal government, at least tentatively, has granted naturopaths, Western herbalists, and traditional Chinese medicine practitioners belonging to certain professional associations an exemption from the General Sales Tax for services rendered to patients. In effect, this means that such approaches are viewed by the government as therapeutic systems rather than forms of quackery. The fact that both the federal government and certain state governments have commissioned inquiries into various aspects of CAM constitutes also a de facto form of legitimation.

Although the vast majority of Australian naturopaths in the past probably were men, in more recent years both naturopathy and the natural therapies have attracted large numbers of women to the point where they constitute the clear majority in these fields—a fact that Baer observed directly during his visits to various schools and activities of complementary medicine in Australia, such as the School of Natural and Complementary Medicine at Southern Cross University and the meeting of the National Herbalists Association of Australia. Some time ago, Wiesner (1989:19) reported that naturopaths, homeopaths, and herbalists "generally are barely able to make a living." While this assertion may not be as true today, Bensoussan et al. (2004:22) found in a survey of naturopathic and Western herbal practitioners that 38.2 percent of their respondents earned less than $40,000 Australian a year. Furthermore, despite the popularity of CAM in Australia, the large number of students graduating from natural therapies training programs in both public and private institutions has probably saturated the CAM marketplace with practitioners.

## Lay or Direct-Entry Midwifery

There are a large number of nurse-midwives in Australia, as in other Western societies. The women's liberation movement stimulated development of the natural childbirth movement in Australia. Organizations that grew out of this development include the Childbirth Education Association, Parents Centres Australia, and the Nursing Mothers Association of Australia. Several public universities, including Flinders University in Adelaide and Monash University in Melbourne, came to offer direct-entry programs in which midwifery is offered as an undergraduate degree. Organizations that promote lay midwifery care in both hospitals and homes include the Australian College of Midwives, the Australian Society of Independent Midwives, a consumer group called Maternity Coalition, and the Community Midwifery Program, which since 1990 has been funded by the government to seek alternative models of childbirth for low-risk women (Sutton 2004:6–7).

## Teaching CAM

Other alternative therapeutic systems such as homeopathy, massage therapy, reflexology, aromatherapy, Reiki, polarity therapy, kinesiology, and various other CAM therapies constitute limited or marginal heterodox medical systems in Australia. Many of these systems function as specific treatment modalities that are taught in schools of natural therapy or that are used as adjuncts by naturopaths or natural therapists in their practices. Furthermore, when the tenets of these subsystems are taught at a school of natural therapy as a specialized program of study or at a training institution that focuses on a specific therapy, such as homeopathy or reflexology, they often entail a shorter period of study and the granting of a "diploma" or "certificate" rather than a "degree" or "advanced diploma."

At the next level, one finds various Euro-Australian religious healing systems, such as Christian Science, Spiritualism, Seventh-Day Adventism, the Liberal Catholic Church, Scientology, New Age healing, and Pentecostalism. Finally, as a multiethnic society, Australia has numerous folk medical subsystems. Of these, Aboriginal healing systems in particular have received considerable attention, particularly from anthropologists. In contrast, the folk medical systems of various European and Asian immigrant groups have received relatively little attention. Han's (2000) examination of the health status of Korean immigrants in Sydney reveals that most of them take *hanbang* (which, in Korean, means Chinese medicine) herbal medicine and health food, such as ginseng and deer antlers, but also rely heavily on biomedicine.

## CAM and Biomedicine

In the past, the Australian Medical Association (AMA) had been a virulent opponent of CAM. While the AMA admitted that chiropractors might provide patients with some relief from back pain, it argued "that chiropractors' use of manipulation to treat pain in the musculoskeletal system involves no more than the application of techniques well known to the medical and physiotherapy professions" (AMA 1992:8). It argued that chiropractic should not qualify for either public or private health insurance funding. Despite the policies of the AMA, many biomedical general practitioners have been adopting

CAM therapies, especially acupuncture, or are now willing to refer patients to CAM therapists. Discussion of CAM reportedly has been introduced into the undergraduate curriculum of several biomedical schools. Moreover, in 1992, various biomedical physicians formed the Australian Integrative Medicine Association. Ironically, as a result of the increasing popularity of CAM, the AMA has in recent years relaxed its long-standing dismissal of CAM systems (Easthope et al. 2000).

In addition to the growing interest of biomedical physicians in CAM, various policymakers, politicians, and public servants have been giving increasing attention to it in Australia. As in other developed societies, the corporate class and the state in Australia have since the 1970s come to express concern about rising health care costs. Najman (2003) notes that between 1989–1990 and 1999–2000, health care costs rose from 7.5 percent to 8.5 percent of the Australian gross domestic product. While it is rarely mentioned in the health economics literature, the growing support in various ways for CAM exhibited by the Australian government may constitute a covert strategy for curtailing rising health costs. An observer at the Alternative Medicine Summit in Canberra in 1996, for example, noted that "one calculation estimated savings to government over an election period of around $640 million if just 10% of people with non-serious, self-limiting conditions visited a naturopath rather than a doctor" (Arachne 1997:14). Given that CAM subsystems often emphasize individual responsibility for health, they are compatible with the strong interest among government health administrators, health policymakers, and academics in preventive medicine and health promotion. Since the 1970s, both Labor and Coalition (Liberal and National parties) governments have encouraged citizens to obtain private health insurance and have sought to make them more self-reliant and responsible (White 2002:95). The government's support for CAM is an integral part of its neoliberal effort to divest itself of as much health care expenditure as the Australian public will tolerate. While the federal government provides support for complementary medicine programs, which tend to be relatively inexpensive compared to biomedical schools because of their low-tech approach, for the most part it does not provide reimbursement under the guidelines of Medicare—the Australian national health plan—to complementary practitioners for services rendered.

Periodically, the issue of whether the government should reimburse complementary practitioners for their services arises. Several years ago, Medicare created new regulations that all patients with a referral from a biomedical general practitioner could receive free chiropractic or osteopathic treatment. However, the Enhanced Primary Care plan permits reimbursement for only five visits per year. As Weir (2005:33) so aptly observes, "The referral requirement for this treatment places control over the provision firmly in the hands of the medical profession." Given that chiropractors in particular are prone to treat patients on a quite-regular basis, the patient will be forced to either pay for additional visits out of pocket or receive a partial rebate (perhaps around 20 percent) from a private health plan.

The future of CAM as well as integrative medicine in Australia is difficult to predict but will be subject to numerous larger political, economic, and social structural forces in the larger society. So long as CAM is not fully incorporated into Medicare, it will tend to serve primarily the more affluent sectors of Australian society. As health sociologist John Gray (2006:245) observes, patients who use CAM "represent a generally more privileged segment of the Australian population." Furthermore, although chiropractors, osteopaths, naturopaths, Western herbal medicine practitioners, homeopaths, and Chinese medicine practitioners view themselves as primary care practitioners, so long as they cannot practice in hospitals on a regular basis, they will remain subordinate partners in the Australian dominative medical system.

## TYPOLOGIES OF PLURAL MEDICAL SYSTEMS

A number of social scientists have created typologies to help understand the nature of medical pluralism in complex societies of the sort described in the three cases that were presented here. Drawing on the meaning-centered perspective, Chrisman and Kleinman (1983), for example, created a widely used model that delineates three overlapping sectors in the health care system. The popular sector consists of health care performed by patients themselves along with their families, social networks, and communities, or what Janzen (1978:4–5) terms the "therapeutic management group." It includes a wide range of therapies, such as special rituals, diets, prohibitions on certain behaviors, herbs, teas, exercise, rest, baths, and massage, as well as, with the rise of commercial pharmacies, articles such as over-the-counter drugs, vitamin and nutritional supplements, humidifiers, heating pads, and hot water bottles. Based on his research in Taiwan, Kleinman estimates that 70 to 90 percent of the illness treatment episodes on the island occur in the popular sector.

MEDICARE AROUND THE WORLD

When Americans think of Medicare, they think of the U.S. government's health program for citizens over the age of sixty-five. In contrast to the United States, which, along with South Africa, is the only developed country in the world lacking national health insurance, both Canada and Australia have national health plans that are also called Medicare. The Canadian system was implemented in 1968 and consists of ten provincial health plans that must abide by certain national standards and are funded jointly by federal and provincial governments through corporate taxes, personal taxes, property taxes, and taxes on gasoline, tobacco, and liquor. In Australia, a national health plan called Medibank was created in 1974 after the Labor Party under Prime Minister Gough Whitlam came to power. The Liberal Party eventually dismantled Medibank when it assumed power in 1977, but the Labor Party reinstated a national health plan renamed Medicare, a largely federally operated system, when it again assumed power in 1983. While the coalition government under Prime Minister John Howard has made concerted efforts to privatize health care in Australia, between 1996 and 2007, it did not attempt to dismantle it because, despite its inadequacies, Medicare is an institution that the great majority of Austrailians support. However, Labor governments since 2007 have left privatized health plans and hospitals intact.

The second level of this typology, the folk sector, encompasses various healers who are self-trained or undergo an apprenticeship and tend to practice independently, often out of their home on a quasi-legal or illegal basis. These include shamans, mediums, magicians, herbalists, bonesetters, lay midwives, psychics, and faith healers, such as the Maprofeita healer from Mozambique shown in Figure 5.1. An example of the folk sector was described in chapter 2 in the case of Brodwin's study of *houngans* in Haiti and the ways in which people make decisions about which type of healer to consult when they feel ill.

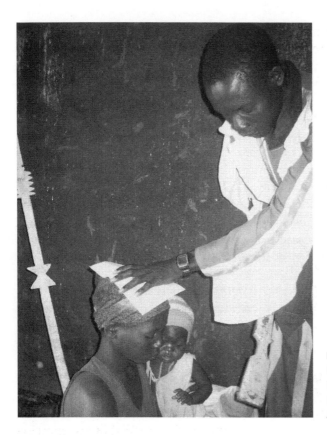

FIGURE 5.1
Maprofeita faith healer
in urban Mozambique.
Photo by Ippolytos
Andreas Kalofonos.

The professional sector includes the practitioners and bureaucratic structures, such as clinics, hospitals, and associations, that are associated with
both biomedicine and professionalized heterodox medical systems, such as
Ayurveda and Unani in South Asia; acupuncture and herbalism in China;
homeopathy, osteopathy, chiropractic, and naturopathy in Britain; and *Heilpraktikers* (naturopaths) in Germany. The department of surgery studied by
Katz that was presented in chapter 2 is an example of one part of the professional sector in biomedicine.

### Healing and History

In the previous chapter we introduced Fabrega's biocultural approach to
medical systems, in which he maintains that medical pluralism is first manifested in chiefdom societies, prestate societies, and early state societies and

then develops an even more elaborate form in more complex societies, starting out with empires and civilizations, such as ancient China, ancient India, ancient Greece, and medieval Islamic societies, followed by European societies and finally postmodern societies.

According to Fabrega, in state societies, sickness and health adaptation (SH) is characterized by two tiers: (1) an official, scholarly, academic medical system oriented to the care of elites and (2) a wide array of less prestigious physicians and folk healers who treat subordinate segments of the society. The state, with its various government bodies, plays an increasing role in medical care by hiring practitioners for elites and providing free or nominal care for the poor, especially during famines and epidemics. The literate or "great" medical tradition, such as in traditional Chinese medicine or Ayurveda in South Asia, includes the formation of a medical profession, the beginnings of clinical medicine, and increasing commercialization (and technologicalization) of the healing endeavor.

The ancient city-state of Sumer and its hinterland exemplifies the existence of medical pluralism in an early state society. Sumeria, which existed between 4000 and 3000 B.C., possessed three categories of cuneiform texts that included various kinds of medical information: therapeutic or medical texts per se, omen collections or "symptom texts," and miscellaneous texts that included information on ailments and medical practices (Magner 1992:19). Sumerian physicians diagnosed symptoms by taking health histories rather than performing direct physical examination. Conversely, the "conjurer," "diviner," or "priest-healer" in Sumer society conducted a direct physical examination and used the patient's symptoms and life circumstances as omens to help diagnose disease. The Sumerian pharmacopoeia included 250 medicinal plants and some 120 mineral substances as well as alcoholic beverages, fats and oils, animal parts and products, honey, wax, and various kinds of milk.

In the centuries after Sumer, various empires and civilizations developed particularly elaborate corpora of medical knowledge, such as manifested in traditional Chinese medicine and Ayurveda in South Asia, that are incorporated into writings and commentaries which over time both exhibit an internal order and also include numerous inconsistencies. While much has been written about medical systems in Old World ancient empires and civilizations, out of which biomedicine ultimately developed, including those of Egypt, Greece, and Rome, far less has been written about the medical systems of New World civilizations and empires, such as those of the Mayas, Aztecs, and Incas.

The Aztecs, who developed an extensive empire in central Mexico that was brought to an end with the Spanish conquest in the early sixteenth century, had a complex medical system that combined naturalistic and supernaturalistic elements and included priests, shamans, and physicians (Ortiz de Montellano 1989). The state-sanctioned presence of both priests and shamans was a unique situation worldwide because of the strong antagonism that generally exists between the two. The Aztecs believed that the human body contains several souls, each with a specific function affecting growth, development, physiology, and fate in the afterlife. The three primary souls were the *tonally*, situated in the head; the *teyolia*, located in the heart; and the *ihiyotl*, found in the liver. Health depended on the relative size of each soul at any point in time and the degree of balance among the three souls. Diet and personal behavior influenced the size of each soul. Offended deities, particularly the creator god Tezcatlopoca (or one of his many manifestations), or certain animals could inflict disease on an individual. Aztec astrology posited that the equilibrium of the universe affected the human body. The Aztecs also believed that disease could be inflicted by a sorcerer through certain rituals.

The Aztec priesthood became more elaborate and specialized as the Aztec civilization and empire expanded. According to Wolf (1999:153), "Various kinds of priests organized and officiated at rituals, including those featuring human sacrifice; managed the wealth that was accumulating in temple treasuries; taught school; and took confession and prescribed penance." Priests conducted worship of the Aztec pantheon that consisted of numerous deities, each of which had one or more temples where its idol was kept. The vast majority of priests were males, but there were some female priests who generally served briefly before marrying.

Aztec shamans were capable of sending their *tonally* on magical flights back to the time of creation or, alternatively, transforming them into the appearance of an animal. This process of spiritual transformation by the shamans was assisted by the use of various hallucinogenic plants. Shamans focused on curing ailments caused by imbalance in the relationships between the gods and humans or by the intrusion of beings from other cosmic realms into the sufferer's body.

Aztec physicians could be either male or female. Sahagun, a Catholic priest who chronicled many aspects of Aztec culture following the Spanish conquest, provides this description of a good general practitioner:

> The true doctor. He is a wise man; he imparts life. A tried specialist, he has
> worked with herbs, stones, trees, and roots. His remedies have been tested; he

examines, he experiments, he alleviates sickness. He massages aches and sets broken bones. He administers purges and potions; he bleeds his patients; he cuts and he sews the wound; he brings about reactions; he staunches the bleeding with ashes. (quoted in Smith 2003:255)

Aztec medicine also had an array of medical specialists who focused on diagnosing specific ailments by identifying the offended deity who had induced the disease and prescribing the appropriate propitiatory ritual, which could be making an offering, confessing a wrongdoing, engaging in acts of penance, or praying. It included, as well, empirical knowledge about hundreds of medicinal plants that were applied by herbal specialists. The Aztec medical system relied on highly sophisticated surgeons, including those who served in the many battles that the Aztecs fought while enlarging their empire, some of whom even practiced plastic surgery. Aztec society also had fortune-tellers who could be either male or female and who divined by casting maize kernels and gazing in water.

Sickness and health adaptation in modern state societies worldwide is characterized by the emergence of biomedicine as a dominant and hegemonic profession. Biomedicine, in turn, is characterized by patterns of secularization, including the weakening of the role of institutional religion in public life; scientific knowledge, with its embrace of biological reductionism, including the tendency to view disease as due primarily to biological factors, such as germs; the emergence of the hospital as the center of healing and research; and the universalization of categories of sickness. For Fabrega and many other social scientists, modernity is generally associated with the rise of advanced technology, conventional Western science, the notion of progress, rationalism, efficiency, and secularization. In this scenario, the hospital emerges as the center of healing and the "clinical gaze" in which the body is subjected to close probing and scrutiny, such as in the use of the stethoscope and surgery.

Biomedicine during the modern era became increasingly specialized with the appearance of practitioners who focused on certain parts of the body, such as the heart, the lungs, and the immunological system. Furthermore, in keeping with a pattern of medical specialization is the "growth of the discipline of psychiatry and the increasing importance given to mental illness in the society and in conceptions of social disability, welfare, and crime" (Fabrega 1997:136). At the same time, medical pluralism in Western societies and Japan manifests itself in the continuing existence of alternative practitioners, such as homeopaths, herbalists, osteopaths, chiropractors, and naturopaths, who are held in contempt by many biomedical physicians.

Despite persisting biomedical dominance, the pursuit of alternative therapies, including ones based on Western spirituality or Eastern mysticism, manifests itself most profoundly in what Fabrega and other social scientists term postmodern societies. The postmodern world is associated with corporate globalization involving the diffusion of corporate control over economic, political, and cultural processes throughout the world; a sense of social fragmentation and uncertainty about social institutions and values; an emphasis on consumerism; a growing faith in intuition; and "hybridity," which is the blending together of elements from different cultures and parts of the world. Many individuals in postmodern societies, particularly those belonging to higher socioeconomic categories, regard health as an achieved status obtained through education, prevention, and lifestyle. Further, postmodern societies manifest an "obsessive preoccupation with health and fitness" (Fabrega 1997:137), thus resulting in the phenomenon of the "worried well."

### Patients of CAM

These patterns result in "dissatisfaction with physicians, with 'establishment' medicine, with the escalating costs of a more routinized and procedural approach to healing, and with tentacles of medical insurance companies," all leading to an "increasing interest in holistic medical traditions and the growth of health-promoting and life extension industries that compete with orthodox biomedicine" (Fabrega 1997:244)

Numerous patient utilization studies conducted in the United States, Canada, Britain, Australia, and various Western European countries have sought to identify the types of people who tend to turn to complementary and alternative therapies and practitioners. These studies indicate that users of CAM, aside from various folk medical systems, tend to be female, relatively young, employed, highly educated, and often but not necessarily involved in alternative lifestyles. At the same time, CAM has found some reception among working-class people in developed societies. Connor (2004), for example, found that many of her respondents in Oceanport (pseudonym), a suburb of an Australian city, reported that they and other household members followed a "mixed therapy regimen" in which they used a CAM therapy either prior to or in combination with biomedical treatment.

Based upon interviews with forty CAM practitioners and three hundred patients of CAM clinics in Denmark, Helle Johannessen delineates three principal actor-networks: a technocrat network, a social-democratic network, and a neoliberal network. The technocrat network exhibits body praxis that operates with a plumbing model in which the body is viewed as a series of pipes that "reflects technologies of drainages systems, circulation of water, heat and electricity in the house so familiar to contemporary people" (Johannessen 2007:270). In Danish CAM clinics, reflexology in particular, which entails the massage of reflex zones on the feet that are purportedly linked with various organs, follows the plumbing model associated with the technocrat network. The social-democratic network model seeks to achieve an internal balance among body organs reflective of the need for a more macroscopic balance between the body's immune system and external disease agents, such as allergens, pollutants, bacteria, and viruses. CAM therapies focused upon proper nutrition and the technologies of biopathy illustrated, for instance, by use of an "electrical apparatus showing signs of light and sound" exemplify this model, which is characterized by "principles of democracy, consultancy, and uniqueness" (Johannssen 2007:273). Finally, the neoliberal network model views the body as a computer governed by the brain that can be corrected through a process of reprogramming when an autonomous individual begins to malfunction. In order to reprogram the patient's body-mind, kinesiology with its tests of muscle strengths operates on the basis of this model in that its practitioners administer bodywork based upon patients' responses to questions about their experiences in childhood and even previous lives, substance intolerance, malfunctioning organs, and strained social relations. Patients may prefer one or another actor-network, but in reality they move between them, thus following a sort of mixed therapy regimen within the confines of CAM.

While CAM systems have, since the 1970s, become increasingly popular in developed societies, the high cost of biomedicine and the fact that it tends to be based in urban areas means that many people in developing societies, particularly in rural areas but also in cities, continue to rely heavily on "traditional" medical systems or on new healers who combine aspects of folk medicine and biomedicine. As Pfeiffer (2005:277) demonstrates in his examination of indigenous and church-based healers in Mozambique, "traditional healing had already been substantially modified by the intrusion of the modern for some time as it responded to the convulsions of colonialism and deeper integration within wider markets over at least the last 100 years in that country and much of the developing world." Men, in particular, in poverty-stricken Mozambique have responded to structural adjustment policies imposed on their country by the World Bank and the International Monetary Fund in 1987 by turning to traditional healing as a means of making a livelihood. Indeed, the Mozambique Association of Traditional Healers, a government-based body to which many *curandeiros* belong, lists the availability of numerous treatments, including ones to help a client obtain a job, avoid mishaps, contact ancestral spirits, and cope with a wide array of problems of living. Some traditional healers, however, view the association as a government ploy to tax them. In response to the growing pecuniary orientation of many traditional healers, a large number of people in Mozambique have turned to Pentecostal sects and African independent churches, which syncretize or blend elements of traditional African religions and Christianity, to create healing rituals designed to help them cope with their plight.

**CAM and Class**

In keeping with Navarro's (1986:1) assertion that classes as well as ethnic groups and genders within capitalist societies "have different ideologies which appear in different forms of culture," it may be argued that these social categories also construct different health understandings, behavior patterns, and medical subsystems to coincide with their respective views of reality. Regarding gender differences, for example, various medical anthropologists concerned with reproductive health have argued that men and women do not always share reproductive goals and strategies. As Sargent (2006:32) observes, "Contested reproductive interests may derive from women's and men's differing experiences of pregnancy and birth, varying domestic and productive responsibilities, or discrepant material interests." How men influence women's reproductive behaviors, in fact, remains an understudied issue. The reason for this, according to Carole Browner (2001:773), is that "those who would be expected to be interested in the topic, anthropologists . . . have historically seen reproduction as a 'woman's topic' and therefore not central to the field," a telling comment on how social factors influence the course of social research within and beyond medical anthropology.

Class differences in health understandings, behaviors, and medical subsystems are also of considerable importance. Critical medical anthropologists, for example, argue that the patterns of medical pluralism found in state societies tend to reflect hierarchical and unequal social relations based on class, caste, ethnicity, region, religion, and gender distinctions found in the larger society. Thus, critical medical anthropologists argue that national medical systems in the modern world should be described as "plural" rather than "pluralistic" inasmuch as biomedicine enjoys a dominant status over both heterodox (e.g., chiropractic and naturopathy) and folk medical systems (e.g., *curanderismo* and African American Spiritualism). In reality, plural medical systems may be best described as "dominative" in that one subsystem within the larger complex of coexistent medical traditions generally enjoys a preeminent status over the 'others. As noted earlier, within the modern context, it is biomedicine that exerts dominance over all other complementary and alternative medical subsystems (see chapter 1), although people are quite capable of "dual use" of distinct medical subsystems, either simultaneously or sequentially (Romanucci-Ross 1977). Thus, it is not unusual for a patient to be treated during a period of time for the same or different health problems by a folk healer and a biomedical physician (with or without the knowledge of one or both healers).

In the United States, as a result of financial backing for its research activities and educational institutions, initially from corporate-sponsored foundations and later the federal government as well, biomedicine evolved into the dominant medical system. It then asserted scientific superiority and clearly established authority over professionalized heterodox medical systems, such as homeopathy (a medical system developed by Samuel Hahnemann, a disenchanted German physician), eclecticism (a hybrid of regular medicine and botanical medicine), hydropathy (an elaborate system of water cures), osteopathy, and chiropractic. Homeopathy and eclecticism have been somewhat absorbed by biomedicine at both the organizational and the therapeutic level. Osteopathy initially constituted a manual medical system created by Andrew Taylor Still, a dissatisfied regular physician who viewed the spine as the key to good health. It evolved into osteopathic medicine and surgery and achieved full practice rights in all fifty states and the District of Columbia by the early 1970s. Chiropractic, another manual medical system developed by D. D. Palmer, an American magnetic healer, evolved into the leading professionalized heterodox medical system in the United States (and in a growing number of settings in the United States is being practiced as a junior partner to orthopedics). At the beginning of the twentieth century, hydropathy became part of naturopathy, a highly eclectic medical system that incorporated botanical medicine, exercise, dietetics, and colonic irrigations. Naturopathy declined in the 1930s but underwent a rejuvenation with the emergence of the holistic health movement during the 1970s and 1980s.

Biomedical dominance over rival medical systems has never been absolute. In capitalist societies, the corporate class historically has come to exert greater and greater influence over politicians and government bureaucrats through processes such as lobbying, campaign contributions, and the dissemination of information favorable to its positions. Nevertheless, despite the fact that the state serves the interests primarily of the wealthiest class in society, it must periodically make concessions to subordinate social groups in the interests of maintaining social order and the capitalist mode of production. As a result, certain complementary and alternative practitioners, with the backing of clients and particularly influential patrons, were able to obtain legitimation in the form of full or limited practice rights. Lower social classes, ethnic minorities, and women have often used CAM therapies as a forum for challenging not only biomedical dominance but also, to a degree, the hegemony of the corporate class or state elites. CAM systems sometimes resist, at least subtly, the elitist, hierarchical, and bureaucratic patterns of biomedicine. In contrast to biomedicine, which is dominated ultimately by the corporate class or state elites, folk healing systems are more generally the domain of common people. Biomedical physicians often have significant representation on the registration boards of other health practitioners, tend to be overrepresented on hospital and health policy advisory boards and in government health departments, and dominate health research funding.

As was the case in Australia, the growing interest in CAM therapies by corporate and government elites around the world is related to the cost of high-technology biomedicine. Even in countries where explicit financial and/or legal support is absent, governments often prefer to support CAM approaches because they focus on self-limiting diseases, that is, diseases that tend to run their natural course without treatment. While some anthropologists have commended efforts to integrate aspects of biomedicine and CAM practitioners as constituting a key to more comprehensive and culturally sensitive health care, Philip Singer (1977) views the therapeutic alliance between biomedicine and folk healers as a manifestation of a "new colonialism." An emancipatory therapeutic alliance ultimately requires an egalitarian relationship between various medical systems, one that transcends the hierarchical structure of existing dominative systems associated with modern societies.

Societies vary considerably in the degree to which they tolerate medical pluralism. This reality is effectively captured in a scheme depicted in Table 5.2, developed by Murray Last (1996:380), which depicts the "range

**Table 5.2. Plural Medical Systems in Terms of the Officially Accepted Range of Medical Subcultures**

**Exclusive systems**
    Soviet model
    French model
    American model
  **Tolerant systems**
    British model
    German model
**Integrated systems**
**Third World systems**

INTEGRATIVE MEDICINE

Just as has been the case in the term "complementary and alternative medicine" (CAM), certain biomedical physicians who are favorably predisposed have created the term "integrative medicine" to refer to the integration of biomedical and CAM therapies, either on the part of a biomedical physician or in a clinical setting where both biomedical physicians and CAM practitioners collaborate in the provision of health care. While on the surface such an arrangement appears to be commendable, various scholars have argued that integrative medicine in essence is another example of biomedical hegemony in that biomedical physicians tend to be in positions of dominance in most integrative medical settings.

of subcultures permitted within a national medical culture." In the case of the exclusive system, the national power structure recognizes and tolerates only one medical subculture, namely, biomedicine, as acceptable or at least dominant over alternative systems. Such a system existed in the former Soviet Union and former Soviet-bloc countries where alternative healers were viewed as feudalistic anachronisms associated with superstition and economic backwardness. In the French model, which is followed not only in France but also in francophone Africa and parts of Latin America, the national power structure recognizes only biomedical practitioners and defines alternative medical systems as illegal. In the American model, which theoretically is based on free market principles, the national power structure defines "hospital medicine" or biomedicine as the dominant medical subculture legally and in terms of funding for medical education and research. Conversely, this variant permits a restricted tolerance of alternative medical systems, some of which, such as chiropractic and acupuncture, enjoy more official acceptance than others, such as herbalism and various forms of bodywork.

While giving preeminence to biomedicine, tolerant systems adopt a more or less laissez-faire policy toward alternative medical systems. The British system, which is followed not only in Britain but also in Australia, New Zealand, and many developing nations, operates on the basis of common law, which essentially states that if the law does not specifically restrict certain procedures, such as prescribing legally defined drugs, performing surgery, and signing death certificates, as exclusively the domain of the biomedical practitioner, individuals may practice an alternative medical system, such as herbalism or naturopathy. While this policy applied for a long time to both osteopaths and chiropractors, both of these healing groups obtained statutory recognition, in Australia in the early 1980s and in Britain in the early 1990s. Another example of the tolerant system is the German model mentioned earlier. While biomedical physicians may work within the traditions of both *Schulmedizin* and *Naturheilkunde*, Germany has a diverse group of practitioners called *Heilpraktikers* (the counterparts to naturopaths in North America, Britain, Australasia, and India) who vary tremendously in terms of their training but are permitted to practice a wide array of natural therapies as long as they have passed an examination indicating that they understand the laws regulating medical practice.

The integrated system is especially characteristic of India and China. In India, the government permits practitioners of various ancient healing systems, such as Ayurvedic, Siddha, and Unani medicine, to establish their own professional associations, training institutions, hospitals, and pharmaceutical industry and provides these systems with statutory recognition and funding. Unfortunately, the increasing commodification of indigenous medicinal substances in recent times "threatens to rob the poor sections of Indian society of access to Indian medicine because they cannot afford the relatively expensive Ayurvedic and Unani brands" (Bode 2006:233). The poor farmer from Bankura district in West Bengal, India, in Figure 5.2, is an example of the part of Indian society whose access to Indian medicine is becoming more limited. The People's Republic of China officially recognizes both biomedicine and traditional Chinese medicine and has integrated both of them to a certain degree in state-operated institutions, including some clinics, hospitals, and colleges. During the Maoist era, barefoot doctors, who were highly touted as paragons of revolutionary dedication, served as medical auxiliaries trained in both biomedicine and Chinese medicine. China also has made provisions for incorporating various indigenous or folk healers.

Finally, the Third World model is situated in many developing societies, particularly the poorest ones in which biomedicine is primarily urban based, poorly financed, and largely a privilege of elites and a small middle class. While the power structure privileges biomedicine and even makes it available on a restricted basis to the masses, it tolerates a wide array of alternative medical systems consisting of local folk healers, bonesetters, injectionists (folk healers who use syringes to inject vitamins, antibiotics, or other drugs), barber-surgeons, and midwives who serve the majority of people—a fact recognized by the World Health Organization. For example, in Mozambique,

FIGURE 5.2
Impoverished small farmer dries grains in Bankura District in West Bengal, India. Photo by
Anna Marie Nicolaysen.

which has one biomedical physician for some fifty thousand people, there
is a traditional healer available for every two hundred people. Furthermore,
pharmacists in developing nations often serve as a major source of medical
information and dispense drugs freely that generally require a prescription
written by a biomedical physician in developed societies. In many developing
societies, folk and indigenous healers have organized themselves into professional associations in their efforts to obtain greater legitimation and recognition (Last 1996).

## NEW DIRECTIONS IN THE STUDY OF MEDICAL PLURALISM
Whereas the early work on medical pluralism tended to focus on levels in
plural medical systems, more recent research on this phenomenon recognizes
that, as Stoner (1986:47) asserts, "pluralism can now be examined as a multiplicity of healing techniques, rather than of medical systems." In a similar
vein, Pool and Geissler (2005:45) maintain:

Rather than trying to reveal "[medical] systems" we should focus on studying practice (what people people actually do when they are ill or suffer misfortune). Health-seeking behavior is not simply enactment of "beliefs" within the confines of "culture" or a "system," but a creative process in which we must recognize the role of invention, innovation, and disorder.

In reality, practitioners from various specific medical systems borrow therapies or modalities from other systems, such as when folk healers in developing societies prescribe manufactured biomedical drugs or even inject them. In South Kanara, India, healers often mixed Ayurvedic medicine with biomedicine and traditional healing techniques (Nichter 1989:187–215).

In response to the growing popularity of CAM in various developed societies, biomedical physicians have increasingly been incorporating various therapeutic techniques from homeopathy, herbalism, acupuncture, and bodywork into their regimen of treatment in an effort to creative an "integrative medicine." In essence, while biomedicine continues to enjoy dominance and preeminence worldwide, it increasingly has come to find itself challenged by CAM practitioners of various sorts, including professionalized heterodox ones (e.g., chiropractors and naturopaths), partially professionalized heterodox ones (e.g., herbalists and bodyworkers), and religious and folk healers. Some biomedical practitioners continue to resist the inroads being made by CAM practitioners, yet an increasing number of them are choosing to collaborate with them, but in a manner in which the CAM practitioners later face the danger of cooptation by being transformed into medical auxiliaries similar to nurses, physicians' assistants, and physical therapists.

Brodwin (1996), whose research in Haiti was discussed in chapter 2, asserts that analysis of medical pluralism has reached a theoretical impasse because categorization efforts produced static functionalist typologies or employed incomparable terms. Medical anthropologists turned to concerns such as the political economy of health, biomedical domination, CAM systems in developed societies, reproduction, the mindful body, biotechnology, substance abuse, and AIDS. Despite the validity of Brodwin's comments on the shortcomings of much of the research on medical pluralism, various critical medical anthropologists, as we have seen, developed an interest in how power relations shape plural medical systems. In essence, medical pluralism is a topic that continues to be of central concern in medical anthropology.

In keeping with increasing globalization, medical anthropologists have come to find a growing pattern of *syncretism* or *hybridization*—a process in which two relatively distinct medical systems merge to form an essentially new one or at least elements of different medical systems are blended together in the treatment of a specific health problem (Pool and Geissler 2005:44-45). Ayurvedic acupuncture constitutes a fascinating example of medical hybridization, one which entails the blending together of Ayurveda, a Hindu medical system based on Sanskrit medical texts, and traditional Chinese medicine or Taoist medicine. Alter (2005:25) maintains that the "popularity of acupressure and acupuncture therapy in modern India" has resulted in the "construction of something called Ayurvedic acupuncture." Both Ayurveda and Chinese medicine contend that the unimpaired flow of bioenergy, *Prana* in the case of the former and *chi* in the case of the latter, are essential to health maintenance. *Prana* flows through each and every organ of the body much in the same way that *Tying* and *chi* flow through channels or twelve regular meridians and eight subsidiary meridians, respectively.

Another example of medical hybridization entails the simultaneous use of the biomedical drug Viagra and herbal medicine in China in the treatment of male sexual impotence. Viagra initially officially entered the Chinese market in July 2000, yet for ages Chinese medicine has used *zhuangyang* herbal tonics that purportedly nourish kidney yang in order to cure impotence. Anthropologist Everett Yuehong Zhang interviewed some two dozen physicians, both biomedical and Traditional Chinese medical, and about 350 patients suffering from impotence or other sexually related diseases. While very few men relied exclusively on Viagra in treating their impotence, many of them engaged in a pattern of switching between the use of Viagra and herbal tonics in their treatment regimen. This switching pattern is illustrated in the case of Mr. Wang (pseudonym) who took ten herbal *yikanwan* pills (in batches of five twice a day) each day over the course of four months and took only two Viagra pills, apparently to give him an extra sexual boost (Zhang 2007:65). Even some biomedical physicians advise that herbal medicine be taken in conjunction with Viagra. While biomedicine does not support the notion that Viagra directly affects sexual desire, only the ability to have a penile erection, some Chinese patients took Viagra to increase their sexual desire. Based upon his study, Zhang (2007:82) argues:

> Medical pluralism now operates not only *between* medical systems but also *within* those systems, not only in the consultation room but also in the lab, not

only in the advice given by physicians but also in patients' perceptions of that advice. My fieldwork experience in China shows that it is no longer possible to study traditional Chinese medicine without taking account its intensified relationship with biomedicine.

Thus, in seeking to achieve and provide sexual potency in China, both male patients and physicians essentially hybridize traditionalism, which has drawn from an ancient civilization, and modernity, which has been heavily shaped by the West. Such incidences and other incidences of the blending of bio-medicine and traditional Chinese medicine can be referred to as a "mangle of practice" (Pickering 1995, Scheid 2002).

Elsewhere in East Asia, Korean medicine also has undergone a process of hybridization as it has sought out scientific validation for its herbal formulas. In efforts to prove the efficacy of Korean medicines, "K[orean] M[edicine] doctors blend traditional medicine with several techniques and theories of biomedicine" (Kim 2009). Korean medicine doctors and South Korean businessmen have joined to transform Korean medicine into a "transcultural medical system" that is marketed abroad, including in China, Taiwan, and the United States.

# 6

# Health Disparity, Health Inequality

Ch 6

The causes of many diseases are a complex interplay of multiple factors, many of which are due to social injustice.

—*Barry Levy and Victor Sidel (2006:11)*

ealth and disease are unequally distributed across populations. Malaria is found in some places but not in others; some segments of a population are much more likely to get tuberculosis than others. Moreover, access to health care and treatment within health care settings is not uniform; many studies of health care in the United States, for example, show that African Americans get different—generally poorer—health care than white Americans. These differences have been variously labeled health disparities or health inequalities. As will be seen in this chapter, these terms are not fully synonymous. Addressing inequalities in health and health care is becoming an important arena of work in medical anthropology. In this chapter, we (1) define health disparity and health inequality; (2) examine the nature of disparities in health within the context of U.S. society; (3) review the debates about the causes of health disparities; (4) closely scrutinize three key issues in U.S. health disparities: asthma, access to health insurance, and the development of culturally competent health care; (5) move from the United States to a cross-cultural examination of health disparities; (6) discuss methods and approaches in ameliorating disparities and inequalities in health; (7) discuss the roles that medical anthropologists are playing in addressing health disparities; and (8) conclude with a discussion of the issue of the biological concept of "race" as a factor in health disparities.

## WHAT IS HEALTH DISPARITY?

Jack Geiger (2003:417), a professor at the City University of New York Medical School, reports, "At no time in the history of the United States has the health status of minority populations—African Americans, Native Americans, and, more recently, Hispanics and several Asian subgroups—equaled or even approximated that of white Americans." Even though important scientific and technical advances in biomedicine have occurred over the past several decades, for many people of color these have not contributed to an equalization of health and well-being with other groups in society. In other words, certain groups have not benefited fully or equitably from the growth of medical knowledge and medicine's expanded capacity to heal. As noted by the Institute of Medicine (2002:34),

> Significant health disparities continue to exist across diverse populations, despite efforts to reduce or eliminate those disparities. The problem is likely to grow if predictions of increasing social and cultural diversity in the United States over the next 50 years are correct.

The term "health disparities," in short, refers to disproportionate or excess morbidity, mortality, and decreased life expectancy as well as unequal access to health care and other health-supportive resources (e.g., insurance or access to good nutrition) in disadvantaged groups in society or in the world at large. This has emerged as a major public health issue worldwide as well as a topic of considerable importance in medical anthropology. While the term "health disparities" references differences in health across groups, the term "health inequalities" points also to underlying structural causes in disease distribution, namely, that social inequalities produce health inequalities.

## HEALTH DISPARITY IN THE UNITED STATES

Although the United States is the richest country in the world and the most technologically advanced, this has not translated into having the best health or the greatest life expectancy for either men or women. Overall life expectancy in the United States for the total population, however, masks significant differences by subgroups. For example, while the life expectancy on average is 76.7 years for white males, among African American males it is 67.8 years, almost eight years less than white men. Among white females, the average life expectancy is 79.9 years, while for African American females it is 74.7 years, about five years less than white women. African Americans have been found to be at significantly greater risk of death, including premature death, than whites, with most existing studies showing a 30 percent higher age-adjusted risk of mortality among African Americans. Higher prevalence of several diseases, including hypertension, HIV infection, ischemic heart disease, stroke, and cancer, accounts for the higher death rate of African Americans. Much of the difference in this burden of disease—but not all of it—is explained by differences in the socioeconomic status (SES) of African Americans compared to whites. In an analysis of several national studies, for example, Franks and his colleagues (2006:2472) found that

> African-Americans experience about 67,000 more deaths than they would have had their mortality rates been similar to whites. This translates into 2.2 million more YLL [annual years of life lost]. After adjusting for SES, these numbers drop to about 38,000 lives and 1.1 million YLL. Thus, roughly 29,000 of the lives lost and 1.1 million years lost annually may be attributable to differences in income and education between the groups.

The additional burden of morbidity and mortality among African Americans after statistical adjustment for SES is believed to be a consequence of the health damage done by racism, including its direct and indirect effects on stress and chemical changes in the bodies of stressed populations. African Americans who perceive they are being subjected to racism have been found to have higher blood pressure than those who do not (Kreiger and Sidney 1996). Moreover, SES and being the object of racism have been found to interact, increasing the adverse health effects of each. As these data suggest, ethnicity appears to be an important factor in health in the United States.

In fact, researchers have found that there are considerable and consequential inequalities in the distribution of health, disease, and access to health care across populations, subgroups, and regions of the United States. While the issue of health disparity has received a growing level of public health, policy, media, researcher, and public attention in recent years, it remains a topic of considerable debate, especially with regard to the causes of disparity and its social solutions. Studies have found multiple indicators of health disparity; for example, with reference to the impact of ethnicity on access to health care, the Institute of Medicine (2002) reported the following:

- Research on diagnostic tests and surgeries in ten states, with controls for geographic access, has found that health care providers appear to give less intensive care to African American patients compared to white patients.
- A study of 1.7 million hospital discharge records for seventy-seven disease categories found that African Americans were significantly less likely than whites to receive a major therapeutic procedure; overall, African Americans were found to receive fewer services than whites.
- A study of Mexican Americans with myocardial infarction found that they were 40 percent less likely than whites to receive thrombolytic therapy.
- In a study of ethnic variation in care, African Americans were found to be less likely to receive even low discretionary care (e.g., for clinically urgent health problems like appendicitis and abdominal aortic aneurysm).
- Even with adjustment for SES, in a three-state study Latinos were found to be less likely than non-Latinos to undergo major medical procedures.
- In a study of diabetics and nondiabetics, African Americans were found to be significantly more likely to undergo amputations and less likely to receive lower-limb arterial revascularization.
- In a teaching hospital study, Latinos with long-bone fractures were found to be twice as likely as non-Latinos to receive no medication for pain, and minority cancer patients were found to be less likely to receive adequate analgesic medication for pain.

In short, the care you receive in biomedicine is determined by many factors, including who you are in terms of the social construction of ethnicity.

## GASPING FOR BREATH

These various studies of the health care system—and many more that could be mentioned—affirm considerable inequity based on ethnicity. Similarly, there are major inequalities in the distribution of diseases. Consider, for example, asthma. More than seventeen million people in the United States suffer from asthma, about a third of whom are children under eighteen years of age. Asthma has been identified as one of the most common chronic illnesses of childhood in the nation; however, this breath-robbing disease is not equally distributed among children of different ethnicities. Recent national surveys report an overall lifetime asthma prevalence of 12.2 percent for children (under eighteen years of age), although there are dramatic differences across ethnic groups and subgroups (Dey et al. 2004). Rates of asthma are especially high among African Americans and Latinos. Among Latinos, Puerto Ricans have the highest lifetime asthma rate (19.6 percent), more than three times the rate for Mexican Americans (6.1 percent). Additionally, they exceed those for non-Latino African Americans (13.8 percent) and are almost double those of non-Latino whites (11.1 percent) (National Center for Health Statistics 2002). Houston, Texas, the fourth-largest city in the United States and the home of large numbers of Latinos and African Americans, for example, is one of the most polluted cities in the country and exhibits high rates of respiratory ailments, including asthma, in large part because of air pollution from motor vehicles and petrochemical plants (Harper 2004). Indeed, in the Houston metropolitan area, people of color and working-class people in general tend to live in closer proximity to freeways and petrochemical plants than do affluent whites.

While distressing, reported rates of asthma among Puerto Ricans probably underestimate the actual prevalence of the disease in this population because many symptomatic children are not diagnosed. Research by Whitman and coworkers (2004) in Chicago, for example, found that when cases of "possible asthma" based on a report of patient symptoms rather than actual medical diagnosis were added to cases of physician-diagnosed asthma, the prevalence level for Puerto Rican children jumped to an alarming 34 percent (Joseph et al. 1996). This higher rate suggests the potential overall significance of asthma among Puerto Ricans. In a study of asthma among children in East Harlem, New York, Puerto Rican children with asthma were found to be more likely to miss school because of asthma than children of other ethnic groups from the same neighborhoods (Findley et al. 2003). This study also found that low-income Latino families that have young children with asthma lack the necessary information, training in asthma management, and medical resources for good asthma control. The problem, however, is not simply one of the health care system failing to adequately prepare Latino parents in asthma management. Notably, the Childhood Asthma Severity Study (Ortega et al. 2002), which surveyed 1,002 children and their families, found that Latino and African American children were given fewer beta2-agonists, which is a standard medicine in asthma management, and, further, that Latino children received fewer inhaled steroids than white children.

## CAUSES OF HEALTH DISPARITY:
## LIFESTYLE VERSUS SOCIAL INEQUALITY

The public debate over health disparities in the United States encompasses many different factors, but of central importance is a heated discussion of lifestyle versus social structural causation of health disparities.

## Living Right

The lifestyle view asserts that differences in health are a consequence of eating right, exercising, avoiding smoking, avoiding illicit drugs, drinking moderately, learning to overcome stress, getting proper rest, and getting good medical care—that is, taking personal responsibility for your health. It emphasizes individual-level decision making and behavior as the primary factor in poor health. This perspective flows from very core American values concerning individual hard work and achievement and a tendency to believe that we are personally responsible for our own life situation, social standing, and success or failure.

In his book *Real Age: Are You as Young as You Can Be?*, Michael Roizen (2001), a physician, provided a formula for people to calculate how many months of life they were losing because of their own behaviors (e.g., eating fatty foods or not flossing) based on the questionable assumption that individuals are the primary determinant of their own longevity. By 2001, Roizen's book was outselling Harry Potter on eBay.

## Structural Explanation

By contrast with the lifestyle perspective, the social structural view holds that health disparities are more than the consequences of individual decisions and actions; they are the products of social inequality in many spheres of life, from opportunities in education and housing to treatment in the criminal justice system and access to health care. From this perspective, the key issue is not health disparity per se but health inequity and social injustice. As Scott (2005:1) has noted with reference to the role of social class in health,

> Class is a potent force in health and longevity in the United States. The more education and income people have, the less likely they are to have and die of heart disease, strokes, diabetes and many types of cancer. Upper-middle-class Americans live longer and in better health than middle-class Americans, who live longer and better than those at the bottom. And the gaps are widening, say people who have researched social factors in health. As advances in medicine and disease prevention have increased life expectancy in the United States, the benefits have disproportionately gone to people with education, money, good jobs and connections.

Adds Kreiger (2005:15),

> Social inequality kills. It deprives individuals and communities of a healthy start in life, increases their burden of disability and disease, and brings early death.

Poverty and discrimination, inadequate medical care, and violation of human rights all act as powerful social determinants of who lives and who dies, at what age, and with what degree of suffering.

These patterns can be readily seen by examining the relationship between being in poor health and income, as reported by the Healthy People 2010 report.

Moreover, health adversities due to structural factors are often lifelong despite improved socioeconomic conditions. As the organization Voices for Children (Canny et al. 2002:29) notes with reference to women's health,

> Women from lower income conditions as children [are] 58 per cent more likely to show high insulin resistance than those who lived under higher income conditions as children. Women living in better social and economic circumstances as adults still had a 29 per cent greater chance of being insulin resistant if they grew up in low-income families. Women who grew up poor [also are] more likely to . . . have higher levels of bad cholesterol and obesity than those who lived under better socioeconomic circumstances as children. These relationships remain . . . after taking into account adult social and economic conditions.

Consequently, there is a need to study the expressions and interconnections of health disparities across the life span (Adler and Stewart 2010).

While poverty appears to be a critical factor in health disparities, household income is not the only issue involved. While health disparities are strongly influenced by poverty, disparity is greatest among poor people who live in areas with a high percentage of poor people in the local population. Thus, poor people in cities with smaller impoverished populations are at lower risk of dying than those in cities with large impoverished populations. In other words, the density of poverty in an area appears to be a crucial determinant of the health status of the poor.

Moreover, studies of differences by location among the poor show that the sociophysical environment in which people live—that is, their experience of their surrounding community, including issues of danger, stress, comfort, and appeal—is also an important determinant of their health. Feelings of hopelessness and powerlessness in a community have been found to be good predictors of health risk and health status. One direction the study of health among the poor has been developed by anthropologists involves the investigation of human biological responses to impoverishment, or what has been called the biology of poverty (Thomas 1998).

## BIOLOGY OF POVERTY

Poverty is known to cause increased exposure to biological stressors such as undernutrition, diverse infectious pathogens, toxic substances in the living and working environment, and environmental extremes because of inadequacies of clothing and shelter. As a result, there are identifiable biological patterns associated with impoverishment. In his study of poor people living in the Andes of Peru, Carey (1990), for example, found that they work under hypoxic conditions and are regularly exposed to extreme cold. They are forced to live in areas with poor sanitation and to regularly take health risks in order to survive. Further, they are malnourished, their growth is retarded, and they have comparatively high rates of morbidity and mortality. Their bodies, in short, can be analyzed as corporal expressions of the biology of poverty. Poverty, quite literally, is inscribed on and in their bodies. One of the consequences of the biology of poverty is that, to the degree that poverty-induced bodily defects and diseases are increased in a population, the challenge for that population of overcoming conditions of poverty without outside resources is greater.

Recalling the disparities in health care reported earlier, it is also evident that ethnic discrimination by health providers, whether conscious or unconscious and whether driven more by individual or institutional bias, is another important structural cause of disparities in health. In an analysis of existing research, Gary King (1996) concludes that the key factor is "institutional racism," a systemic tendency to view ethnic minorities as less worthy patients, an ideology that is grounded in power imbalances between minorities and professional elites in medicine. In their contribution to the Institute of Medicine review of health disparities, anthropologist Mary-Jo DelVecchio Good and coworkers (2003) emphasized the importance of the "culture of medicine," including how medical students and residents are trained in the perpetuation of institutional racism in medicine.

### INSURING DISEASE

Health insurance coverage has become an important measure of access to health care in the United States. Yet tens of millions of Americans, especially ethnic minorities, have never had access to insurance coverage. As Figueroa (2004:i) aptly points out,

> Not having health insurance is deadly and costly. Even those with health insurance suffer from the insecurity of inadequate coverage and care. . . . [P]roposals to reform the nation's health care system over the last several decades have succumbed to partisan politics and intensive lobbying campaigns by insurance companies. Meanwhile, more than 44 million Americans are without health insurance.

Nationally, Latinos consistently have been found to be the group most likely to lack health insurance across all age groups. Thus, Latino children are the most likely not to be covered by health insurance, with only 8.8 percent of non-Latino white children lacking coverage in 1999 compared to 27.1 percent of Latinos under eighteen years of age. In the same year, while 68.4 percent of non-Latino whites had employer-based health insurance, among Latinos this figure was only 43.4 percent. Despite some improvements, by 2003 only 79 percent of Latino children had health insurance compared with 93 percent of white children and 86 percent of African American children (Holahan et al. 2003). Poverty, discrimination, parental lack of awareness of eligibility, language barriers, enrollment barriers, and fear (especially among undocumented immigrants) of repercussions for using publicly funded insurance have been cited as factors to explain why so many Latino children do not have health insurance. Thus, for example, the fact that in 2003 at least 30 percent of Latino children nationally lived in households with incomes below the federal poverty line, compared to 10 percent of white children, is likely an important factor in health insurance disparities faced by Latino youth (Interagency Forum on Child and Family Statistics 2005).

Significantly, the Commonwealth Fund (Doty 2003) found that the number of uninsured Latinos has steadily gone up, doubling between 1990 and 2002. Lack of health insurance coverage is a significant determinant of both being able to be seen by a doctor when in need and having a primary care provider. Moreover, the uninsured are much more likely to report that they are in poor or only fair health than are the insured. The Robert Wood Johnson Foundation (2005) reported that nationally 37.7 percent of uninsured Latinos are unable to see a physician at a time of need compared to about 10 percent of insured Latinos. Notably, among the insured, Latinos were the most likely to report inability to be seen by a physician at a time of need. Additionally, uninsured Latinos are the ethnic group most likely to lack a personal physician, and, whether they are insured or not (but especially among the uninsured), Latinos are the most likely to report being in poor or only fair health. While 69.6 percent of uninsured Latinos nationally lack a personal physician (compared to 48.8 percent of uninsured whites), almost one-fourth (24.5 percent) of insured Latinos also do not have a personal provider. Lacking personal physicians results in Latinos being the group most likely to rely on a community or public clinic for whatever health care they do receive (Doty 2003), with Spanish-speaking Latinos being almost five times more likely than whites to get care in a community or public clinic. While 85 percent of whites receive care in a doctor's office, this is true of only 43 percent of Spanish-speaking Latinos. In short, many Latinos have little or no choice of where to go for medical care.

Additionally, lack of health insurance coverage is a significant barrier to preventive health care for Latinos in the United States. Thus, the Commonwealth Fund (Doty 2003) found that comparatively low rates of insurance among Latinos limits their access both to routine preventive care, including visits to the dentist, routine Pap tests among women, routine mammograms, routine prostate examinations, and help with management of diabetes, and to acute care at the same levels as the insured. As a result, the health of Latinos is further compromised, with the resulting development of a number of significant chronic health problems.

On March 23, 2010, after a protracted political struggle (described by sociologist Katherine Newman as a "firestorm of opposition"), President Barack Obama signed the Patient Protection and Affordable Care Act (H.R. 3590) and the Health Care and Education Affordability and Reconciliation Act (H.R. 4872) into federal law. Together these two bills constitute a significant reform of health insurance access and coverage in the United States, although they do far less to achieve true health equity than the types of reforms called for by some sectors of the population, including many medical anthropologists. Many important components of the new law do not go into effect for many years, and legal challenges by opponents will continue to try to block enforcement of the law's provisions. Nevertheless, the intended goals of these bills, as explained by the White House, are the following:

- to make health insurance more affordable by providing a significant tax cut for health care and reducing insurance premiums for millions of families and small business owners
- to enable thirty-two million Americans to afford and have health care
- to establish a competitive health insurance market

- to increase accountability by established rules intended to keep insurance premiums down and prevent insurance industry abuses and denial of care
- to end discrimination in access to care against people with preexisting health conditions

## CULTURALLY COMPETENT CARE

Health disparity research suggests that ethnic minority groups like African Americans, Latinos, and Native Americans suffer a triple burden in seeking health care: (1) they are significantly less likely to have health insurance than whites, so accessing care is a major challenge, and while adequate acute care is hard enough to come by, preventive care is all but impossible for those who are not insured; (2) in the health care system, ethnic minority patients face individual and institutional discrimination at every level; and (3) culturally competent health care is in especially short supply.

What is culturally competent health care? It has been defined by the Commonwealth Fund (Betancourt 2006:1) as the "ability of systems to provide care to patients with diverse values, beliefs and behaviors, including tailoring delivery of care to meet patients' social, cultural, and linguistic needs." In other words, from a medical anthropology perspective, culturally competent care begins with the perspective of the patients, their culturally conditioned understandings, attitudes, expectations, and feelings; more precisely, its starting point is patient experience and the often emotionally charged cultural meanings attached to that experience (G. Becker 2004). At present, there are major gaps between the health care systems in place around the country and what would be considered culturally competent care in light of local ethnic diversity. Yet the need for health care providers to meet the needs of ethnic minority patients is inescapable, as seen in the changing ethnic composition of the U.S. population.

While individuals of white European and related heritage accounted for about 75 percent of the U.S. population at the time of the 1990 national census, current trends suggest that by 2030 whites will make up only 60 percent of the population. At that point, almost one in five norteamericanos will be Latino. Since culturally competent health care is seen as being better health care, unless health care systems adapt, the quality of care will continue to drop as the American population diversifies.

Recognizing these realities, there has been a push in health care systems to (1) develop principles and standards of culturally competent care, (2) implement curricula to train health care providers in culturally competent care and to evaluate their adherence to learned approaches, (3) conduct research on the contribution of cultural competency to reducing disparities in health and health care provision, (4) publish and disseminate reviews of best and promising culturally competent practices, (5) identify strategies to overcome linguistic and cultural barriers, and (6) develop organizational structures to support culturally competent care. Reflecting these trends, the Office of Minority Health of the U.S. Department of Health and Human Services has established national standards for health care institutions such as hospitals and clinics to follow in responding to the medical needs of their culturally diverse clients. These standards include the following:

- ensuring that patients receive effective, understandable, and respectful care that is provided in a manner compatible with their cultural health beliefs and practices and preferred language
- implementing strategies to recruit, retain, and promote a diverse staff and leadership that are representative of the social and demographic characteristics of people living in the area served by the health institution
- ensuring that staff at all levels and across all disciplines receive ongoing education and training in culturally and linguistically appropriate service delivery

Given their focus on the role of culture in health, illness, and healing, medical anthropologists recognize the value and support the adoption of such standards, although—often citing the costs they might entail—health care providers are not always immediately receptive to changing their practices. Medical anthropologists have found that it is important to demonstrate that culturally and linguistically appropriate services, or what is called culturally competent health care, is, in fact, more effective in terms of producing better health outcomes, which is generally an accepted and valued goal among health care providers.

One expression of the new medical sensitivity to culture is the notable popularity of Ann Fadiman's (1997) compelling and very touching book *The Spirit Catches You and You Fall Down: A Hmong Child, Her American Doctors, and the Collision of Two Cultures*, which has become the most widely used text in cultural competence training for health care practitioners, including many first-year medical students, in the United States. The book recounts the story of Lia Lee, a Hmong child who was born in Merced, California, in 1982. At three months of age, Lia began having intense seizures, which were interpreted as signs of "soul loss" by her parents and a Hmong shaman but diagnosed by her biomedical doctors as epilepsy. Convinced that Lia's parents were not administering the medicines they prescribed because of their faith in Hmong ethnomedicine, Lia's doctors launched a successful effort to remove her to foster care. Only after a year of battling the system were Lia's parents able to have their daughter returned home. Ultimately, Lia suffered a massive seizure that left her permanently brain damaged. By poignantly describing a fatal clash of cultures in medicine, Fadiman's book has made clear to many why culture is so important in the practice of medicine (though some have criticized the book for presenting an overly static "fixed-in-time" view of culture rather than seeing it as a moving process that is created and changed as it is used).

As the importance of culturally competent care has begun to catch on in biomedicine, a number of organizations concerned with the education of physicians and other health care providers have begun to develop medical and nursing school curricula that reflect an awareness of the importance of paying close and sensitive attention to the patient's cultural and linguistic heritage and its role in their health. For example, the Society of Teachers of Family Medicine has developed "Recommended Core Curriculum Guidelines on Culturally Sensitive and Competent Health Care" (see http://stfm.org/group/minority/guidelines.cfm), and the California Endowment has created "Principles and Recommended Standards for Cultural Competence Education of Health Care Professionals" (see www.calendow.org/pub/frm_pub.htm). Various medical and other health education institutions in the United States and elsewhere have adopted elements of these tools into their educational curricula.

These changes, at least in part, reflect the impact of medical anthropologists who work in clinical settings within the subfield of medical anthropology called clinical anthropology or clinically applied anthropology, as described in chapter 4. Exemplary of the anthropological contribution to cultural competence in health care is a three-volume set produced by the California Endowment. Edited by anthropologist M. Jean Gilbert of California State University, Long Beach, these three manuals include a set of principles and recommended standards for culturally competent health care education, a resource guide, and a manager's guide for running a culturally competent health care institution. The manuals illustrate once again an important way in which medical anthropology is a discipline in action actively seeking to address pressing issues in health. Another example, from Australia, demonstrates the practical collaboration of anthropology with people from the health professions and public agencies. The Intercultural Interaction Project in the School of Occupation and Leisure Sciences at the University of Sydney, established in 1992, is directed by Maureen H. Fitzgerald, an anthropologist, and Colleen Mullavey-O'Byrne, an occupational therapist. This collaborative project, which involves health science students and organizations such as the Transcultural Mental Health Centre in Sydney, has resulted in classroom and workshop training materials and a teaching model to enhance the cultural competence of health professionals. From this work has developed the idea that cultural competency can be considered as being of three types: culture specific, intercultural, and culture general (Fitzgerald 2000). The emphasis in this work on culture general competence highlights issues particularly in relation to multicultural societies where there is a need to recognize that cultural issues in the provision of health care and social services arise and must be addressed for all people, not just minority ethnocultural communities.

## HEALTH AND SOCIAL DISPARITIES CROSS-CULTURALLY

Health disparities are not peculiar to the United States or to the Western world but are a global problem. Internationally, there are two expressions: disparities between wealthier and less wealthy nations and disparities within the populations of all nations around the world. With regard to the first of these, the Health Evidence Network of the World Health Organization (World Health Organization 2006b) notes that over the past several decades the number of people in the world living on less than $2 per day has grown to almost three billion. Further, income disparities between the rich and the poor around the world are growing. While the income of the richest 20 percent of the population in the world was thirty times that of the poorest 20 percent of the population in 1960, today it is eighty-two times greater. Within this context of an ever-wider gap between the rich and the poor, health disparities are driven by factors such as social exclusion and discrimination, inadequate diet and malnutrition, a rapid reemergence of both waterborne and bloodborne infectious diseases, poor housing, low-status employment, unhealthy early childhood living conditions, degradation of the physical environment, disinvestment in the public health and health care infrastructure serving the poor, escalating violence, and lack of health insurance (Figure 6.1).

One way to get a better understanding of health disparities across nations is to compare the top causes of death between a wealthy nation such as the United States and the world as a whole, as seen in Table 6.1. It is evident from reviewing this table that, aside from the high ranking of heart disease and cerebrovascular disease (stroke) as well as unintended injuries, the primary causes of death in the United States and the world as a whole are quite different. Of even greater significance from the standpoint of health disparities is the fact that while chronic conditions dominate the United States, a number

FIGURE 6.1
Backyard pond in East Medinipur District, West Bengal, India, in which this family must
bathe, fish, clean fish, and wash dishes and clothes. Photo by Anna Marie Nicolaysen.

of acute conditions and diseases that could be treated if appropriate health
care were available (e.g., diseases marked by an asterisk in the table) dominate
the global list. In other words, if health care were equitably distributed in the
world, millions of people around the planet would not be dying of diseases for
which cures and treatments already exist.

A critical factor contributing to health disparities around the world is the
emergence of new infectious diseases and new vector-borne diseases. Infectious diseases—diseases whose immediate cause is a pathogen, such as viruses,
bacteria, protozoa, or helminthes—are on the rise and kill millions of people
each year, particularly in resource-poor nations. The era of "new diseases"
began with the appearance of AIDS in the early 1980s, followed quickly by the
emergence of Ebola, hantavirus, Rift Valley fever, and a rising tide of other new
or renewed infections (i.e., diseases that had been brought under some control but have since reemerged, often in more virulent form, and are resistant
to the drugs that had once controlled them). One such reemergent disease,

**Table 6.1. Top 10 Causes of Death in the United States and Worldwide**

| United States | Worldwide |
|---|---|
| 1. Heart disease | 1. Heart disease |
| 2. Cancer | 2. Cerebrovascular disease |
| 3. Stroke (cerebrovascular disease) | 3. Acute lower respiratory infections* |
| 4. Chronic lower respiratory diseases | 4. Chronic obstructive pulmonary disease |
| 5. Unintentional injuries | 5. Diarrheal diseases |
| 6. Diabetes mellitus disease | 6. HIV/AIDS* |
| 7. Pneumonia and influenza | 7. Tuberculosis* |
| 8. Alzheimer's disease | 8. Lung/bronchial/tracheal cancer |
| 9. Nephritis | 9. Unintentional injuries |
| 10. Septicemia | 10. Premature birth and low birth weight |

* Acute diseases that are treatable if health care is available.
Sources: Centers for Disease Control and Prevention and World Health Organization.

tuberculosis, often associated with AIDS (a combination most frequently seen in the poorest populations), has become one of the world's greatest causes of mortality linked to an infectious agent. Vector-borne diseases (those spread by a blood-sucking arthropod such as a mosquito), including malaria, dengue, yellow fever, plague, filariasis, louse-borne typhus, trypanosomiasis, and leishmaniasis, also have become an ever more important source of health disparities in the world. By the mid-1990s, for example, there were between three hundred million and five hundred million clinical cases of malaria each year, 90 percent of them in Africa, with the rate of malaria-related deaths, mostly of children, on the rise (World Health Organization 1996). Various factors have contributed to the changing profile of infectious diseases in the world, including the breakdown of public health prevention systems in poorer countries; the social disinvestment in health in debt-ridden nations under pressure from development banks and wealthy lender nations; the increased concentration of people living in mega-cities with huge impoverished population sectors living in overcrowded, unhygienic conditions; the frequent movement of populations fleeing low- and high-intensity wars and other military threats; the rapidity of global travel made possible by jet aircraft; the global movement of consumer products that can harbor infectious agents; the environmental discard of nonbiodegradable products such as worn-out tires that become mosquito breeding sites in the rainy season; deforestation; and environmental change associated with global warming.

### Child and Maternal Health Disparities

An important measure of health internationally, one that is used commonly to assess the health status of a nation, is the general health and well-being of young children and their mothers. The WHO reports that more than ten million children and more than five hundred thousand mothers die each year, mostly from preventable causes. These numbers suggest the painful significance of health problems in the world today, usually rooted in social marginality, poverty, and powerlessness, despite tremendous national and international efforts to make the world a healthier place (Figure 6.2). As the anthropologist Judith Justice (2000:24) notes,

> By the late 1970s, children's health was given increasing attention by the international health community. At the time the focus was on factors contributing to infant mortality rates and the high number of deaths from diarrheal-related diseases. . . . By the early 1980s, infant survival began receiving priority attention at international conferences and in the development literature.

In addition to reducing diarrhea-related diseases through the distribution of a simple oral solution for rehydrating children with diarrhea, international health efforts focused on childhood immunization against major infectious diseases such as tuberculosis, diphtheria, pertussis, tetanus, measles, and poliomyelitis.

FIGURE 6.2
Family awaiting the demolition of their home in slum clearance in Dhaka, Bangladesh. Photo by Sabina Faiz Rashid.

As Justice (2000:25) observes, these "two technological interventions—oral re-hydration and immunization—emerged as the twin-engine approach to child health and reducing infant mortality" (Figure 6.3).

As a result of these efforts and the investment of resources in child survival, the rate of mortality of children under five years of age fell throughout the world during the latter part of the twentieth century, going from 146 per 1,000 population in 1970 to 79 per 1,000 population in 2003. Between 1990 and the present, the rate of childhood death dropped by about 15 percent, resulting in the lives of two million children being sheltered from death in 2003 alone. As the millennium was coming to a close, however, the general global downward trend in childhood mortality began to level off. In the years between 1970 and 1990, the mortality rate of children under five years of age dropped by 20 percent every decade; by contrast, between 1990 and 2000, it dropped by only 12 percent. This slowdown signaled shifts in relations among richer and poorer nations, a fact that is revealed by moving from global averages to an assessment of regional differences in child mortality. In two regions of the world, Africa below the Saharan Desert and the western Pacific, the

FIGURE 6.3
Two mothers with sick children from the Dani people of Papua, Indonesia. Photo by Leslie Butt.

slowdown in the tempo of deaths among children under five years of age began during the 1980s. Sub-Saharan countries of Africa began the last thirty years of the twentieth century with the highest levels of under-five child mortality, witnessed the smallest reductions (about 5 percent per decade between 1980 and 2000), and displayed the most marked slowdown in the process of improving children's health by the end of the century. By contrast, progress in reducing childhood mortality continued or even accelerated in the Americas, Europe, and Southeast Asia throughout the period of concern.

As reflected in these statistics, disparities in the health of children in richer and poorer countries around the world have been growing in recent years. The mortality rate for children under five years old is now seven times higher in sub-Saharan Africa than it is in Europe. In 1980, it was just over four times higher. Indeed, child death in the world increasingly is concentrated in sub-Saharan Africa, where 43 percent of the global total of child mortality is found, reflecting an increase of 13 percent between 1990 and 2003. Another 28 percent of child deaths occur in Southeast Asia. Indeed, more than half of all child deaths in the world occur in just six countries: China, the Democratic Republic of the Congo, Ethiopia, India, Nigeria, and Pakistan.

Even short of actual mortality, disparities in children's health cross-culturally are telling. For example, 6 percent of children around the globe are born with serious birth defects. More than 90 percent of births with serious defects are found in middle- to low-income countries (March of Dimes 2006). Poverty has been found to be one of the most important factors in birth defects internationally; other factors include the mother's age, marriage among close blood relatives, and living in the "malaria belt" of countries with significant levels of malaria in which inherited diseases such as sickle cell disease, thalassemia, and glucose-6-phosphate dehydrogenase deficiency are most common. Similar sociogeographic disparities are found in childhood nutritional status and nutrition-related health conditions, according to the WHO. From 1990 to 2000, the global prevalence of both growth stunting (due to poor diet) and being underweight dropped by 20 and 18 percent, respectively. But high rates of malnutrition among children and other nutrition-related health and physical symptoms continue in southern and central Asia and sub-Saharan Africa. For children in particular, the planet increasingly is a world divided between comparatively wealthy and comparatively poor places, and where you are born is a major determinant of what will happen in your life, including the likelihood that you will live beyond your fifth birthday.

One of the key forces impacting the health of children around the world is the condition of the environment in which they live, including the quality of the air they breathe, the water they drink, the food they eat, and the hidden threats that lurk in the areas in which they play, issues that will be addressed more fully in chapter 7. Children are at particular risk from environmental toxins because their brains, nervous systems, and immune capacities are still developing and because exposure to environmental poisons can cause lifelong damage and chronic disadvantage. Air pollution, for example, both outdoors and within the home, is a primary cause of acute lower-respiratory infections in children, especially pneumonia (Figure 6.4).

Such infections are among the major sources of mortality among young children, causing more than 2 million deaths each year, the vast majority in resource-poor nations. Similarly, lack of access to clean water is common in poorer countries. Each year, diarrhea disease, a consequence in part of unclean drinking water, takes the lives of 1.5 million children. Moreover, it is estimated by the WHO (2006a) that 2.5 billion people, most of them in poor countries, lack access to adequate sanitary facilities.

War and internal conflict are also forces impacting children's health internationally (Figure 6.5). Countries that have been ravaged by internal wars, such as Sierra Leone, Angola, Afghanistan, Liberia, and Somalia, tend to have the highest child mortality rates in the world. In Sierra Leone, for example, 250 of every 1,000 children die before they reach their fifth birthday, compared to 8 per 1,000 in the United States, according to UNICEF. Since 1990,

FIGURE 6.4
Factory air pollution is a source of respiratory disease. Photo by Merrill Singer.

FIGURE 6.5
Tibetan orphan in front of the Medical Care Unit at the Tibetan Homes
Foundation in Uttarakh, India. Photo by Anne Marie Nicolaysen.

90 percent of conflict-related deaths have been civilians, and, of these, 80
percent have been women and children. UNICEF reports that in a typical war,
the death rate among children under five years of age goes up by 13 percent.
Wars often take a significant toll on health facilities and other societal infrastructure, loss of which is especially damaging to the most vulnerable sectors
of a population. Moreover, many children are left orphaned, and others are
abducted to be used as soldiers or are raped or otherwise injured. The emotional scars from exposure to violence, loss of family members, dislocation
from their homes, and resulting impoverishment can be lifelong. Typical is

Sumaya, a fifteen-year-old girl from Sudan whose village was attacked by an Arab tribal militia force called the Janjaweed. Sumaya was interviewed by UNICEF workers in the Kalma refugee camp in South Darfur:

> "I was at school when they attacked us," says Sumaya. "My sisters ran back to the village, and I ran with some friends. My cousin Mona was running ahead of me when she was shot. I stopped and held her hand. When she died, her hand slipped out of mine. Some boys came and told me that I had to run, so I did." Along the way Sumaya found her grandmother and her 4-year-old brother, Mozamel (whom everyone calls Baba). She took the little boy in her arms and started running. "We ran and ran until I felt that I couldn't go on any longer," remembers Sumaya. "I thought about throwing my brother in the grass because he was so heavy, but my grandmother took my hand and told me that we should all stay together." Two agonizing weeks went by before Sumaya and Baba were reunited with the rest of the family. Together, they walked 147 kilometres to Kalma Camp [along with 70,000 other refugees]. (UNICEF 2006)

Among women of childbearing age, the health risks associated with pregnancy and childbirth are the leading causes of death, disease, and disability internationally. More than three hundred million women in poorer and less-developed countries suffer from short-term or long-term illness brought about by pregnancy and childbirth, according to the WHO, and there are few indicators that improvements are occurring in these areas. Indeed, in some parts of the world, the health of mothers is falling. Not surprisingly, maternal death is especially common in poorer countries, especially in sub-Saharan Africa, with less than 1 percent of maternal deaths in the world occurring in wealthy countries. While the lifetime risk of maternal death is 1 in 16 in the world's poorest nations, it is 1 in 2,800 in the world's wealthiest nations.

In short, despite major international efforts and significant initial improvements in maternal and child health, rates of success have not been sustained, nor have they been equitably distributed across the nations of the world. In Justice's (2000) assessment, several factors are important:

- While international funds were made available to cover initial costs of improving maternal and child health, individual countries were required to use their own resources to implement programs at the local level. Poorer countries with limited human and financial resources were unable to meet all the local challenges of program implementation.

- The international community failed to recognize the fragile nature of the health systems and scarcity of resources (e.g., availability of trained personnel in local settings) in poorer countries.
- Immunization was tested in a number of small-scale pilot projects without full consideration of how to scale up immunization in resource-poor nations.
- The international health priorities and programs shift from year to year, leaving earlier programs, such as childhood immunization, on their own without international support, leading to drops in immunization rates in many countries.

In other words, from Justice's perspective as a medical anthropologist trained to shift her analytic lens between the macrolevels and microlevels in human social systems, overemphasis on a top-down approach, inadequate attention to disparities in national health resources, and failure to recognize local diversity within nations became important barriers to sustained improvements in maternal and child health. In the following section on globalization, we will consider some other factors as well.

One final indicator of health disparities across nations is access to health insurance. Lack of health insurance among the poor globally is an especially damaging problem. According to Julio Frenk of the WHO,

> Insurance protects people against the catastrophic effects of poor health. What we are seeing is that in many countries, the poor pay a higher percentage of their income on health care than the rich. . . . In many countries without a health insurance safety net, many families have to pay more than 100 percent of their income for health care when hit with sudden emergencies. In other words, illness forces them into debt. (World Health Organization 2000)

## ADDRESSING HEALTH DISPARITIES

In a keynote address at the 2004 International Conference on Overcoming Health Disparities: Global Experiences of Partnerships between Communities, Health Services and Health Professional Schools, David Satcher, the former surgeon general of the United States and director of the Morehouse School of Medicine, noted that to eliminate health disparities globally, we must "know enough" (i.e., carry out much-needed research on existing health disparities and their causes), "do enough" (i.e., deliver desired outcomes in terms of removing barriers to health care access, eliminating the social causes of poor health among disparity populations, and implementing culturally competent care), "care enough" (i.e., have the commitment needed to accomplish desired goals), and "persevere enough" (i.e., recognize that the elimination of health disparities is a long-term objective and avoid discouragement). Each of these agenda items for achieving global health equity represents a major challenge for policymakers, health care providers, consumers, and the field of medical anthropology.

Health disparities have become an area of concern to the work of a growing number of medical anthropologists. In particular, medical anthropologists who are active in this arena have been attempting to understand biocultural and biosocial interactions as causes of health inequality and marshaling research findings on these connections in the development of targeted intervention programs intended to reduce or eliminate disparities.

### Addressing Health Disparities in the Community

What can medical anthropologists do to address health disparities? At the Hispanic Health Council, for many years a number of anthropologists and colleagues from various other disciplines regularly worked on community-based health disparities issues, such as addressing unequal access to quality and appropriate health care as well as the underlying social conditions that create disproportionate health problems among the poor. One issue that continues to come up in this kind of work is the lack of health insurance among so many people who are at or below the official federal poverty line. Is the federal implementation of universal health care coverage the answer to this problem as it has been in countries such as Canada, the United Kingdom, and Australia? A related question that applied medical anthropologists must ask is whether it is possible to achieve universal health care in the United States. It would seem so, given the vast resources of the nation and the fact that other countries have been able to implement programs designed to cover the health care costs of all residents. There has been tremendous resistance to this idea historically in the United States, especially from the powerful insurance industry.

As this example suggests, the elimination of health care disparities is not easy because it would involve significant social changes that are not supported by sectors of the society that benefit from the existing way society is organized. As Peter Townsend (1986) argued in what is now a classic article in the literature on health disparities, it is not simply the case that there are rich and poor in the world; instead, there are rich precisely because there are poor. Consequently, to eliminate health disparities he argues it is necessary "to restrict the power and wealth of the rich, to dismantle the present structures of social privilege, and to build social institutions based on fair allocation of wealth and on social equality" (Townsend 1986:29). More recently, Chernomas and Hudson (2010) have argued that historical broad health and social inequality was justified by the claim that the poor are intellectually and behaviorally inferior to the rich. While this assertion is no longer made, at least publicly, the wealthy maintain that redistribution of wealth is unnecessary because a free market will efficiently and justly distribute income among members of society. This neoliberal argument, which Chermomas and Hudson refer to as "the myth of conservative economic policy," has not proven to eliminate either health or social disparities, suggesting a reconsideration of Townsend's proposition.

### Upstream Analyses of Health Disparities

A very different role that medical anthropologists can play in addressing the issue of health disparities emerges from the broad, holistic perspective of anthropology. To date, much of the work that has been done on health disparities that addresses the "social determinants of health" tends to frame its discussion of causal factors in terms of intermediate-level issues, such as poverty, local or neighborhood conditions, malnutrition, and SES, without embedding these variables in a more expansive macroscopic context. Two very important books, however, have moved beyond an intermediate-level focus. The first of these, *Dying for Growth*, emanated from the collaborative work of an interdisciplinary team based at the Institute of Health and Social Justice in Cambridge, Massachusetts (Kim et al. 2000). One of the editors of this volume is Jim Yong Kim, a physician, medical anthropologist, and president of Dartmouth College, and another editor, Joyce V. Millen, also a medical anthropologist, is on the faculty of Willamette University. This important anthology explores the linkages between neoliberalism or late global capitalism and health problems among the poor in various countries. In its various essays, *Dying for Growth* argues that the World Bank's policy of "structural adjustment," which has fostered privatization of social and health services in developing countries, has in turn adversely affected the poor around the globe. Further, the book explores the adverse impact of the practices of transnational corporations (those that have operations in multiple countries) on the health of the poor, such as in the case of the 1984 Bhopal gas disaster in India and the harsh working conditions experienced by maquiladora workers who are employed in factories owned by American companies just over the border in Mexico.

The second book that provides a macroscopic perspective on health disparities is *Global Inequality and Human Needs* by Laurie Wermuth (2003), a medical sociologist who adopts a political economic perspective in her examination of regional trends in world health; the impact of gender, race, and ethnicity on both physical and mental health; and the relationship between economic development and health. She argues,

> Among the social factors that influence health and life chances is location in the global economy. Economic projects designed by capitalists in affluent parts of the world have ripple effects in the countries where the production occurs. . . . A person's location in this global economic web of production and consumption is likely to influence how well he or she is fed, clothed, and housed, and what kinds of educational and occupational opportunities he or she has. (45–46)

Obviously, social factors such as food, clothing, shelter, and educational and occupational background play an important role in people's health and access to health care. By "looking upstream" to the factors and social relationships that ultimately determine health disparities, medical anthropologists can help seek effective responses to health inequality.

### Focusing on Disparity in Diseases

One medical anthropologist who has been quite active in addressing health disparity issues is Deborah Erwin, the director of health disparities at the Division of Cancer Prevention and Population Sciences at the Roswell Park Cancer Institute in Buffalo, New York. The focus of Erwin's career has been on reducing and preventing health disparities in cancer. She has worked for many years developing culturally appropriate programs to enhance access and screening for cancer among minority and underserved populations. As part of this work, Erwin helped develop the Witness Project, a breast cancer education and screening intervention specifically targeted to African American women. The Witness Project, developed originally in Arkansas, has been replicated in more than thirty sites in twenty-two states. At the heart of the project are African American women living with cancer who share their personal narratives with patients with a more recent diagnosis of cancer. These narratives affirm that "African American women are not helpless as patients in the biomedical system [and stress] the fact that other sisters can help navigate the process, much like shaman traversing unknown worlds." Moreover, they call attention to the need "to recognize and address the social justice issues and social determinants integrated into cancer detection, treatment, and causation" (Erwin 2008:144–45)

Another medical anthropologist who works on cancer as a health disparity issue is Christine Makosky Daley of the University of Kansas Medical School. In addition to working on other applied medical anthropology projects, Daley is the project director on an American Lung Association–funded assessment of a smoking cessation program culturally tailored for American Indians and Alaska Natives. Although American Indians and Alaska Natives have the highest smoking rates in the country, few smoking cessation interventions are specifically targeted to these populations. The Muscogee Indian Nation of Oklahoma developed one such program, called Second Wind, which was based on the American Cancer Society's FreshStart smoking cessation model. While the program was thought to be quite effective in helping participants quit smoking, the actual impact of the program had not been formally evaluated. Toward this end, Daley conducted six focus groups with forty-one Native Indian adult smokers at the Haskell Health Center in Lawrence, Kansas (Choi et al. 2006). These group interviews were developed to assess beliefs, attitudes, and behaviors related to smoking cessation and to better understand the perceptions of participants concerning the cultural appropriateness and feasibility of Second Wind for a diverse group of Native Americans. The research team conducted content analysis of audiotapes of the focus groups. Participant responses were categorized into three major themes: traditional tobacco use, quitting smoking and quit attempts, and attitudes toward the Second Wind program. The researchers found that participants who reported that traditional tobacco use is important to them were less inclined to use tobacco recreationally. Additionally, they offered a number of suggestions for modifying the Second Wind intervention, including addressing the meaning of tobacco to American Indian cultures and emphasizing the importance of integrating recreational-smoking cessation with support for traditional uses of tobacco. In addition to this work, Daley is helping to develop a touch-screen computer system to increase patients' open and relaxed discussion of colorectal cancer screening with their physicians.

### Multidisciplinary Approaches

In his work at Northwestern University, Thomas McDade focuses on understanding health and human development in the context of social and cultural processes, with a particular emphasis on the role of stress in the development of disparities in health. For example, McDade (2003) has studied the impact of stressful life events on the function of the immune system among Samoan adolescents. Additionally, McDade helped develop Cells to Society (C2S), a center for innovative, multidisciplinary approaches for studying health disparities. Specifically, C2S was developed to unite the social, life, and biomedical sciences in expanding the understanding of the origins and consequences of health inequalities in the United States and using this information to generate policy solutions. Of special interest to McDade and other researchers at the center is how broad social, ethnic, and economic disparities "get under the skin," such as through the impact on the immune system, and affect human development, psychological well-being, and longevity.

**Studying Place**

A final example of the roles medical anthropologists play in health disparities is seen in the work of Lee Pachter, who, in addition to being a medical anthropologist, is a member of the Department of Pediatrics at the University of Connecticut School of Medicine and a pediatrician on the clinical staff of Saint Francis Hospital and Medical Center in Hartford, Connecticut. Pachter's research has focused on accounting for patterns of health disparities among children, among other related topics (Pachter 2006). In his research with inner-city populations, he has argued that purely economic indicators, such as household income, do not fully account for the unequal distribution of health and illness among children. In addition, he has shown that residential segregation and the number of urban poor families living in concentrated poor neighborhoods is of critical importance. Pachter has identified three mechanisms through which residential segregation magnifies child health disparities: (1) having to pay higher prices in smaller neighborhood stores while having limited employment opportunities, (2) the breakdown of interpersonal cooperation for mutual benefit with resulting loss of interpersonal trust and community participation, and (3) enduring exposure to structural violence (e.g., racism and discrimination) giving rise to psychological deficits, such as low self-esteem, a low sense of self-efficacy, and disempowerment. It is the interconnectivity and mutual reinforcement of these factors that produces heightened rates of poor health among the children of households in highly concentrated poor neighborhoods. As a pediatrician, Pachter is able to translate his findings into hospital-based programs to improve the health of poor children.

As this discussion suggests, with reference to public health, "place matters." Indeed, this is the title of one of the seven episodes in the widely viewed public health documentary video *Unnatural Causes: Is Inequality Making Us Sick?*, produced by California Newsreel (see www.unnaturalcauses.org/episode_descriptions.php?page=5). As this educational program emphasizes, people's street address is a good predictor of their health status. Exemplary is the economically depressed city of Richmond, California. During World War II, Richmond had been a boomtown, with the local shipyards turning out ships for the war effort twenty-four hours a day. But at the end of the war the shipyards shut down, throwing workers into unemployment. White families were able to take advantage of federally backed home loans and move to the suburbs, but because of overt discrimination this was not the case for ethnic minorities. The result was the emergence of a legacy of poverty and poor health in places like Richmond. Today Richmond has high rates of asthma hospitalization and diabetes and a lower life expectancy than suburban areas. Research indicates that in places like Richmond, there is a 50 to 80 percent increase in risk for heart disease related to chronic stress. Additionally, while fresh fruits and vegetables are hard to find locally, tobacco, liquor, and fast foods are readily available.

## "RACE" AND HEALTH DISPARITY

One of the debates over health disparities concerns the role of genetics and race as determinants of health status. For example, it is known that throughout the Americas, "people of African ancestry have higher blood pressures and higher rates of hypertension than do others in the same societies" (Gravlee et al. 2005:2191). Hypertension plays a major role in lowering the life expectancy of African Americans in the United States—more so than cancer, diabetes, stroke, or AIDS—and this is true elsewhere in the Americas among people of African origin. Moreover, among African Americans, those with darker skin color tend to have higher blood pressure than those with lighter skin color. One hypothesis about why this might be so is that dark skin color is a visible marker of African ancestry and reflects a genetic, race-based predisposition for higher blood pressure. To test this hypothesis, Gravlee and coworkers (2005) conducted a study in Guayama in southeastern Puerto Rico in which they first used cultural consensus analysis to determine local study participants' assessment of the color of seventy-two standardized facial portraits that varied by skin tone, hair texture, nose shape, and lip form. This led to the identification of five different color groups (e.g., Blanco, or white; Trigueño, or wheat colored; and Negro, or black) that represented meaningfully different groups based on color in the local community. One hundred individuals, one-fourth drawn from each of four neighborhoods in Guayama, were recruited to participate in the study. Based on their observation of each participant's appearance, interviewers assigned them to one of the five color groups. Additionally, a narrowband reflectometer was used to objectively determine each participant's color. Then an automatic blood pressure monitor was used to measure each participant's blood pressure three times during the course of an hour-long interview. These researchers found that objectively measured skin color was associated neither with blood pressure nor with which culturally defined color group a person was assigned to. However, the culturally defined color group was associated with blood pressure, with those labeled Blanco or Trigueño having statistically lower blood pressure than those labeled Negro. In other words, the key factor associated with blood pressure was not one's actual skin pigmentation (which would reflect genetic influence) but rather how people in the community culturally defined someone's "race." Rather than finding support for a racial determination of health

RACE

In recent years, anthropologists increasingly have dropped the term "race," which traditionally was used to refer to biologically distinct groups, from their lexicon of scientific terms. As the American Anthropological Association affirmed in its 1998 "Statement on 'Race,'" most physical variation, about 94 percent, lies within so-called racial groups. Conventional geographic "racial" groupings differ from one another only in about 6 percent of their genes. This means that there is greater variation within "racial" groups than between them. In neighboring populations, there is much overlapping of genes and their phenotypic (physical) expressions. Throughout history, whenever different groups have come into contact, they have interbred. The continued sharing of genetic materials has maintained all of humankind as a single species. Importantly, while anthropologists no longer believe it is empirically valid to use the term "race," they nonetheless recognize that racism—bias based on assumed biological differences between populations—is quite real and does significant damage to the health of those who are subject to it.

disparity, this study provides support to the primary competing hypothesis, namely, that having perceived darker skin subjects individuals "to racial discrimination, poverty, and other stressors related to blood pressure" (Gravlee et al. 2005:2191).

In sum, in the arena of health inequalities, social factors (including social inequality) rather than genetic factors tend to be most important. From an applied perspective, this means that health inequalities will be limited or eliminated to the degree that social disparities are limited or eliminated. As succinctly summarized by Nancy Krieger (2007:662): "social justice + human rights = health equity."

# 7

# Health and the Environment

*Toward a Healthier World*

It is no measure of health to be well adjusted to a profoundly sick society.

—*Krishnamurti*

This chapter focuses attention on the impact of both the natural environment and the socially constructed environment on human health, placing special emphasis on the impact of global warming on the environment, human settlements, and health. Further, the chapter discusses the ways in which corporate globalization is playing a crucial role in not only creating health disparities and global warming but also contributing to diseases such as cancer and even AIDS. Finally, and in conclusion, the chapter reviews the need for an alternative world system to replace the present global economy in creating a healthy planet for both humanity and the environment.

The health of a population related to the environment in which the population lives has been central to medical anthropology for many years. Many medical anthropologists have attempted to answer this question for specific populations, and some have attempted to develop general ecological theories of human health that apply across local situations. From an epidemiological perspective, as McMichael and Beaglehole (2003:4–5) observe, population health is rooted in "a stable and productive natural environment that: yields assured supplies of food and fresh water; has a relatively constant climate in which climate-sensitive physical and biological systems do not change for the worse; and retains biodiversity (a fundamental source of both present and future value)." This is an ideal that no human populations experience in full. The reasons they do not, the nature and determinants of alternative human-environment relations, variations in environment-related health status within and between ecological zones, and the causes and health implications of environmental change are the concerns of this chapter.

The "natural environment" refers to the earth's surface and atmosphere, including biological organisms (of which humans are one species), along with air, water, soil, and numerous other resources required to sustain life. As a result of having developed cultures that include technoeconomic, social structural, ideological, and attitudinal components, humans are able to survive in a wide diversity of habitats, indeed, in most habitats on land surfaces around the planet. They do not do so passively by merely adapting to the contingencies in the physical conditions around them. Rather, humans are capable of having a profound impact on the natural world, and in this sense the environments humans inhabit are, to varying degrees, not really natural in the sense of being pristine and free of human influence. At the same time, human health is significantly affected by the environment produced by the daily interaction of natural and sociocultural forces. To take one vitally important and increasingly pressing example—one that, because of its significance, we will return to in greater detail later in the chapter—the World Health Organization estimates that the earth's warming climate causes 150,000 deaths and five million illnesses each year, and this toll could double by 2020. Global warming is contributing to rising rates of malaria, diarrhea (a common cause of death among children in developing nations), and malnutrition. For instance, higher temperatures in South Asia have caused elevated rainfall levels and contributed to improved breeding opportunities for mosquitoes. As a result, diseases spread by mosquitoes, such as dengue fever and malaria, have skyrocketed. Notably, rising temperatures on the planet have a disproportionate impact on poorer nations, those that have through their limited production of industrial pollution or other environmental effects of human technology contributed the least to causing global warming. As Jonathan Patz of the Gaylord Nelson Institute for Environmental Studies of the University of Wisconsin has observed, "Those most vulnerable to climate change are not the ones responsible for causing it. . . . Our energy-consumptive lifestyles are having lethal impacts on other people around the globe, especially the poor" (quoted in Elperin 2005:2). In short, humans both make and are made (and, in the case of disease and death, are unmade) by their environment. As this discussion suggests, the relationship between human health and the environment is complex, and it has certainly been an arena of debate within medical anthropology.

## MEDICAL ECOLOGY AND CRITICAL MEDICAL ANTHROPOLOGY ON THE ENVIRONMENT

Two perspectives within medical anthropology—medical ecology and critical medical anthropology—have especially concerned themselves with human-environment interactions. As noted in chapter 1, medical ecology, a biocultural perspective in medical anthropology, views health and disease within an elaborate ecosystem, one that includes physical, biological, and cultural components (McElroy and Townsend 2003). The physical, or abiotic, environment includes climate, energy sources, and material resources, such as those that can be converted into tools for procuring food, building shelters, and making clothes to protect people from the natural elements. The biotic environment includes plants and animals that can be converted into food, clothing, and even shelter as well as predators, vectors, and pathogens that can endanger the life of the individual or the group. Finally, the cultural environment includes technology, social organization, and ideology, all of which serve to sustain health and counteract disease, which is not to say that culture does not play a large role as well in producing illness and death. According to McElroy and Townsend (2003:24–25),

> The parts are interdependent and continually in interaction, a change in one variable frequently leads to a change in another (this is what a system means). Although we usually focus on the separate parts and think of them as causes and effects of change processes, it is also possible to imagine all these individual spheres and variables functioning as single unit.

According to McElroy and Townsend, changes in any of the components of their model can cause imbalances in the other components (e.g., new subsistence strategies can lead to exposure to new risks), and a very severe imbalance can generate stress and disease. Built into the medical ecology model are the following assumptions:

- There are no single causes of disease (e.g., a virus); rather, disease ultimately flows from human-ecosystem imbalances.
- Health and disease develop within the interface of physical, biological, and cultural subsystems.

- The environment is not only physical habitat but the human-made environment of villages, towns, and cities.
- Perceptions of the environment are shaped by culture.

While there are points of overlap between medical ecology and critical medical anthropology in their respective approaches to health and the environment, there are notable differences in emphasis as well. Both of these perspectives in medical anthropology overlap with a multidisciplinary approach called "political ecology," which incorporates political economy but goes beyond examining the relationship of social inequality to health to also consider the impacts of social inequality on the environment and, through human interactions with the environment, on human health. Contributors to political ecology come from many fields, including sociology, anthropology, political economy, and geography (J. Foster 2000; Robbins 2003). Parsons (1977:xii) provides a succinct overview of the basic premises of political ecology in his assertion that

> economy is a matter of ecology: it has to do with the production and distribution of goods and services in the context of human society and nature. . . . [It recognizes] that under the practices of ecological practices of monopoly capitalism, the natural environment is being destroyed along with the social environment.

Scholars interested in the political economy and political ecology of health have considered a wide array of politically and ecologically induced health problems, including malaria, tuberculosis, occupational hazards, and cancer. To fully understand the political ecology of health in the contemporary world, it is necessary to recognize, as does Waitzkin (2000:8), that "the analysis of illness, work, and the environment must consider the connections between these issues and the contradictions of capitalism," as this is the world system in which, in varying ways, almost all people on the planet participate.

In assessing the role of the environment in human health, the critical perspective in medical anthropology draws on the notion that nature has been affected by human events. In other words, the political economy of specific sociocultural systems and the world system generally has profoundly shaped the actual physical reality of nature. This approach differs notably from the common view of nature as an autonomous reality that operates in terms of its own principles separate from human society, a perspective that is reflected in the separation of "natural history" and "human history" into two different and largely separate fields of study but also is seen, more mundanely, in

Western ideas about getting back to nature or escaping to nature as refreshment from life in a human-made environment. The critical perspective, in contrast, attempts to consider "the relation of people to their environment in all its complexity" (Turshen 1989:48) and to treat political economy and political ecology as inseparable.

Crosby (1986), who uses the term "ecological imperialism" to label the biological expansion of European life forms (including European peoples, their plants, animals, parasites, and pathogens) into all corners of the globe, has contributed an important concept for the exploration of the impact of capitalist political economy on "nature." He asserts that this impact involves "a condition of continual disruption: of plowed fields, razed forests, over-grazed pastures, and burned prairies, of deserted villages and expanding cities, of humans, animals, plants, and microlife that have evolved separately suddenly coming into intimate contact" (Crosby 1986:291–92). Crosby argues that the ability of earlier civilizations—such as the Sumerians and, much later, Europeans—to conquer indigenous peoples often had more to do with the fact that they had exposed the latter to a multiplicity of alien diseases than with technological and military superiority. For example, shortly after the First English Fleet arrived in the harbor of Sydney, Australia, in 1788, small-pox spread like wildfire both up and down the coast and inland among the Aboriginal peoples, eventually affecting even residents in the remote outback of New South Wales, Victoria, and South Australia.

## HEALTH AND THE ENVIRONMENT IN THE PAST

Ancient populations developed fitness to resist environmental threats, including climatic ones, periods of food shortage, microbial parasites, and predators, particularly during the Paleolithic era. Most skeletal remains from the Mesolithic (10,000 to 8,000 years B.P.) and the Upper Paleolithic (40,000 to 10,000 years B.P.) eras depict vigorous adults who were relatively free from organic diseases. Cohen (1989) maintains that people in indigenous societies have enjoyed cleaner environments and better health than the majority of people in agrarian civilizations. Even today, indigenous people exhibit a scarcity of cancers, cardiovascular diseases, and other degenerative diseases, although researchers often have observed that few people live long enough to contract them, in large part because they are vulnerable to parasites, predators, poisonous snakes, accidents, warfare, and unexpected harsh climatic conditions that may cause periods of food and water shortage or otherwise lead to illness and death.

All human societies encroach on and modify the natural environment. Bodley (2001) points out that human societies have created environmental crises of greater or lesser degree throughout their long evolution. Foragers contributed to the creation of grasslands, pastoralists overgrazed their lands, and peasants caused deforestation. Each of these levels of social and techno-logical complexity in human social evolution probably contributed to the extinction of certain species. While there is a tendency in Western society to romanticize indigenous peoples, such as pre-Columbian Native Americans, various species, such as indigenous small horses, camels, and large game animals in North America, disappeared after the arrival of the first humans in the Americas, perhaps in small or large part because of overhunting. Jared Diamond (2005) argues that environmental degradation was one of the prin-cipal factors contributing to the demise of the Anasazi ("the ancient ones," as they are referred to by contemporary southwestern Native Americans) horticultural villages of Chaco Canyon in western New Mexico, the chiefdom societies of Easter Island, and the Norse settlements in Greenland.

The emergence of social mechanisms for harnessing large amounts of energy from the environment contributed to the emergence of what Ruyle (1977:623) has called "predatory ruling classes." In addition to the role of class conflict in contributing to the demise of the earliest state societies (e.g., ancient Sumer, Egypt, and Rome), as Hughes (1996:29) observes, "their fail-ure to maintain a harmonious balance with nature" was a significant factor in their demise. In the New World, environmental devastation created by the classic lowland Mayan civilization contributed to a yellow fever epidemic that may have played a significant role in the collapse of the Mayan state structure and unifying institutions.

The dangers of ecological self-destruction that plagued ancient state soci-eties became even more pronounced with the advent of industrial capitalism beginning around 1800, and it has been growing ever greater with the pas-sage of time. In contrast to the smaller-scale environmental modifications resulting from the intervention of indigenous societies, global capitalism, with its treadmill of production and consumption, introduces a new array of industrial and chemical pollutants that disrupt the natural environment and have devastating effects on human health. The Industrial Revolution allowed for the harnessing of nonrenewable fossil fuels, namely, coal, petroleum, and natural gas, and humans came to rely increasingly on machine power rather than the energy derived from humans and animals.

In order to meet the needs of the capitalist system for functionally healthy workers, the development of water supplies, sanitation, and agricultural practices dramatically improved health conditions and longevity worldwide, but these benefits were unevenly distributed: some societies benefited far more than others, and within societies some social classes profited dispropor- tionately. Conversely, capitalists often ignored the health of their workers if they had access to a surplus labor pool and could increase profits by ignoring the physical environment of the workplace, the pace of the work itself, and the housing and living conditions of the workers. One consequence is the significantly substandard housing found among the poor and working people of a highly marginalized country like Haiti, as seen in Figure 7.1.

Within the context of the global economy, any effort to create a healthy global community must come to grips with what has been called "the pro- ductivist ethic," a belief that continual economic expansion is necessary, socially beneficial, and natural, as summarized in folk sayings such as "you can't stop progress." Closely tied to the productivist ethic is a "culture of consumption" that assumes that humans have insatiable material needs and live in an environment with endless resources. The productivist ethic, which is part of the ideology that rationalizes the capitalist mode of production, historically helped drive many of the key social changes that despoiled and continue to despoil the ecologically fragile biosphere while channeling an

FIGURE 7.1
*Poor-quality housing in Cité Soleil, Haiti, reflects the overall poverty of the country. Photo by Merrill Singer.*

increasingly large share of the planet's limited resources to the privileged few at the expense of the masses of people. The global economy has been transforming more and more of the natural environment—including water, forests, beaches, and plants—into private commodities to be purchased and sold on the market.

## HEALTH AND THE ENVIRONMENT TODAY

The fossil fuel–based technologies that make up industrialization brought about sweeping environment-reshaping changes, including the growth and pollution of heavily populated urban centers. These changes have had a profound impact on human health. During the twentieth century and continuing in the present century, the world has witnessed the emergence of teeming metropolitan areas such as Mexico City, São Paulo, Mumbai (Bombay), Beijing, and Los Angeles, places that environmental scientists call unhealthy "heat islands" because of the elevated temperatures their technology and population densities produce. Rapid industrialization and technological innovation, including changes in transportation and telecommunications, are part of a process that has come to increasingly be referred to as "globalization" or, perhaps more appropriately, "corporate globalization." A global energy-intensive food production system, the ever-increasing adoption of motor vehicles and air-conditioning systems, oversized houses, a myriad of consumer items for the affluent, the increasing use of air transport for business and pleasure, and other "developments" act to strain a fragile ecosystem and ultimately threaten human health. Environmental degradation, as a result, has become a primary public health issue internationally in the contemporary world.

In their drive for profits, private multinational corporations in the West and state corporations in state capitalist societies such as China have created not only a global factory but also a new global ecosystem that has resulted in the burning of fossil fuels, motor vehicle pollution, acid rain, toxic chemical and nuclear radioactive waste, desertification, defoliation, ozone depletion, and greenhouse gases. The last of these, which include chlorofluorocarbons, methane (largely from vast cattle breeding facilities), and carbon dioxide (a direct product of fossil fuels) emitted by motor vehicles, airplanes, ships, and coal- or oil-fired electric generators, have been contributing to ozone depletion and global warming. Carbon dioxide acts like the glass covering of a greenhouse in that it allows heat from the sun to pass through to the earth's surface while preventing much of it from escaping from the planet.

### Infectious Diseases in a Globalizing World

One of the consequences of corporate globalization has been the emergence of new infectious diseases and the rapid spread of infectious diseases (new and old) to previously uninfected populations. The discovery of new pathogens, some of which are already widespread by the time they are recognized as a threat to human health, is now occurring at a swift pace. Approximately three new human infectious diseases are identified every two years, and a new pathogen is reported on in the health literature weekly. New diseases in human communities commonly have their origin in nonhuman animal species (and hence are called zoonotic diseases). This process of cross-species infection involving humans has been going on at least since the earliest domestication of animals, and it continues to occur today. HIV/AIDS, for example, transferred to humans from chimpanzee populations (perhaps as long as a century ago), but the disease did not come to human attention until it spread around the world as a result of the global movement of people as tourists, on business, as refugees, as armies on the move, and so forth. Severe Acute Respiratory Syndrome (SARS) is another global pandemic that had its origin in nonhuman animals and later spread to and adapted to living in human bodies (as a result of mutation and natural selection).

The possible role of corporate globalization in the spread of infectious disease is illustrated by the influenza pandemic that began in April 2009. This zoonotic disease developed in pigs, and the initial epicenter of the outbreak among humans was in a part of Mexico that is home to the massive Smithfield Foods hog production center, which supplies approximately one million animals annually to the world food market. Smithfield, a global corporation, is the world's largest pork processor and hog producer, with revenues that exceeded $11 billion in fiscal 2010. Industrial farm animal production (known as IFAP) centers, like Smithfield's operation in Veracruz, Mexico, have been found to produce more than livestock. They also generate vast quantities of animal waste that are too large, concentrated, and toxic to be converted into reusable manure. The Pew Charitable Trusts and Johns Hopkins Bloomberg School of Public Health have reported that livestock centers like Smithfield are a grave potential source of land and water pollution with toxic and potentially infectious animal waste products. Among the prominent concerns explicitly raised by these institutions is whether large-scale corporate livestock production creates a risk environment that fosters the emergence of novel viruses like H1N1 that could lead to human infections, sickness, and death.

**The Impact of Global Warming on Health**

The 2007 United Nations Intergovernmental Panel on Climate Change (IPCC) synthesis report states that there was a 0.75 degree Centigrade (1.35 degree Fahrenheit) rise in global temperature and a 22 centimeter rise in sea levels over the course of the twentieth century. While this may not sound particularly serious, ongoing economic development, coupled with the increasing demands of an ever-growing population—which, in part, is a response to the conditions of poverty that push people in particularly developing countries to have more children in order to have enough laborers to meet their subsistence needs—further aggravates the problem. The U.S. Environmental Protection Agency projected a rise in global temperature of between 1.6 and 6.3 degrees Fahrenheit by 2100, which, in turn, would result in a significant rise in the level of the oceans and a devastating impact on human populations living near coastlines and beyond. The IPCC, consisting of some two thousand climate scientists, economists, and other scientists around the world, predicts that global temperatures could rise further between 1.1 degrees Centigrade (2.0 degrees Fahrenheit) and 6.4 degrees Centigrade (11.5 degrees Fahrenheit) by 2100 and that sea levels could rise between 28 centimeters and 79 centimeters by 2100, or even more if melting of Greenland and Antarctica would accelerate. Worldwide, 2010 was the wettest year on record but also a very hot year, despite very cold winters in Europe and North America. The World Meteorological Organization maintained that 2010 was the hottest year since records began in 1850 and the National Aeronautical and Space Administration and the National Ocean and Atmospheric Administration reported that 2010 tied with 2005 as the hottest year on record. Every single year of the twenty-first century has been among the top ten warmest years since instrumental records began, with winters warming faster than summers. Increases in temperature vary considerably around the planet. For example, a global temperature rise of 5.4 degrees Fahrenheit (3 degrees Centigrade) could translate into an increase of only 1 to 2 degrees Centigrade (1.8 to 3.6 degrees Fahrenheit) over most of the oceans but an increase of 7.1 to 8.0 degrees Centigrade (12.8 to 14.4 degrees Fahrenheit) in the Arctic (Paskal 2010:68). Various prominent climate scientists, such as those at a 2009 congress in Copenhagen, have asserted that the IPCC reports have been on the conservative side, that the global climate is changing faster than previously thought, and that global emissions must not rise after 2015 (Pittock 2009).

Forty percent of the Arctic icecap has retreated during the past several decades; glaciers in the Himalayas, Andes, high African mountains, the North American Rockies, and sub-Antarctic island mountains have been rapidly retreating; much of the tundra of Arctic areas has been melting and releasing a growing level of methane gas into the atmosphere; and portions of the Antarctic icecap also have been breaking up. Because of global warming, plants and animals are moving into regions closer to the poles because these regions are becoming warmer. Animals, such as polar bears, are in danger of extinction due to the contraction of the Arctic ice pack and a reduction of the animals, such as seals, upon which they feed. Coral reef damage is occurring all over the world, including in the Greater Barrier Reef off the coast of Australia.

While climate scientists debated for many years whether global warming was primarily a natural phenomenon or a human-created one, the vast majority now agree that it has been induced by the emission of various greenhouse gases, particularly carbon dioxide, which has increased from 280 parts per million at the time of the Industrial Revolution to about 390 parts per million in 2010. While some climate scientists contest this conclusion, a number of these are employed by the fossil-fuels industry. A global economy that relies heavily on fossil fuels, namely, coal, petroleum, and natural gas, has played a significant role in the emission of carbon dioxide into the atmosphere. The sources of global warming, however, are numerous and include a growing global population clamoring for both basic and prestige resources, a growing number of airplane flights around the world, overheating and overcooling of larger and larger dwelling units (particularly in the developed countries), deforestation, animal production, and the production of a seemingly endless array of consumer products that in part serves to alleviate the alienation of social life in the modern world. It has been found that 56.5 percent of greenhouse gases came from carbon dioxide emitted by fossil fuels, such as coal-fired power plants, motor vehicles, and airplanes; 17.3 percent from carbon dioxide emitted from land use alterations, such as deforestation; 14.3 percent from methane emitted by biomass decomposition, coal mining, natural gas and oil systems leakages, livestock production, wastewater treatment, cultivation of rice, and burning of savannah; 7.9 percent from nitrous oxide released by agricultural soils; and 1.1 percent from other highly active greenhouse gases (McKeown and Gardner 2009:189). In 2005, in terms of total greenhouse gas emissions, the United States and China tied for number one with 18.3 percent each; the European Union emitted 12.6 percent, the former Soviet Union 8.4 percent, the OPEC countries 4.7 percent, India 4.6 percent, Southeast Asia and South Korea 4.3 percent, Japan 3.5 percent, Canada 2.0 percent, Indonesia 2.0 percent, Australia 1.5 percent, South Africa 1.3 percent, and the rest of the world 18.5 percent (Garnaut 2008). Although various studies have indicated that the China has superseded the United States in total greenhouse gas emissions, one must bear in mind that China has a population of about 1.3 billion in contrast to about 300 million for the United States. While the global financial crisis of 2008 to 2009 resulted in significant reductions in carbon dioxide emissions in the United States, the United Kingdom, Germany, and Russia, such reductions did not take place in China and India, and emissions have started to spiral upward again in most countries around the world.

Global warming is already having serious impacts on human, animal, and plant life around the world. South Pacific islanders in particular face a threat to their traditional horticultural lifestyle because of rising sea levels that inundate their fields and water supplies and threaten to submerge their islands. The Inuit of Arctic Canada and Alaska are experiencing a contraction of the polar bear populations that they have traditionally hunted, and they are unable to access seals because the icepack is freezing later than it once did. Andean peoples face the possibility of the eradication of their way of life as glaciers from which they have drawn water for themselves, their fields, and their animals retreat. Peoples living in coastal areas around the world face the possibility of increased flooding and hurricanes because of the rise and warming of the oceans. A growing number of prominent climate scientists now believe that global warming contributed to the devastating effects of hurricanes Katrina, Rita, and Wilma in 2005. Among these is Judith Curry of Georgia Tech University, whose research has shown that an ever greater percentage of hurricanes are of the most intense kind, in no small part, she believes, because global warming is increasing the temperature of the world's oceans. According to Curry, Hurricane Katrina was the "the 9/11 of global warming. . . . The melting of polar ice caps is fairly remote. It's hard to get upset about it. But everybody personally felt Katrina" (quoted in Lang 2006:4).

Further, many climate scientists contend that the droughts that people in parts of sub-Saharan Africa and Australia have been facing are related to global warming as well. Moreover, global warming appears to be the primary impetus behind the spread of infectious diseases to environments north and south of the equator and heat waves that threaten the lives and health of vulnerable populations, such as the elderly and the sick.

Berger (2000:36–37) provides the following overview of the impact of global warming on the prevalence of certain diseases:

> Milder temperatures have contributed to the spread of mosquito-borne diseases in Africa. Richards Bay, South Africa, for example, which was once malaria-free, had 22,000 cases in 1999. Malaria has also reached highland

regions of Kenya and Tanzania where it was previously unknown. In the Andes of Colombia, disease-carrying mosquitoes that once lived at altitudes no higher than 3,200 feet have now appeared at the 7,200-foot level.

While global warming is not the only factor involved, today it is estimated that there are 300 million to 500 million cases of malaria in Africa each year, resulting in between 1.5 million and 2.7 million deaths, more than 90 percent occurring among children under five years of age. Global warming also has been implicated in the resurgence of various other epidemics, including cholera in Latin America in 1991, pneumonic plague in India in 1994, and the outbreak of a hantavirus epidemic in the U.S. Southwest also in 1994. Tony McMichael, a physician-epidemiologist based at the Centre of Epidemiology and Population Health at the Australian National University in Canberra and a pioneer in the study of health consequences of global warming, presents the following sobering observations:

> The main anticipated impact of climate change on the potential transmission of vector-borne diseases would be in tropical areas. In general, populations on the margins of endemic areas in tropical and subtropical countries would be most likely to experience an increase in transmission. . . . This appears to reflect a combination of increasing population mobility, urbanization, poverty and regional warming, along with a slackening of mosquito control programmes. Meanwhile, in temperate zones, climate change may also affect diseases such as tick-borne viral encephalitis (which occurs in parts of Western Europe, Russia and Scandinavia) and Lyme disease. (McMichael 2001:302)

Additionally, global warming may endanger people's health and even their lives through heat exhaustion, as was the case during the summer of 2003 in Europe. The estimated mortality of some 35,000 people during the heat wave was associated not only with the high temperatures but also with the fact that nighttime low temperatures have been rising nearly twice as fast as daytime temperatures. The lingering nighttime warmth deprived people of normal relief from blistering daytime temperatures and of the opportunity to recuperate from heat stress. Air pollution linked to longer, warmer summers particularly affects those suffering from respiratory problems, such as asthma. Given the health consequences of global warming, we can speak of diseases of global warming. These would not necessarily be new diseases, although they might be, but would include any "tropical" disease (e.g., malaria and dengue fever) that spreads to new places and peoples because of global warming as well as diseases linked to poor nutrition due to desertification of pastoral areas or flooding of agricultural areas.

Singer (2009, 2010) developed the term *ecosyndemic* to label the role of anthropogenic changes in the environment that increase the frequency of adverse disease interactions and, as a result, increase the health burden of affected populations. Ecosyndemics are likely to concentrate among the poor and other marginal communities, who are least able to obtain adequate nutrition, sanitation, adequate shelter, low-stress life experiences, and access to preventive and curative health care. Global warming is disrupting natural ecosystems and contributing to the geographic diffusion of disease-causing viruses, bacteria, fungi, and other pathogens. Diseases that have increased in range because of global warming include malaria, dengue, Rift Valley fever, West Nile disease, Chikungunya fever, and yellow fever. Increased planetary warming is also a factor in the spread of disease-bearing rodents (as well as other disease vectors) like those responsible for the outbreak of hantavirus in the U.S. Southwest in 1994 and pneumatic plague in India the following year. Furthermore, water-borne diseases like cholera are spreading because of ever-warmer oceans.

There is growing recognition that the time is overdue for anthropologists, including medical anthropologists, and other social scientists to begin examining the impact of global warming on human populations, including their health. As McMichael (2003:15) aptly observes, "This topic is likely to become a major theme in population health research, social policy development and advocacy during this first decade of the twenty-first century."

Unfortunately, to date very few anthropologists and other social scientists, in contrast to climate scientists (see Pittock 2009) and other natural scientists, have paid much attention to the impact of global warming on humanity, including the impact on many of the peoples that they have studied over the course of the past century and a half. While archaeologist Brian Fagan (1999:76) is correct in his assertion that "global warming is nothing new for humanity," the magnitude of the global warming that the planet has been experiencing over the past several decades and that is predicted will continue for decades to come, even if it is checked by monumental preemptive measures, is on a magnitude never experienced before by humanity. In the introduction to their anthology *Weather, Climate, Culture*, Sarah Strauss and Ben Orlove (2003:10–11) refer to "climate change" only in passing, and none of the essays in their volume focuses on climate change or, more specifically, global warming. In a book chapter titled "Cultural Paradigms: An Anthropological Perspective on Climate Change," Celeste Ray argues that policies about global warming "must employ cross-cultural knowledge of benign environmental practices while maintaining consciousness of traditional family and community structures, labor division, and localized subsistence strategies" (Ray 2001:90). While Ray is to be commended for bringing the anthropological lens to the study of climate change, her analysis is somewhat limited in that it does not discuss the relationship of climate change to the treadmill of production and consumption associated with global capitalism.

Susan A. Crate and Mark Nuttall edited an anthology titled *Anthropology and Climate Change* (2009), a welcome addition to a quickly emerging anthropology of climate change or global warming. Their book includes eleven case studies that focus on the impact of climate change on various local populations and their efforts to adapt to it. None of these chapters, however, discusses specifically the impact of climate change on health per se. What is missing from *Anthropology and Climate Change* is a clear-cut recognition of the critical anthropology of global warming, a perspective that has been delineated in a number of publications, including *Global Warming and the Political Ecology of Health* (Baer and Singer 2009).

Global warming (or climate change) constitutes one of the most important issues of the twenty-first century, along with the growing gap between the affluent and the poor within most nation-states and between nation-states, thanks to corporate globalization and ongoing conflicts in many parts of the world. The latter in part can be attributed to various states, led by the United States but also including the United Kingdom and Australia, doing the bidding of multinational corporations in what Klare (2002) calls the "resource wars." We have called for the development of a critical medical anthropology of global warming that recognizes its relationship to the treadmill of capitalist production. We maintain that, ultimately, global warming or climate change is a problem that is part and parcel of global capitalism with its drive for profits that results in a pattern of ever-increasing production and consumption. As John Bellamy Foster (2005:14–15), a critical sociologist, argues,

> The ecological crisis engendered by the capitalist world economy . . . threatens the collapse of world civilization, and irreparable damage to the entire biosphere from which human society and the planet as we know it may never recover—if current trends are not reversed. The latest scientific reports indicate that global warming is, if anything, increasing faster than we previously thought, leading to fears of unpredictable and cumulative effects and of abrupt climate change. . . . The removal of environmental regulations as a part of neoliberal economics has only served to heighten this ecological crisis.

There is much debate on how to adapt to and mitigate global warming, ranging from turning to alternative energy sources (such as wind, solar, biomass, and even nuclear, which many argue would be an utter ecological and health disaster) to planting trees and developing environmentally friendly technology and energy-saving devices. Many of these proposals would be steps in the right direction, but others, particularly schemes such as carbon trading, carbon offsetting, growing biofuels on land that could produce food, or eliminating forested areas to clear land for biofuel crops, are dubious. Conversely, there would be a significant drop in global warming if the majority of people in the developed world and the affluent in the developing world were to opt to live simpler lifestyles by restricting the use of motor vehicles; relying more on mass transit, bikes, and their feet for transportation; and consuming less. Ultimately, as we state at the end of this chapter, an authentic program of mitigation to reverse the trend toward global warming will require transcendence of global capitalism.

Moreover, as Spratt and Sutton (2008:xi) point out, global climate change is only the exposed "tip of [a] broader global-sustainability iceberg" that includes a litany of environmental degradations that are now "converging rapidly in a manner not previously experienced." All of these threats (e.g., acid rain, air pollution), which are connected to the transformation of the earth's biomass into an ever-growing human population, have vital implications for a host of human diseases and other threats to health (e.g., exposure to toxins). Even more significant than the number of health-related degradations that are occurring is the issue of *ecocrises interaction*. Rather than the various environmental calamities we face and their respective configurations of health indicators being stand-alone threats to human well-being—which is the conventional but limited outlook that leads to fragmented and even competitive mitigation efforts—adverse human impacts on the environment intersect and the resulting interaction significantly exacerbates the overall human (as well as other animal and plant) health consequences; these interacting ecocrises create the potential for catastrophic outcomes (M. Singer 2009).

### Other Environmental Impacts on Health

Chlorofluorocarbons also play an important role in ozone depletion, which has allowed a significant increase in the amount of ultraviolet light striking the earth's surface, especially in portions of the Southern Hemisphere nearest the pole, namely, southern Australia, New Zealand, Argentina, and Chile. While skin cancers are a well-known health consequence of ozone depletion—and rates of these diseases have been rising steadily (e.g., skin cancers account for around 80 percent of all new cancers diagnosed in Australia each year)—increased ultraviolet radiation at ground level also can lead to mutations, especially among viruses, whose only protection from the air is a thin layer of protein.

As a reflection of the underlying productivist ethic that led to their creation, national indices of growth and development, such as the gross domestic product, count only the production of goods and services that are sold in the marketplace (i.e., commodities) but do not take into account the impacts of their production, such as environmental degradation. While the emergence of global capitalism has ensured plentiful (if far from equitably distributed) food resources (including nutritionally dubious ones), modern sanitation, and biomedicine for some, these material benefits have often been obtained at the expense of the masses of people in developing nations and the working class in the developed world. Even the privileged few in the developed world face the danger of ecocide. As Stavrianos (1989:153) argues,

> Today, . . . the ecological impact of humans on their planet has become explosive because of three major interrelated factors: the exponential growth of human populations, the imperatives of the new global capitalist economy, and the hardly foreseen consequences of a seemingly uncontrollable technology.

McMichael and Beaglehole (2003) delineate two categories of health risks posed by corporate globalization: (1) primary health risks stemming from changes in the social and natural environment and (2) more specific forms of health risks. The former includes the following:

- growing socioeconomic disparities both within and between nation-states, a topic that we discussed in the previous chapter
- the fragmentation and weakening of labor unions as multinational corporations attain greater influence over governments around the world and thereby endanger occupational health in their insatiable drive for profits
- the depletion of the biodiversity of plants and animals, as reflected in vast acres devoted to a single plant, such as wheat or corn, and the destruction of the habitats that support many species
- the spread of "invasive" species, most notably humans themselves, resulting from imbalances in biodiversity and the dispersal of persistent organic pollutants

The latter include the following:

- the spread of tobacco-related diseases and dietary diseases resulting from food consumption patterns shaped by marketing campaigns intended to convince people to eat nutritionally dubious foods that are high in carbohydrates, starches, and fat but low in protein and vitamin content
- the proliferation of motor vehicles, including more recently in developing societies, such as China
- the rise of obesity in urban populations where most people follow a relatively sedentary lifestyle
- the expansion of international drug trafficking related in part to demoralization among socioeconomically disadvantaged populations, including youth, searching for an escape from the alienation of modern life
- the spread of infectious diseases due to increased global travel
- the increasing prevalence of depression and other mental ailments in aging and socially isolated people, particularly in urban areas

Although public health measures and secondarily biomedicine have done much, although by no means enough, to counter the threat of infectious diseases, there has been growing concern in recent years about what have been termed "emerging diseases." There exist four types of emerging infectious diseases: (1) newly described conditions that have been discovered or recognized only within the past few decades (e.g., HIV and SARS, or sudden acute respiratory syndrome), (2) expansion of a familiar disease into a new region or habitat (what have been called "reemerging diseases," such as malaria), (3) marked increase in the local incidence of a disease, and (4) increased severity or duration of an older disease or its increased resistance to previously effective treatment (e.g., tuberculosis). The spread of emerging diseases appears to be a consequence of several factors. These include major environmental changes such as deforestation and reforestation, intensification of agriculture, dam construction and irrigation, mining, and housing and road construction; the increasing concentration of people in overcrowded and densely packed cities (particularly in the developing world); the global movement of people due to migration, business, and tourism; and the development of pathogen resistance to overused and misused antibiotics.

**Water and Globalization**
In terms of health and illness, particularly with reference to infectious diseases, whether of the older variety or the new emerging variety, access to clean

freshwater is crucial, perhaps more than most of us in the developed world think, because, as it is available at the turn of a faucet handle in so many places, we often take it for granted. Despite the fact that water covers more than 70 percent of the world's surface, particularly in the form of oceans, less than 1 percent of the water on the planet is available for human consumption, thus making it a precious natural resource that has increasingly become commodified within the context of corporate globalization. A growing number of anthropologists have addressed this issue, as reflected in the book *Globalization, Water, and Health*. In this volume, Linda and Scott Whiteford (2005:9–10) delineate four categories of diseases related to water: (1) waterborne diseases, such as cholera, typhoid, and hepatitis, emanating from the ingestion of water containing pathogenic organisms; (2) water-washed diseases resulting from a lack of water for washing or personal hygiene; (3) water-based diseases, such as schistosomiasis, resulting from exposure to nonhuman parasitic hosts in activities such as bathing, swimming, or washing clothes; and (4) water-related diseases, such as dengue, West Nile fever, malaria, and yellow fever in which humans come into contact with water that an insect vector uses as a breeding ground. Many of these diseases could be prevented if people had access to clean water for drinking, cooking, washing, and recreational purposes as well as access to sanitary living conditions and adequate nutrition. Whereas for eons access to water, particularly in indigenous societies, was viewed as a human right, with the spread of global capitalism, water is being redefined as a commodity. In today's world, increasing competition for clean water has been contributing to a tremendous increase in the number of deaths and diseases that could be easily avoided if world resources were not so inequitably distributed.

Clear water supplies increasingly are being threatened by global warming, mining, agriculture (which uses about 69 percent of the world's freshwater supply), deforestation of mountainous woodlands, and urban sprawl. With respect to the last issue, in his contribution to the volume mentioned previously, Carl Kendall (2005) discusses the impact of Lima's rapid growth on the availability of fresh clean water in an arid coastal plain. The Rimac River, Lima's primary water source, has become heavily polluted with heavy metals from nearby mines, high levels of nitrates and other organic compounds, and untreated sewage. Furthermore, the Lima aquifer has become polluted with fecal matter and other pollutants. Lima residents experience high rates of diarrhea that are intimately related to a shortage of water and contamination of their water supply. While limitations of space do not permit discussion of the other case studies in the volume, the following thoughts by the Whitefords are important:

Protecting the physical environment and human health must be part of a deeper change in societal values. For anthropology and other social sciences to participate in this transformation through methodologically rigorous, theoretically informed, and socially relevant research is the biggest challenge. . . . In this era, social science must make new theoretical understanding relevant to world problems, or it will be too late. (S. Whiteford and L. Whiteford 2005:265)

## THE POLITICAL ECOLOGY OF CANCER

Cancer is an ancient disease that was little understood in the past, and its prevalence prior to the nineteenth century is not known. Whereas many infectious diseases have been on the decline, although AIDS and some other emerging diseases are notable exceptions, cancer rates rose dramatically during the twentieth century and have continued to do so into the present century. Cancer is largely a disease of development rather than underdevelopment, as indicated by the World Health Organization's estimate that about one-half of cancers occur in the most industrialized fifth of the world's population (Proctor 1995:2). Within specific nation-states, cancer rates vary in terms of the type of cancer, regionally, between the sexes, and among ethnic and religious groups.

Cancer etiology is a frequently debated topic, one about which scientists find themselves adopting diametrically opposing interpretations. Some argue that cancer is caused primarily by an array of environmental factors, others that it is related to lifestyle, and still others that it is related to stress, emotions, hereditary factors (referred to as "genetic susceptibility"), aging, and hormonal disturbances. Very likely, each of these factors plays some role in cancer etiology, and which ones are more significant varies greatly from person to person and by type of cancer. Nevertheless, each of these theories ultimately has political implications that have contributed to the "cancer wars," which include disagreements about the most effective way to treat it, ranging from the conventional approaches of radiation, chemotherapy, and surgery to a wide array of alternative therapies.

Several epidemiologists and public health scholars have sought to address the narrow reductionism they find inherent in prominent approaches to disease etiology generally and cancer etiology specifically by adopting a multicausal model that shows that a huge number of phenomena go together to produce illnesses. Within medical anthropology, Peter Brown and colleagues (1996), proponents of the biocultural approach, identify six factors contributing to disease: genetics, nutrition, the environment, psychogenesis, iatrogenic forces, and infection. As Tesh (1988:62) so aptly argues, however, the multicausal model tends to lead to political inaction because "prevention policy has to attack all possible causes at once—a strategy that could stretch available resources far beyond their capacity and end up by devoting only pittance to each." Furthermore, the multicausal model fails to come to grips with the issue of primacy—that is, whether certain factors play a more important role in disease etiology. Notes Turshen (1989:24),

> Health and disease are products of the way society is organized, of the way subsistence is produced as well as surplus, and of the way subsistence and surplus are distributed among the members of society. . . . The consequences for prevention and cure that follow from this theory of disease are the need for fundamental social organization.

There exists considerable evidence that a disproportionate incidence of cancer occurs among members of lower-income groups and workers exposed to industrial carcinogens, although there are some exceptions. For instance, higher breast cancer rates among professional women in affluent communities, such as San Francisco and the Upper West Side of Manhattan, may be related in part to the fact many of these women postpone bearing children until later in their lives. Theories that emphasize political economic and environmental factors in cancer etiology have tended to receive short shrift in health policy and cancer prevention circles, such as in the National Cancer Institute and the American Cancer Society, largely because addressing them would require major social structural changes that ultimately would require transcending the existing global economy.

Wilhelm C. Hueper, the director of the National Cancer Institute's Environmental Cancer Section from 1948 to 1964, was an early proponent of the argument that exposure to industrial chemicals was a major factor in cancer causation (Proctor 1995:36). Samuel Epstein, a progressive biomedical physician and professor of occupational and environmental health at the University of Illinois School of Public Health, followed in his footsteps by authoring *The Politics of Cancer* (1978), in which he documents links between industrial pollutants and rising cancer rates. He estimates that 70 to 90 percent of cancers are induced by exposure to environmental and occupational exposure to carcinogens. More recently, Epstein (2005:281), on the basis of data from the Northeast, has argued that breast cancer, as well as other cancers, has been associated with living near hazardous waste sites:

> Most recently, the high increase in breast cancer incidence and mortality in Connecticut and suburban New York counties, especially Nassau and Suffolk,

has been associated with consumption of milk and water contaminated over the last two decades with nuclear fission products, the short-lived radioactive iodine and the long-lived bone-seeking strontium-90, from the Millstone and Indian Point civilian nuclear reactors. An additional environmental risk in Nassau and Suffolk Counties may reflect past exposure from extensive agricultural use of carcinogenic soil fumigants.

In light of these findings, Epstein (1979, 2005) argues that industry has adopted an elaborate strategy that seeks to exonerate itself from its contribution to cancer etiology, including blaming the victims by postulating the existence of "hypersusceptible workers," who allegedly are more prone to contract cancer, and moving hazardous chemical facilities to developing nations when labor unions and environmental groups have managed to convince politicians to pass environmental legislation.

### Cancer in the Community

Anthropologist Martha Balshem (1993) was intimately immersed in the debate between the lifestyle and environmental theories of cancer etiology when she worked as a health educator at the Fox Chase Cancer Center in Philadelphia, a role in which she found herself feeling increasing uncomfortable. Her highly engaging and readable book *Cancer in the Community* explores "cancer control" in a European American working-class inner-city neighborhood in Philadelphia that Balshem calls Tannertown (pseudonym). The Fox Chase Cancer Center focuses on the prevention of suffering, namely, lowering cancer morbidity and mortality, by encouraging its clients to change their lifestyles, including ceasing smoking, following certain dietary regimens, and having regular cancer screening examinations. Expressive of this approach, with funding from the National Cancer Institute, the Fox Chase Cancer Center initiated Project CAN-DO, a five-year cancer education campaign between 1983 and 1988 in Tannertown. According to Balshem, Tannertowners tend to reject the assertion that their high cancer rates were a result of their lifestyles but instead viewed air pollution emanating in large part, but not entirely, from nearby chemical plants, occupational exposures in the plants, motor vehicle pollution, and the chemical adulteration of their food and water as the primary sources of cancer. Balshem (1993:75) found that

respondents express anger, frustration, and even disdain in reaction to the perceived arrogance of the scientist. On one hand, goes the discourse, science tells us that everything in our environment causes cancer; and on the other, it says that we can prevent cancer through changes in our lifestyle. . . . Control, fate, victimization—these are issues into which talking about cancer leads.

In twenty-five one-on-one interviews and eight focus groups, Balshem found that while her respondents tended to view cancer as resulting from both lifestyle and environmental factors, they believed that making lifestyle changes would be a useless preventive measure in lowering cancer risk. The health educators at the center followed the official health prevention paradigm that stresses individual responsibility for good health. Balshem (1993) maintains that the skepticism that Tannertowners expressed about the views of scientific experts and health educators on cancer constitutes a manifestation of the loss of control that they feel over their daily lives. Interestingly, she goes on to argue "that the community critique of medical science mirrors that of critical studies in medical anthropology" (Balshem 1993:89). This is only partly true in that Tannertowners often assume that God or fate plays a role in whether they develop cancer. In coping with their sense of powerlessness, they—particularly the men—had come to view themselves as being tough and determined to beat the odds. Perhaps if scientists, who undoubtedly Tannertowners view as privileged members of society, were more willing to join forces with them in challenging corporate power, of which the former had some sense, they might not feel so powerless as a collectivity and have to resort to individualistic coping mechanisms rooted in U.S. culture.

### Cancer and Industry

In contrast to Balshem's cultural interpretive account of Tannertowners' view on cancer etiology, David Michaels, who teaches in the Department of Epidemiology and Social Medicine at Montefiore Medical Center in the Bronx, conducted a provocative political economic analysis of corporate policies toward bladder cancer in the U.S. dye industry—one that appears in a special issue of *Medical Anthropology Quarterly* on "Health and Industry" that was guest edited by Ida Susser, a well-known critical medical anthropologist. Despite the fact that European scientists demonstrated in the early twentieth century that beta-naphthylamine and benzidine, two chemicals commonly utilized in dye production, are deadly bladder carcinogens, Michaels (1988) contends that the U.S. dye industry has systematically ignored and suppressed these and later findings concerning the link between these two chemicals and bladder cancer. His study focuses on four corporations: E. I. du Pont de Nemours and Company, Allied Chemical, Cincinnati Chemical Works, and the Upjohn Company. According to Michaels (1988:226–27),

There are striking parallels between the history of dye production and that of the industrial production of asbestos products . . . and tetraethyl lead. . . . Workers employed in the manufacture of these products were exposed to extremely toxic materials, while corporate managers and scientists ignored scientific evidence (much of it gathered by the industry itself) about the hazardous nature of the exposures. Furthermore, in each of these cases, corporate scientists played an important part in justifying management's production policies, and attempted to limit the epidemiologic information released to the scientific community and the public.

## THE POLITICAL ECOLOGY OF AIDS: ASSESSING A CONTEMPORARY SYNDEMIC

Acquired immune deficiency syndrome (AIDS) has emerged as one of the most devastating diseases in human history. Caused by a contagious virus known as the human immunodeficiency virus (HIV), the disease has spread rapidly to all human populations in all corners of the planet. The actual origins of HIV are not precisely known, but it appears to have evolved from similar viruses, called simian immunodeficiency viruses (SIVs), that infect monkey and ape species. Genetically, HIV is most similar to the SIV found among chimpanzees, our closest relative in the animal kingdom. Current thinking is that SIV underwent a mutation that allowed it to infect human hosts (a not-uncommon occurrence in nature) some time in the late nineteenth or early twentieth century. The political ecological context for this transition was the expansion of human settlements into previously forested areas in Africa, associated with the population explosion, deforestation, expanded agriculture, and more rapid transportation produced by colonialism and neocolonial economies. Expansion into previously unsettled areas in tropical zones—where the concentration of microscopic life is highest on the planet—appears to have been the source of a number of the emerging infections of recent decades. Whatever its point of origin, HIV found the human body, especially components of the blood system, a habitable environment; human sexual contact and pregnancy initially and other routes of transmission eventually (e.g., injection drug use and blood transfusion) all proved to be effective mechanisms for moving between hosts and led to its rapid spread within and across populations.

The global count of people living with HIV/AIDS infection reached forty million by the end of 2004; millions more had already succumbed to the disease. Although HIV/AIDS is now found everywhere, it is unequally distributed among the populations and subpopulations of the world. One way of understanding the unequal spread of this disease is by examining the number of people living with HIV/AIDS disease along a geographic continuum. At one end of the continuum is sub-Saharan Africa, which remains the region hardest hit by the disease, with approximately 25.5 million people now living with HIV/AIDS infection and an adult (ages fifteen to forty-nine) prevalence rate of 7.4 percent. Near the opposite end of the continuum falls North America, with about a million people living with HIV/AIDS and an adult prevalence rate of 0.6 percent, which is not significantly above that of Oceania, the region of the world with the lowest prevalence rate. Between these two epidemiological regions lie the island nations of the Caribbean, with less than half a million cases and a prevalence rate of 2.3 percent. After sub-Saharan Africa, the Caribbean is now the second most intensely impacted region of the world (UNAIDS 2004). To get some sense of the impact of HIV/ AIDS, in Caribbean countries such as Haiti and Trinidad it is believed that by 2010, life expectancy will be nine to ten years shorter than it would have been without the disease. In other words, while life expectancy is increasing in the United States and Europe despite the presence of HIV/AIDS, in many Third World countries the disease is significantly shortening how long people live on average. How can we understand the significant disparities found in HIV/ AIDS prevalence and impact among countries of the world?

A starting point in answering this question is to examine disparities in HIV/AIDS in the United States because of the great differences in the social conditions that exist for different populations in the country. Wealth is highly concentrated in the United States, with the wealthiest 2 or 3 percent of the population controlling 40 percent of the nation's wealth and the poorest 20 percent of the population controlling hardly any wealth at all. These disparities in wealth are matched, as discussed in chapter 6, by great disparities in health. Moreover, these inequalities of wealth and health reflect important contrasts across ethnic populations.

Based on frozen human tissue samples, the oldest confirmed case of HIV/ AIDS in the United States was a fifteen-year-old African American boy from St. Louis who was hospitalized in 1968 with an aggressive form of the skin cancer called Kaposi's sarcoma, which until that time had been considered a disease of the elderly. Twenty years later, this boy's stored blood sample tested positive for HIV antibodies, which is diagnostic for bodily exposure to HIV/ AIDS (Garry et al. 1988). Today, the AIDS case rate (for all ages) per 100,000 population in the United States is 6.1 among non-Hispanic whites compared to 58.2 among African Americans. HIV/AIDS is more prevalent—and significantly so—among African Americans than any other ethnic population in the country, a pattern that holds across age and gender subgroups. Among men, for example, the AIDS case rate is more than eight times greater among African Americans than non-Hispanic whites (Centers for Disease Control and Prevention 2003). Among women, the difference is even greater. In terms of the actual number of cases, almost twice as many African Americans have contracted HIV/AIDS than non-Hispanic whites. Importantly, while the number of deaths among whites living with HIV/AIDS fell steadily between 1999 and 2003, among African Americans a clear trend has not emerged, with the number of deaths due to AIDS going up and down from year to year. Overall, however, while African Americans make up about 12.3 percent of the total population of the United States, they accounted for more than 50 percent of the people who died of AIDS from 1999 through 2003. By the end of 2003, almost two hundred thousand African Americans had died of AIDS. In other words, while compared to some other parts of the world the HIV/AIDS prevalence is low in the United States, HIV-related sickness and death are heavily concentrated in the African American sector of the U.S. population. Moreover, in 2002, African Americans who died from HIV/AIDS had more than ten times as many age-adjusted years of potential life lost before age seventy-five than did whites who had died from HIV/AIDS. In short, there is a distinct parallel between disparities in the distribution of HIV/AIDS between the wealthier and poorer nations of the world and between the wealthier and poorer populations within the United States.

This parallel suggests that HIV/AIDS does not exist in isolation from other diseases or from the social and political economic environment that shapes a population's health, access to food and shelter, and availability of medical treatment. To help frame an understanding of these interrelationships, medical anthropologists introduced the concept of "syndemic" in the early 1990s (M. Singer and Clair 2003). While biomedical understanding and practice traditionally have been characterized by the tendency to isolate, study, and treat diseases as if they were distinct entities that existed separate from other diseases and independent of the social contexts in which they emerge, a syndemic model directs attention to social and biological interconnections in health as they are shaped and influenced by inequalities within society. At its simplest level, the term "syndemic" refers to two or more epidemics (i.e., notable increases in the rate of specific diseases in a population) interacting synergistically with each other inside human bodies and contributing, as a result of their interaction, to an excess burden of disease in a population beyond what would otherwise be expected. It refers not only to the temporal or locational co-occurrence of two or more diseases or health problems but also to the health consequences of the biological interactions among copresent diseases, such as between HIV and tuberculosis. HIV-positive individuals infected with tuberculosis (TB), for example, are 100 times more likely to develop active disease than those who are HIV negative with TB. Similarly, research has shown that individuals coinfected with hepatitis C (HCV) and HIV have higher HCV viral loads (i.e., levels of infectious agents in their bodies) than those infected with only HCV.

Beyond the notion of disease clustering in a social location or population and the biological processes of interaction among diseases, the term "syndemic" also points to the critical importance of social conditions in disease interactions and consequences. As Farmer (1999:51–52) has emphasized, "The most well demonstrated co-factors [for HIV] are social inequalities, which structure not only the contours of the AIDS pandemic but also the nature of outcomes once an individual is sick with complications of HIV infection." Living in poverty, for example, increases the likelihood of exposure to a range of diseases, including HIV. Given the impacts of (1) stress that is associated with poverty, unemployment, population density, and exposure to unsafe environments; (2) poor diet (especially early in life); and (3) heightened exposure to man-made toxics in local environments—which tend to be disproportionately common in lower-income areas where populations are more densely populated and opportunities to escape exposure to toxins are lower (e.g., high concentrations of lead in older homes and poor heating systems leading to sealed windows and poor ventilation)—diseases tend to concentrate among impoverished populations. The concentration of multiple diseases in one population increases the biological likelihood of disease interaction of various kinds (e.g., gene swapping or "assortment" among co-occurring pathogens or opportunistic infection by one pathogen because of damage done by another) as well as the adoption of behaviors to cope with and medicate the emotional injuries of oppression and relative deprivation, such as abusive drinking and illicit drug use, which damage the human immune system. Additionally, poverty and discrimination place the poor at a disadvantage in terms of access to diagnosis and treatment for HIV as well as ability to adhere to treatment plans because of structurally imposed residential instability and the frequency of disruptive economic and social crises in poor families.

Haiti, for example, is by far the most impoverished country in the New World, and it is not coincidental that it is the country in the Western Hemisphere that has been hardest hit by AIDS thus far. The cause is not anything biologically or behaviorally unique about Haitians but rather the consequence of being an especially impoverished nation and one used for sexual tourism by non-Haitian visitors at the point of takeoff of the HIV epidemic.

Racism is another critical social condition that appears to contribute to higher levels of HIV risk and infection. In Brazil, for example, while race-based oppression is denied officially and at the popular level, studies show that "the structures of racism are present in everyday experience" (Goldstein 2003:105). Consequently, writing of internalized racism in Brazil, Neusa Santos Souza (1983) notes that dark-skinned Brazilians commonly feel inferior and ugly because of all of the subtle reminders to which they are subjected each day that whiteness equals beauty. Internalized racism, no less than open color-based discrimination, is linked with heightened levels of HIV risk and infection (Baer et al. 2003). Ultimately, social factors, such as poverty, racism, sexism, and marginalization, may be of far greater importance in HIV morbidity and mortality between and within countries than the nature of the virus. Poor populations and populations of color encounter HIV/AIDS not as a single life-threatening disease but as part of a set of interacting diseases and toxic social and biological conditions with a resulting significant toll on their health and well-being.

## STRATEGIES AND VISIONS FOR A HEALTHIER WORLD

While global capitalism has resulted in impressive technological innovations, including ones in biomedicine, it is a system fraught with contradictions, including, as Barone (2004:142) asserts,

> economic instability, perpetual unemployment for millions, militarism and imperialism, profound inequality and poverty in the face of plenty, deadening work and oppressive work conditions, perpetuation of racism and sexism, irrational materialism, environmental destruction, lack of democratic control of economic destiny, constraints on political democracy, and barriers to attainment of community, solidarity, and cooperation.

Needless to say, these contradictions entail numerous consequences for people's health and access to health care.

Students and others reading this text may feel overwhelmed by the enormity of the issues that we have been discussing, as we ourselves often do. Conversely, as Pirages and colleagues (2000:183) observe,

> In many respects, the urgent environmental and health issues confronting humanity on the frontier of the twenty-first century are the same as those it has always faced: epidemic disease, resource limitations, poverty, affluence, and the unintended consequences of new technologies. It is principally the scale and complexities of the problem that have grown and changed across time.

## CAPITALISM

Terminology is often tricky. Which terms you use reflects your underlying theoretical or philosophical understanding of the world. Until relatively recently, the term "capitalism" tended to be used by progressive thinkers to refer to an economic system in which capital or productive resources (e.g., a factory, a farm, or a mine) were used to generate privately held profits. Indeed, Karl Marx's most important scholarly work is titled *Das Kapital* ("Capital"). Mainstream or more conservative scholars, by contrast, tended to prefer the term "market economy," which places attention on the distribution of commodities rather than on the social relationships that shape their production. In the wake of the collapse of the Soviet Union, however, an increasing number of conventional economists are now employing the term capitalism. Additionally, progressive scholars often also refer to the contemporary period in the evolution of capitalism as being shaped by neoliberalism, a philosophical perspective (which, to complicate matters, is neither new nor liberal) embraced by conservative economists, policymakers, and corporate officials who urge the minimization of government regulation of the "free market," including the free flow of goods and services across national boundaries. Notably, the free flow of workers across national boundaries, however, is not advocated by neoliberal thinkers, who tend to want strict immigration laws. Moreover, despite opposing government restrictions on markets or the ability to sell their products anywhere and everywhere, corporations strongly demand government support for their own needs, such as in the construction of the transcontinental railroad across North America in the nineteenth century or the development of the military-industrial complex during the twentieth. While complicated, it is important to understand this array of concepts and philosophies because they have such a large impact on health. When tobacco corporations push for the elimination of laws in various developing countries that, for example, restrict the open advertisement and promotion of tobacco products, their success can have a major impact on health. Tobacco-related diseases, after all, are expected to be the primary cause of death in the developing world by 2020.

The challenge before us is determining how we can collectively address these monumental problems and participate in a larger effort to create a just, environmentally sustainable, and healthy global community. The answers are not easy and require collaboration with many individuals and groups outside the relatively small world of anthropology. As active members of an even smaller endeavor within that discipline, medical anthropologists cannot create a healthy planet single-handedly but can do so only in "pragmatic solidarity" with a broad coalition of progressive people, ranging from health practitioners to academics in other disciplines (particularly sociology, political science, policy studies, and public health) and including the staffs of research institutes, government agencies, international health organizations, and nongovernmental organizations as well as people involved in peace, social justice, environmental, anti–corporate globalization, health rights, women's rights, and other social and labor movements around the world.

As proponents of the critical perspective in medical anthropology, we recognize that other theoretical perspectives, including the biocultural and cultural interpretive ones, have provided and continue to provide important insights that elucidate environmental and health issues. Conversely, we strongly believe that the creation of a healthy planet for both humanity and the ecosystem will, over the long run, require the transcendence of the present global economy and a movement toward a more equitable, just, and ecologically sustainable global order. Such movement, however, is dependent on a vision for an alternative to the present global system.

Global capitalism has been around for some five hundred years, but it has so many inherent contradictions that ultimately it must be transcended. Sociologist John Bellamy Foster (2004:10) argues that lifestyle changes, such as biking, walking, or riding public transport rather than driving cars, are not enough to protect environment:

> We need to organize politically to create the social structures—public transport, intercity train systems, flexible work routines, new forms of urban planning and land development, and so on—which will enable a greater number of people actually to make those choices. . . . People will need to address the broader structures of power in some way before they can get more meaningful environmental choices.

We need to start thinking about an alternative world system, one committed to meeting people's basic needs, social equity and justice, democracy, and environmental sustainability. In the nineteenth century, various revolutionaries and reformers sought to develop alternatives to an increasingly globalizing capitalist world order. Efforts at the national level to create such an alternative started out with the Bolshevik Revolution in Russia in 1917 and included subsequent revolutions in other countries, including China in 1949, Vietnam in 1954, Cuba in 1959, and Nicaragua in 1979. Scholars have spilled much ink trying to determine whether these societies constituted examples of "actually existing socialism," transitions between capitalism and socialism, state capitalism, or new class societies and why many of these societies ultimately became fully incorporated into the capitalist world system, beginning with the collapse of the Soviet Union in 1991. Space does not permit a detailed review of why these experiments to provide an alternative to the present global economy fell short of the mark and in many cases ultimately failed. Suffice it to say that their failure to achieve an authentically democratic socialist world system was ultimately related to both internal forces specific to each of these societies and external forces that created a hostile environment for equitable development.

Global capitalism is a well-entrenched system with support from many sides. But there are voices bucking this massive global system from many quarters, including the anti–corporate globalization movement, the most progressive segments of the labor and environmental movements, peace movements, and indigenous and ethnic rights movements, as well as socialists, anarchists, and even left-leaning liberals and social democrats. Indeed, over the course of the past decade or so, a distinct climate movement has emerged in many developed and developing countries, one that has built upon warning about the dangers of global warming emanating over the past two or three decades from climate scientists, environmental groups, and indigenous groups, particularly in the Arctic and the South Pacific. Much of the climate movement in developed countries, including the United States and Australia, has tended to stress climate change mitigation strategies that come under the rubric of *ecological modernization*, that is, an emphasis on renewable sources of energy (i.e., solar, wind, geothermal, and wave), energy efficiency, electric cars, and mass transportation, but has tended to deemphasize social justice issues. In contrast, the climate movement emanating from developing countries has given much more attention to issues of social parity, such as the fact that the developed countries have historically contributed and continue to contribute much more on a per capita basis to greenhouse gas emissions than have or do the developing countries, even China, which has become the leading emitter in the world, even superseding the United States. The Klimaforum at the UN Copenhagen Conference in December 2009 and the World People's Summit on Climate Change and the Rights to Mother

Earth in Cochabamba, Bolivia, in March 2010, posited global capitalism as an economic system of production and consumption that seeks profits without limits and separates humans from nature. The latter assemblage, in particular, called for the development of an alternative world committed to social justice or parity and environmental sustainability.

Numerous proposals for achieving an alternative world system have been proposed and go by labels such as *radical democracy, earth democracy, economic democracy,* and *democratic ecosocialism* (Baer et al. 2003:356–59). It is our sense that the creation of what Boswell and Chase-Dunn (2000) term "global democracy" would entail the following components: (1) an increasing movement toward public ownership of productive forces at local, regional, national, and international levels; (2) the development of an economy oriented toward meeting social needs and environmental sustainability rather than profit-making; (3) a blending of both representative and participatory democratic processes; (4) the eradication of social disparities and redistribution of human resources between developed and developing societies and within societies in general; (5) the curtailment of population growth that in larger part would follow from the previously mentioned condition; (6) the conservation of finite resources and the development of renewable energy resources, such as wind and solar energy, that counteract the present trend toward global warming; and (7) the reduction of wastes through recycling and transcending the culture of consumption.

Many have argued that socialism has been tried in places like the Soviet Union and China, and even Cuba for that matter, and has proven wanting. While of these three societies Cuba comes the closest to embodying socialist ideals and practices, socialism, let alone global democracy or democratic ecosocialism, remains a vision rather than an existing social system per se. Nevertheless, developments in Latin America, particularly Venezuela, Bolivia, and certainly Cuba, raise the hope of creating a "socialism for the 21st century" (Katz 2007). As John Bellamy Foster (2009:276) so aptly argues,

> It is important to recognize that there is now an ecology as well as a political economy of revolutionary change. The emergence in our time of sustainable human development, in various revolutionary interstices within the global periphery, could mark the beginning of a universal revolt against both world alienation and human self-estrangement. Such a revolt, if consistent, could have only one objective: the creation of a society of associated producers rationally regulating their metabolic relation to nature, and doing so not only in accordance with their own needs but also those of future generations and life as a

whole. Today, the transition to socialism and the transition to an ecological society are one.

Although at the present time or in the near foreseeable future the notion that democratic ecosocialism may be implemented in any developed society may seem utterly ridiculous and utopian, history tells that social changes can occur very quickly once economic, political, and social structural changes have reached a tipping point.

The vision of global democracy provides people everywhere with an alternative to the existing capitalist world system that continues to self-destruct due to its socially unjust and environmental unsustainable commitments and practices. Ultimately, a shift to global democracy in any one country would have to be part of a global process or a "permanent revolution" that no one can fully envision. The history of the Soviet Union and Stalinism tells us that socialism cannot be created in "one country." The struggle for a safe climate needs to be part and parcel of a larger struggle for social justice and environmental sustainability, both internationally and within specific nation-states, including the United States and Australia. As Magdoff and Foster (2010:25) so aptly argue,

> Everywhere radical, essentially anti-capitalist, strategies are emerging, based on other ethics and forms of organization, rather than the profit motive: eco-villages; the new urban environment promoted in Curitiba in Brazil and elsewhere; experiments in permaculture, and community-supported agriculture, farming and industrial cooperatives in Venezuela, etc.

While Cuba remains a poor developing country, it has achieved health statistics in terms of infant mortality and life expectancy at birth that rival those of developed societies, and it has the lowest HIV prevalence in the Americas and one of the lowest in the world. Furthermore, Cuba has been exporting biomedical physicians and nurses to other developing countries, such as Venezuela, Timor-Leste, and Pakistan in the aftermath of its tragic earthquake several years ago.

Proposals such as global democracy and democratic ecosocialism constitute longer-term steps in the creation of a better world for both humanity and the health of its inhabitants and the planet. In the meantime, many medical anthropologists, working on different issues in varied places and with differing perspectives, are actively engaged in seeking to use their knowledge, skills, and resources to address pressing health and health-related social and environmental problems. As an applied field, medical anthropology, as we have seen, is action oriented, and, in light of the significant problems facing human populations, research-informed action is critically needed in the struggles for health and a healthier world. We believe that anthropologists and medical anthropologists, as a process of creating a healthier world, need to become politically engaged and work in solidarity with progressive movements that in various often cumbersome and even contradictory ways are seeking to create an alternative to the existing global political economy. In terms of global warming, anthropologists can work in solidarity with indigenous organizations such as the International Forum of Indigenous Peoples and Local Communities on Climate Change, the Inuit Circumpolar Conference, and the Alliance of Small Island States that have been challenging the limited actions of developed countries in responding to a monumental environmental problem that threatens human settlement patterns, subsistence, lifeways, and health.

# Glossary

**Adaptation**—practice that human societies are implementing to adjust to climate change, such as increasing surface temperatures, rising sea levels, storm surges, droughts, heavy rains, and floods

**Allopathic medicine**—medical system that evolved into biomedicine; term commonly used today to differentiate biomedicine from homeopathic and osteopathic medicine

**Anthropogenic**—usually refers to changes in the environment, including the climate, that are a product of human activity

**Ayurvedic medicine**—global system of traditional medicine that originated in India as far back as three to four thousand years ago, based on healthful living throughout the life cycle and maintaining and reestablishing balance among five elements of life: earth, water, fire, air, and ether

**Bioculturalism**—interaction of biological and cultural factors in the creation of health status

**Bioethics**—ethical issues in medical practice

**Biomedicine**—globally dominant medical system often called Western, allopathic, or cosmopolitan medicine

**Biopathy**—emergent perspective on health care that seeks to restore the body to a fundamental harmonious state, including restoration of the body's natural immune and cell repair systems, and that emphasizes avoiding unnatural products (including biomedicines, processed foods)

**Biosocial**—interaction of biological, social structural, and social relationship factors in the creation of health status

**Biotechnology**—broad range of technological devices and procedures, such as reproductive technologies, organ transplants, mechanical ventilators, magnetic resonance imaging devices, X-ray machines, prosthetic limbs, and even Band-Aids and cotton balls

**Blaming the victim**—blaming the behavior of socially subordinated person or groups for their adverse health and social status

**Body theory**—explanatory approach that focuses on the role of the body in societal processes and the role of society in bodily attitudes, experiences, and practices

**Capitalism**—political economic system based on private property ownership of the means of production, profit-making, and continual economic expansion

**Chinese medicine**—ancient medical system based on concepts of energy flow that has diffused to many regions of the world

**Chiropractic**—form of manual medicine developed in the 1890s in Iowa by D. D. Palmer, a magnetic healer

**Climate change**—change in the climate over either a short or long time period that may be related to natural events or human-created (i.e., anthropogenic) activities or even both

**Commodified bodies**—body organs and fluids that are transformed into entities that can be bought and sold, such that they come to be thought of as commodities with a commercial value

**Complementary and alternative medicine**—healing systems other than biomedicine; this expression locates biomedicine as the core of medicine and views other healing systems as potentially complementary to this dominant system

**Consensus analysis**—quantitative research procedure that is used to determine the modal (i.e., most frequent) answers provided by a group to a set of questions about a particular topic (e.g., "what is disease?")

**Contextual approach**—seeing attitudes and behaviors within the influencing natural and social settings in which they emerge and function

**Critical medical anthropology**—theoretical perspective in medical anthropology that emphasizes the importance of the interface between the political economic/ecological system and local cultural patterns in shaping health

**Cultural broker**—role sometimes played by medical anthropologists as intercessors between local and dominant social and/or medical systems

**Cultural competence**—ability of health care providers to understand and work successfully with the cultural traditions of their patients

**Cultural emotions**—culturally shaped feelings that help shape behavior within a society

**Cultural epidemiology**—integration of the anthropological concept of culture into the study of disease outbreaks and epidemics

**Culture of medicine**—shared set of beliefs and practices acquired by medical students and residents that shape day-to-day behavior and understandings among physicians

**Cyborg**—human being who functions with an artificial part or device or even an organ transplant from another person

**Dengue**—mosquito-borne viral disease, known as the "bone crusher"

**Disease**—diagnosis of a sickness made by a biomedical physician or some type of professionalized heterodox medical practitioner

**Dominative medical system**—system under which biomedicine politically, economically, and culturally dominates other medical subsystems, both professionalized and folk

**Ecological modernization**—shift to technological innovations, such as increasing energy efficiency, renewable sources of energy, and public transport, which are being proposed as strategies to create a more sustainable environment and mitigate climate change

**Ecosocialism**—proposed alternative to global capitalism, based upon a commitment to social parity and environmental sustainability that some theorists view as an important form of climate change mitigation

**Ecosyndemic**—syndemic disease interactions caused by human restructuring of the environment (e.g., anthropogenic climate change enables vector-borne diseases to spread to new areas and interact with other diseases found in the new locations)

**Emic**—seeking to learn the insider's perspective (e.g., how folk healers view their role in society)

**Epidemiology**—study of population health patterns and the emergence and spread of disease within and across populations

**Ethnocultural communities**—historic ethnic cultural traditions of subgroups within a larger society, synonymous with "subcultures"

**Ethnomedicine**—culturally constituted medical systems, including biomedicine

**Ethnosemantics**—organized cultural categories in the minds of members of a society that are used to experience and understand the world (e.g., among college students, key cultural categories include exams, courses, professors, assignments, required reading, grades)

**Ethnosemantic elicitation**—type of interview in which the researcher seeks to learn the cognitive categories study participants use to organize their experience and understanding of the world

**Explanatory model**—group's understanding of the nature, causes, and symptoms of a disease

**Folk healing systems**—indigenous and local health care systems; also called complementary and alternative health care systems

**Folk injectors**—folk healers who use syringe injection of medicines that contain pharmaceutical and folk medicine mixtures

**Free listing**—research method in which researchers ask study participants to name all of the kinds of items that exist within a cultural domain (e.g., all of the causes of disease)

**Global warming**—important manifestation of climate change in which the Earth or portions of the Earth experiences increases in temperature due to various greenhouse gases, particularly carbon dioxide, methane, and nitrous oxide

**Health disparities**—differences in health and disease patterns and health care access across populations or segments of populations

**Health inequalities**—differences in health and disease patterns and health care access across populations or segments of populations that are the consequence of social inequalities

**Health transition**—improvements in life expectancy and changes in the relative importance of various causes of mortality that have occurred worldwide since the end of World War II

**Holistic**—core anthropological concept that refers to viewing specific components of the human condition (e.g., health behavior, religious behavior) within a broader social, environmental, and cultural context

**Homeopathy**—form of alternative professionalized medicine in which practitioners administer diluted forms of substance believed to be the cause of adverse symptoms following the principle that "like is cured by like" not, as in biomedicine, by opposites (e.g., antibiotics).

**Hospital ethnography**—relatively new type of ethnographic research in which medical anthropologists conduct observations in various clinics and other care units in a hospital

**Humoral medical system**—set of beliefs and healing practices based on the premise that the organs, body systems, and fluids inside the body parallel elements and structures of the natural world outside the body and that balance must be maintained across elements to remain healthy

**Illness**—label for the patient's experience of sickness

**Illness behavior**—cultural patterning of behavior among the sick

**Illness narratives**—personal, storylike accounts of illness experience

**Integrative medicine**—medicine that theoretically blends together the best elements of biomedicine and complementary and alternative medical systems

**Life course**—stages of life that find expression in differing health issues and configurations

**Life history interview**—method used to illicit detailed narratives of participants' life stories

**Meaning-centered medical anthropology**—theoretical perspective that prioritizes symbolism and meaning in the interpretation of health-related behavior

**Medical anthropology**—study of human health and disease, health-related behavior, and healing and health care from the perspective of anthropology

**Medical ecology**—theoretical perspective in medical anthropology that emphasizes the interface between populations and their environments in the shaping of health

**Medical hybridization**—blending together of elements of various medical subsystems or the borrowing of elements on the part of one medical system from other medical subsystems

**Medical pluralism**—conflation of medical subsystems in complex or state societies that entails competition and even collaboration among the subsystems

**Medical-industrial complex**—profit-making or pecuniary relationship between biomedicine and various businesses, including health insurance, health care, and pharmaceutical companies

**Meme**—small cultural unit (e.g., bit of knowledge and emotion) transmitted through social learning across generations within a society

**Mindful bodies**—conception of the body developed within medical anthropology that sees the body as a nexus of individual experience, social relationship, and a set of representations of the body as a natural symbol with which to think about nature, society, and culture

**Mitigation**—wide set of practices that are being proposed to reduce the impacts of climate change or global warming

**Multi- or mixed-method research**—integration of a suite of methods, qualitative and quantitative, in a research initiative

**Naturopathy**—highly eclectic medical subsystem that relies on a wide array of therapeutic modalities, including herbalism, homeopathy, reflexology, nutritious eating, and exercise

**Neoliberal reforms**—within the health arena, changes in national health care policies that are favored by big development lending institutions that stress privatization of disease treatment and the use of market mechanisms to set the price of health care

**Nurse-anthropologist**—nurse who holds either an MA or PhD in anthropology

**Osteopathy**—manual medical system developed in the mid-1800s in Kansas by Andrew Taylor Still, a disenchanted American regular physician

**Paleopathology**—study of diseases in the past, especially during prehistoric times

**Panopticon**—term introduced by Michel Foucault that refers to an ever-growing ability to observe, internally and externally, and control individuals in society at all times and places

**Physician-anthropologist**—biomedical physician who holds either an MA or PhD in anthropology

**Pile sort**—research method in which study participants are asked to sort into like piles (as seen by participants) a set of behaviors, ideas, objects, and so forth that have been inscribed on a set of cards (e.g., sort disease symptoms into like piles)

**Psychogenesis**—in psychology, the development of a physical disorder resulting from psychological, rather than physiological, sources

**Q-sorts**—research method in which participants are asked to rank (on some criteria) a set of behaviors, ideas, objects, and so forth that have been inscribed on a set of cards

**Racism**—discrimination in health care (or elsewhere) based on an individual's presumed membership in a biologically defined racial category. Because gene distributions are no more uniform within "identified races" than across culturally imposed racial boundaries, anthropologists discount the existence of distinct races among humans

**Scatter plot**—analytic strategy in which a computer program represents the overall picture or pattern in a set of sorted cards, based on an assessment of which cards people tended to put in the same pile or keep apart in different piles

**Self-limiting diseases**–short-term diseases that the body overcomes without treatment

**Semistructured interview**—flexible interview format in which new questions are inserted by the researcher in response to participant responses to previous questions

**Shaman**—part-time religious healer who makes contact with the supernatural realm so as to determine the cause of illness or petition the spirits to release patients from their distress

**Social stigmatization**—situation involving the creation of what are called socially "discredited selves" in which disease sufferers are blamed for their illness and discriminated against for being a sufferer

**Social suffering**—immediate personal and shared experience of group members of broader human problems caused by the unjust exercise of political and economic power

**Syndemic**—adverse interactions between two or more diseases or other health-related conditions (e.g., stress, malnutrition), often promoted by social inequality and subordination, that increase the total disease burden of a population

**Typology**—categorization of items in a cultural domain into two or more tiers of inclusivity based on the degree of relationship of items (e.g., in U.S. society the cultural domain of "pets" consists of dogs, cats, fish, and the like; the subcategory of dogs consist of Labradors, terriers, poodles, and so on; the subcategory of poodles includes standards and miniatures, and so forth)

**Wounded healers**—shamans and other healers, including modern-day psychologists, who initially underwent treatment for some type of illness

**Writing up**—final act of research by the anthropologist that involves the preparation of a report, article, chapter, or book to present a research project and its findings

# References

Ablon, Joan
    1984    *Little People in America.* New York: Praeger.
    1992    Social Dimensions of Genetic Disorders. *Practicing Anthropology* 14(1):10–13.

Adelson, Naomi
    2003    Cree. In *The Encyclopedia of Medical Anthropology.* Volume 2, *Cultures,* ed. Carol R. Ember and Melvin Ember, 614–22. New York: Kluwer Academic/Plenum.

Adler, Nancy, and Judith Stewart
    2010    Health Disparities across the Lifespan: Meaning, Methods, and Mechanisms. *Annals of the New York Academy of Sciences* 1186:5–23.

Agar, Michael
    2006    *Dope Double Agent: The Naked Emperor on Drugs.* Morrisville, NC: Lulu Books.

Ainlay, Stephen
    1989    *Day Brought Back My Night: Aging and New Vision Loss.* London: Routledge.

Alison, Ian, et al.
    2009    *The Copenhagen Diagnosis: Updating the World on the Latest Climate Science.* Climate Change Research Centre, University of New South Wales, Sydney, Australia.

Alter, Joseph S.
  2005    Ayurvedic Acupuncture–Transnational Nationalism: Ambiva-
          lence about the Origin and Authenticity of Medical Knowledge.
          In *Asian Medicine and Globalization*, ed. Joseph S. Alter, 21–44.
          Philadelphia: University of Pennsylvania Press.
American Anthropological Association
  1947    Statement on Human Rights. *American Anthropologist* 49(4):593–643.
  1998    Statement on "Race." www.aaanet.org/stmts/racepp.htm. Ac-
          cessed August 3, 2011.
  1999    Declaration on Anthropology and Human Rights. www.aaanet.
          org/stmts/humanrts.htm. Accessed August 3, 2011.
American Medical Student Association
  2006    Health Disparities Globally. www.amsa.org/AMSA/homepage/about/
          committees/REACH/healthquality.aspx. Accessed April 27, 2006.
American Psychiatric Association
  2000    *Diagnostic and Statistical Manual of Mental Disorders.* Text revi-
          sion. Washington, DC: American Psychiatric Publishing,
Amour, Stephanie
  2006    Illegal Trade in Bodies Horrifies Loved Ones. http://articles.news.
          aol.com/business/article.adp?id=20060427072709990037&cid=
          403?ncid=NWS00010000000001. Accessed April 14, 2006.
Arachne, Jim
  1997    Alternative Medicines Summit: A Consumer's View. *Diversity*
          [Australian Complementary Health Association] 1(10):13–14.
Arcury, Tomas, Sara Quant, Pamela Rao, Alicia Doran, Beverly Snively, Dana
        Barr, Jane Hoppin, and Stephin Davis
  2005    Organophosphate Pesticide Exposure in Farmworker Family
          Members in Western North Carolina and Virginia: Case Com-
          parisons. *Human Organization* 64(1):40–51.
Ascencio, Marysol
  2002    *Sex and Sexuality among New York's Puerto Rican Youth.* Boulder,
          CO: Lynne Rienner.
Australian Bureau of Statistics
  1999    *Chiropractic and Osteopathic Services, Australia, 1997–1998.* Can-
          berra: Australian Medical Association.
Australian Medical Association
  1992    *Chiropractic in Australia.* Pamphlet.

Baer, Hans
    2001    *Biomedicine and Alternative Healing Systems in America: Issues of Class, Race, Ethnicity, and Gender.* Madison: University of Wisconsin Press.
    2004    *Toward an Integrative Medicine: Merging Alternative Therapies with Biomedicine.* Walnut Creek, CA: AltaMira Press.

Baer, Hans, and Merrill Singer
    2009    *Global Warming and the Political Ecology of Health: Emerging Crises and Systemic Solutions.* Walnut Creek, CA: Left Coast Press.

Baer, Hans, Merrill Singer, and Ida Susser
    2003    *Medical Anthropology and the World System.* 2nd ed. Westport, CT: Greenwood Press.
    2009    *Complementary Medicine in Australia and New Zealand: Its Popularisation, Legitimation, and Dilemmas.* Maleny, QLD, New Zealand: Verdant House.

Balshem, Martha
    1993    *Cancer in the Community: Class and Medical Authority.* Washington, DC: Smithsonian Institution Press.

Barone, Charles A.
    2004    *Radical Political Economy: A Concise Introduction.* Armonk, NY: M. E. Sharpe.

Barrett, Ron
    2010    Avian Influenza and the Third Epidemiological Transition. In *Plagues and Epidemics: Infected Spaces Past and Present,* ed. D. Ann Herring and Alan Swedlund, 81–93. Oxford: Berg.

Bazerman, M., and D. Chugh
    2006    Decisions without Blinders. *Harvard Business Review* 84(1): 88–97.

Becker, Anne E.
    1994    Nurturing and Negligence: Working on Others' Bodies in Fiji. In *Embodiment and Experience,* ed. Thomas J. Csordas, 100–15. Cambridge: Cambridge University Press.

Becker, Gay
    1980    *Growing Old in Silence.* Berkeley: University of California Press.
    1994    Metaphors in Disrupted Lives: Infertility and Cultural Constructions of Continuity. *Medical Anthropology Quarterly* 8(2): 383–410.

2004     Phenomenology of Health and Illness. In *The Encyclopedia of Medical Anthropology*. Volume 1, *Topics*, ed. Carol R. Ember and Melvin Ember, 125–36. New York: Kluwer Academic/Plenum.

Bensoussan, Alan, and Stephen Myers
1996     *Toward a Safer Choice: The Practice of Traditional Chinese Medicine in Australia*. Department of Human Services, Victoria.

Bensoussan, A., S. Myers, S. Wu, and K. O'Connor
2004     Naturopathic and Western Herbal Medicine Practice in Australia: A Workplace Survey. *Complementary Therapies in Medicine* 12:17–27.

Berger, John L.
2000     *Beating the Heat: Why and How We Must Meet Global Warming*. Berkeley, CA: Berkeley Hills Books.

Betancourt, Joseph
2006     *Improving Quality and Achieving Equity: The Role of Cultural Competence in Reducing Racial and Ethnic Disparities in Health Care*. New York: Commonwealth Foundation.

Biehl, João
2007     *Will to Live: AIDS Therapies and the Politics of Survival*. Princeton, NJ: Princeton University Press.

Biehl, João, and Amy Moran-Thomas
2009     Symptom: Subjectivities, Social Ills, Technologies. *Annual Review of Anthropology* 38:267–88.

Binswanger, Hans
2000     Scaling-Up HIV/AIDS Programs to National Coverage. *Science* 288:2173–76.

Blaxter, Mildred
2004     *Health*. Cambridge: Polity Press.

Bloom, Frederick
2001     "New Beginnings": A Case Study in Gay Men's Changing Perceptions of Quality of Life during the Course of HIV Infection. *Medical Anthropology Quarterly* 15(1):38–57.

Bluebond-Langner, Myra
1996     *In the Shadow of Illness: Parents and Siblings of the Chronically Ill Child*. Princeton, NJ: Princeton University Press.

Bode, Maarten
2006     Taking Traditional Knowledge to the Market: The Commodification of Indian Medicine. *Anthropology and Medicine* 13:225–36.

Bodenheimer, T.
1985 The Transnational Pharmaceutical Industry and the Health of the World's People. In *Issues in the Political Economy of Health Care*, ed. J. McKinlay, 187–216. New York: Tavistock.

Bodley, John
2001 *Anthropology and Contemporary Human Problems.* 4th ed. Mountain View, CA: Mayfield.

Bolton, Ralph, and Gail Orozco
1994 *The AIDS Bibliography: Studies in Anthropology and Related Fields.* Arlington, VA: American Anthropological Association.

Boswell, Terry, and Christopher Chase-Dunn
2000 *The Spiral of Capitalism and Socialism.* Boulder, CO: Lynne Rienner.

Brentlinger, Paula, and Miguel Hernán
2007 Armed Conflict and Poverty in Central America: The Convergence of Epidemiology and Human Rights Advocacy. *Epidemiology* 18(6):673–77.

Brier, Bob
1998 *The Murder of Tutankhamen: A True Story.* New York: G. P. Putnam's Sons.

Briggs, Charles
2005 Communicability, Racial Discourse, and Disease. *Annual Review of Anthropology* 34:269–91.

Brodwin, Paul
1996 *Medicine and Morality in Haiti: The Contest for Healing Power.* Cambridge: Cambridge University Press.

Brown, Peter, ed.
1998 *Understanding and Applying Medical Anthropology.* Mountain View, CA: Mayfield.

Brown, Peter J., Marcia C. Inhorn, and Daniel J. Smith
1996 Disease, Ecology, and Human Behavior. In *Medical Anthropology: Contemporary Theory and Method*, rev. ed., ed. Carolyn F. Sargent and Thomas M. Johnson, 183–218. Westport, CT: Praeger.

Browner, Carole
2001 Situating Women's Reproductive Activities. *American Anthropologist* 102(4):773–78.

Budrys, Grace
2003 *Unequal Health: How Inequality Contributes to Health and Illness.* Lanham, MD: Rowman and Littlefield.

Buikstra, Jane, and D. C. Cook
   1980    Paleopathology: An American Account. *Annual Review of Anthropology* 9:433–70.
Bulled, Nicola, and Merrill Singer.
   2010    Syringe-Mediated Syndemics. *AIDS and Behavior* 13(6).
Cain, Carol
   1991    Personal Stories: Identity Acquisition and Self-Understanding in Alcoholics Anonymous. *Ethos* 19:210–53.
Campbell, Stephen A., John L. Dillon, and Barbara I. Polus
   1982    Chiropractic in Australia: Its Development and Legitimation. *Journal of the Australian Chiropractors' Association* 12(4):21–30.
Canny, Priscilla, Douglas Hall, and Shelley Geballe
   2002    *Child and Family Poverty in Connecticut: 1990 and 2000.* New Haven, CT: Connecticut Voices for Children.
Carey, James
   1990    Social System Effects on Local Level Morbidity and Adaptation in the Rural Peruvian Andes. *Medical Anthropology Quarterly* 4(3):266–95.
Cassell, Joan
   1998    *The Woman in the Surgeon's Body.* Cambridge: Harvard University Press.
Caudill, William
   1953    Applied Anthropology in Medicine. In *Anthropology Today: An Encyclopedic Inventory,* ed. Alfred Kroeber, 771–806. Chicago: University of Chicago Press.
Centers for Disease Control and Prevention
   2003    *Cases of HIV Infection and AIDS in the United States.* Atlanta: Centers for Disease Control and Prevention.
Chavez, Leo, Allan Hubbell, and Shiraz Mishra
   1999    Ethnography and Breast Cancer Control among Latina and Anglo Women in Southern California. In *Anthropology and Public Health,* ed. Robert Hahn, 142–64. New York: Oxford University Press.
Chernomas, Robert, and Ian Hudson
   2010    Inequality as a Cause of Social Murder. *International Journal of Health Services* 40(1):61–78.
Choi, W., Christine Daley, A. James, J. Thomas, R. Schupbach, M. Segraves, R. Barnoskie, and J. Ahluwalia

2006     Beliefs and Attitudes Regarding Smoking Cessation among Amer-
         ican Indians: A Pilot Study. *Ethnicity and Disease* 16:35–40.
Chopp, Rebecca
1986     *The Praxis of Suffering.* Maryknoll, NY: Orbis Books.
Chrisman, Noel J., and Arthur Kleinman
1983     Popular Health Care, Social Networks, and Cultural Mean-
         ings: The Orientation of Medical Anthropology. In *Handbook of
         Health, Health Care, and the Health Professions,* ed. David Me-
         chanic, 569–91. New York: Free Press.
Christakis, Nicholas, Norma Ware, and Arthur Kleinman
1994     Illness Behavior and the Health Transition in the Developing
         World. In *Health and Social Change in International Perspective,*
         ed. Lincoln Chen, Arthur Kleinman, and Norma Ware, 276–302.
         Boston: Harvard School of Public Health.
Clair, Scott, Merrill Singer, Elsa Huertas, and Margaret Weeks
2003     Unintended Consequences of Using an Oral HIV Test on HIV
         Knowledge. *AIDS Care* 15(4):575–80.
Clouser, K. Danner, Charles M. Culver, and Bernard Gert
2004     Malady: A New Treatment of Disease. In *Health, Disease, and Ill-
         ness: Concepts in Medicine,* ed. Arthur L. Caplan, James J. McCart-
         ney, and Dominic A. Sisti, 90–103. Washington, DC: Georgetown
         University Press.
Cohen, Mark
1989     *Health and the Rise of Civilization.* New Haven, CT: Yale Univer-
         sity Press.
Colfax, Grant, Gordon Mansergh, Robert Guzman, Eric Vittinghoff, Gary
Marks, Melissa Rader, and Susan Buchbinder
2001     Drug Use and Sexual Risk Behavior among Gay and Bisexual Men
         Who Attend Circuit Parties: A Venue-Based Comparison. *Journal
         of Acquired Immune Deficiency Syndromes* 28:373–79.
Connor, Linda H.
2004     Relief, Risk, and Renewal: Mixed Therapy Regimens in an Austra-
         lian Suburb. *Social Science and Medicine* 59:1695–705.
Conrad, Peter, and Joseph Schneider
1980     *Deviance and Medicalization: From Badness to Sickness.* St. Louis,
         MO: Mosby.

Corporate Crime Reporter
   2005    Eli Lilly Pleads Guilty to Illegally Promoting Evista, to Pay $36
          Million. *Corporate Crime Reporter* 1(1), December 21.
Crabtree, Sara, Christina Wong, and Faizah Mas'ud
   2001    Community Participatory Approaches to Dengue Prevention in
          Sarawak, Malaysia. *Human Organization* 60(3):281–87.
Crandon-Malamud, Libbet
   1991    *From the Fat of Our Souls: Social Change, Political Process, and
          Medical Pluralism in Bolivia.* Berkeley: University of California
          Press.
Crate, Susan A. and Mark Nuttall, eds.
   2009    *Anthropology and Climate Change: From Encounters to Action.*
          Walnut Creek, CA: Left Coast Press.
Crosby, Alfred
   1986    *Biological Imperialism: The Biological Expansion of Europe, 900–
          1900.* Cambridge: Cambridge University Press.
Davis-Floyd, Robbie
   1992    *Birth as an American Rite of Passage.* Berkeley: University of Cali-
          fornia Press.
Davis-Floyd, Robbie, Sheila Cosminsky, and Stacey Pigg, eds.
   2001    Daughters of Time: The Shifting Identities of Contemporary Mid-
          wives. Special Issue. *Medical Anthropology* 20(2–3/4).
Desjarlais, Robert R.
   1992    *Body and Emotion: The Aesthetics of Illness and Healing in the Ne-
          pal Himalayas.* Philadelphia: University of Pennsylvania Press.
Dey, A., J. Schiller, and D. Tai
   2004    Summary Health Statistics for U.S. Children: National Health
          Interview Survey, 2002. *Vital Health Statistics* 10:1–78.
di Leonardo, Micaela
   1998    *Exotics at Home: Anthropologists, Others, and American Modernity.*
          Chicago: University of Chicago Press.
Diamond, Jared
   2005    *Collapse: How Societies Choose to Fail or Succeed.* London: Penguin.
Doty, Michelle
   2003    *Insurance, Access, and Quality of Care among Hispanic Populations:
          2003 Chartpack.* Boston: Commonwealth Fund.
Douglas, Mary
   1973    *Purity and Danger: An Analysis of the Concepts of Pollution and
          Taboo.* London: Routledge and Kegan Paul.

Dow, James
    2001    Central and North Mexican Shamanism. In *Mesoamerican Healers*, ed. Brad R. Huber and Alan R. Sandstrom, 66–94. Austin: University of Texas Press.

Easthope, G., B. Tranter, and G. Gill
    2000    General Practitioners' Attitudes toward Complementary Therapies. *Social Science and Medicine* 51:1555–61.

Eddy, David
    1990    The Challenge. *Journal of the American Medical Association* 263:287–90.

Eliade, Mircea
    1964    *Shamanism: Archaic Techniques of Ecstasy.* New York: Pantheon Books.

Elperin, Juliet
    2005    Scientists Link Global Warming, Disease. *Hartford Courant*, November 17, 2.

Epstein, Samuel
    1978    *The Politics of Cancer.* San Francisco: Sierra Club Books.
    1979    *Politics of Cancer.* Rev. and exp. ed. Garden City, NY: Anchor Books.
    2005    *Cancer-Gate: How to Win the Losing Cancer War.* Amityville, NY: Baywood.

Erickson, Pamela
    1998    *Latina Adolescent Childbearing in East Los Angeles.* Austin: University of Texas Press.
    2003    Medical Anthropology and Global Health. *Medical Anthropology Quarterly* 17(1):3–4.
    2008    *Ethnomedicine.* Long Grove, IL: Waveland Press.

Erwin, Deborah
    2008    The Witness Project: Narratives That Shape the Cancer Experience for African-American Women. In *Confronting Cancer: Metaphors, Advocacy, and Anthropology*, ed. Juliet McMullin and Diane Weiner, 63–82. Santa Fe, NM: School of Advanced Research.

Etkin, Nina
    1988    Cultural Constructions of Efficacy. In *The Context of Medicines in Developing Countries*, ed. S. Van der Geest and W. Reynolds, 299–327. London: Kluwer Academic.
    1996    Ethnopharmacology: The Conjunction of Medical Ethnography and the Biology of Therapeutic Action. In *Medical Anthropology:*

*Contemporary Theory and Method*, rev. ed., ed. Carolyn F. Sargent and Thomas M. Johnson, 151–64. Westport, CT: Praeger.

Evans, Sue
    2000    The Story of Naturopathic Education in Australia. *Complementary Therapies in Australia* 8:234–40.

Everett, Margaret
    2006    Doing Bioethics: Challenges for Anthropology. *Human Organization* 65(1):46–54.

Fabrega, Horacio, Jr.
    1997    *Evolution of Healing and Sickness*. Berkeley: University of California Press.

Fadiman, Anne
    1997    *The Spirit Catches You and You Fall Down: A Hmong Child, Her American Doctors, and the Collision of Two Cultures*. New York: Farrar, Straus and Giroux.

Fagan, Brian
    1999    *Floods, Famines, and Emperors: El Niño and the Fate of Civilization*. Cambridge: Cambridge University Press.

Farmer, Paul
    1994    AIDS-Talk and the Constitution of Cultural Models. *Social Science and Medicine* 38:801–10.
    1999    *Infections and Inequalities: The Modern Plagues*. Berkeley: University of California Press.
    2005    *Pathologies of Power: Health, Human Rights, and the New War on the Poor*. Berkeley: University of California Press.

Fassin, Didier
    2007    The Politics of Life: Beyond the Anthropology of Health. In *Medical Anthropology: Regional Perspectives and Shared Concerns*, ed. Francine Saillant and Serge Genest, 252–66. Malden, MA: Blackwell.

Fassin, Didier, and Richard Rechtman
    2009    *The Empire of Trauma: An Inquiry into the Condition of Victimhood*. Princeton, NJ: Princeton University Press.

Ferguson, A.
    1981    Commercial Pharmaceutical Medicine and Medicalization: A Case Study from El Salvador. *Culture, Medicine and Psychiatry* 5(2):105–34.

Ferzacca, Steve
    2001    *Healing the Modern in a Central Javanese City*. Durham, NC: Academic Press.

Figueroa, Juan
    2004    Preface to *Uninsured: The Costs and Consequences of Living without Health Insurance in Connecticut*. Hartford: Universal Health Care Foundation of Connecticut.
Findley, S., K. Lawler, M. Bindra, L. Maggio, M. Pinocchio, and C. Maylahn
    2003    Elevated Asthma and Indoor Environmental Exposures among Puerto Rican Children of East Harlem. *Journal of Asthma* 40(5):557–69.
Fitzgerald, Maureen
    2000    Establishing Cultural Competency for Health Professionals. In *Anthropological Approaches to Psychological Medicine*, ed. V. Skultans and J. Cox, 184–200. London: Jessica Kingsley.
Foster, George M.
    1953    Relationships between Spanish and Spanish-American Folk Medicine. *Journal of American Folklore* 66:201–17.
Foster, George M., and Barbara Gallatin Anderson
    1978    *Medical Anthropology*. New York: John Wiley and Sons.
Foster, John Bellamy
    2000    *Marx's Ecology: Materialism and Nature*. New York: Monthly Review Press.
    2004    Ecology, Capitalism, and the Socialization of Nature. *Monthly Review* 56(6):1–12.
    2005    The Renewing of Socialism: An Introduction. *Monthly Review* 57(3):1–18.
    2009    *The Ecological Revolution: Making Peace with the Planet*. New York: Monthly Review Press.
Foucault, Michel
    1975    *The Birth of the Clinic: An Archaeology of Medical Perception*. New York: Vintage.
Frank, A.
    1995    *The Wounded Storyteller: Body, Illness, and Ethics*. Chicago: University of Chicago Press.
Franks, Peter, Peter Muennig, Erica Lubetkin, and Haomiao Jia
    2006    The Burden of Disease Associated with Being African-American in the United States and the Contribution of Socio-Economic Status. *Social Science and Medicine* 62:2469–78.
Freidson, Eliot
    1970    *Profession of Medicine: A Study of the Sociology of Applied Knowledge*. New York: Harper and Row.

Garnaut, Ross.
  2008    *The Garnaut Climate Change Review: Final Report.* Cambridge;
          Cambridge University Press.
Garry, R., M. Witte, A. Gottlieb, M. Elvin-Lewis, M. Gottlieb, C. Witte, S.
Alexander, W. Cole, and W. Drake Jr.
  1988    Documentation of an AIDS Virus Infection in the United
          States in 1968. *Journal of the American Medical Association*
          260:2085–87.
Gawande, Atul
  2002    *Complications: A Surgeon's Notes on an Imperfect Science.* New
          York: Henry Holt.
Gee, J.
  1985    The Narrativization of Experience in the Oral Style. *Journal of
          Education* 167:9–35.
Geest, T., M. Engberg, and T. Lauritzen
  2004    Discordance between Self-Evaluated Health and Doctor-Evalu-
          ated Health in Relation to General Health Promotion. *Scandina-
          vian Journal of Primary Health Care* 22(3):146–51.
Geiger, H. Jack
  2003    Racial and Ethnic Disparities in Diagnosis and Treatment: A Re-
          view of the Evidence and a Consideration of Causes. In *Unequal
          Treatment: Confronting Racial and Ethnic Disparities in Health
          Care*, ed. Brian D. Smedley, Adrienne Y. Stith, and Alan R. Nelson,
          417–54. Washington, DC: Institute of Medicine.
Goldstein, Donna
  2003    *Laughter Out of Place: Race, Class, Violence, and Sexuality in a Rio
          Shantytown.* Berkeley: University of California Press.
Good, Byron
  1994    *Medicine, Rationality, and Experience: An Anthropological Perspec-
          tive.* Cambridge: Cambridge University Press.
Good, Mary-Jo DelVecchio, Byron Good, and Anne Becker
  2003    The Culture of Medicine and Racial, Ethnic, and Class Dispari-
          ties in Healthcare. In *Unequal Treatment: Confronting Racial and
          Ethnic Disparities in Health Care*, ed. Brian D. Smedley, Adrienne
          Y. Stith, and Alan R. Nelson, 594–625. Washington, DC: Institute
          of Medicine.
Goodale, Mark
  2006    Introduction to "Anthropology and Human Rights in a New
          Key." *American Anthropologist* 108(1):1–8.

Gravlee, Clarence, William Dressler, and H. Russell Bernard
  2005    Skin Color, Social Classification, and Blood Pressure in Southeast-
          ern Puerto Rico. *American Journal of Public Health* 95(12):2191–97.
Gray, D. E.
  2006    *Health Sociology: An Australian Perspective.* Frenchs Forest, NSW:
          Pearson Education Australia.
Grønseth, Anne Sigfrid
  2006    Experiences of Illness and Self: Tamil Refugees in Norway Seeking
          Medical Advice. In *Multiple Medical Realities: Patients and Heal-
          ers in Biomedical, Alternative, and Traditional Medicine,* ed. Helle
          Johannessen and Imre Lázár, 148–62. New York: Berghahn Books.
Hahn, Robert
  1995    *Sickness and Healing: An Anthropological Perspective.* New Haven,
          CT: Yale University Press.
Hahn, Robert, and Arthur Kleinman
  1983    Biomedical Practice and Anthropological Theory. *Annual Review
          of Anthropology* 12:305–33.
Han, Gil Soo
  2000    Traditional Herbal Medicine in the Korean Community in Aus-
          tralia: A Strategy to Cope with Health Demands of Immigrant
          Life. *Health* 4:426–54.
Haraway, Donna
  1991    *Simians, Cyborgs, and Women: The Reinvention of Nature.* New
          York: Routledge.
Harper, Janice
  2002    *Endangered Species: Health, Illness, and Death among Madagascar's
          People of the Forest.* Durham, NC: Carolina Academic Press.
  2004    Breathless in Houston: A Political Ecology of Health Approach to
          Understanding Environmental Health Concerns. *Medical Anthro-
          pology* 23:295–326.
Harris, Anna
  2009    Oversea Doctors in Australian Hospitals: An Ethnographic Study
          of How Degrees of Difference Are Negotiated in Medical Practice.
          PhD thesis, Centre of Health and Society, University of Mel-
          bourne, Australia.
Harris, Judith
  2006    Obesity, the Terror Within. *Hooah 4 Health,* sponsored by the
          Army National Guard. www.hooah4health.com/overview/heal-
          thed/hecorner/obesity.htm. Accessed August 3, 2011.

Harrison, Margaret E.
    2000    Mexican Physicians, Nurses, and Social Workers. In *Mesoameri-can Healers*, ed. Brad R. Huber and Alan R. Sandstrom, 270–306. Austin: University of Texas Press.
Hawass, Zahi, Yehia Gad, Somaia Ismail, Rabab Khairat, Dina Fathalla, Na-glaa Hasan, Amal Ahmed, Hisham Elleithy, Markus Ball, Fawzi Gaballah, Sally Wasef, Mohamed Fateen, Hany Amer, Paul Gostner, Asharaf Selim, Albert Zink, and Carsten Pusch
    2010    Ancestry and Pathology in King Tutankhamun's Family. *Journal of the American Medical Association* 303(7):638–47.
Hogle, Linda F.
    1999    *Recovering the Nation's Body: Cultural Memory, Medicine, and the Politics of Redemption*. Newark, NJ: Rutgers University Press.
Holahan John, Lisa Dubay, and Genevieve Kenney
    2003    Which Children Are Still Uninsured and Why. *Future of Children* 13(1): 68–70.
Horton, Sarah, and Judith Barker
    2010    Oral Health Disparities for Mexican American Farmworker Chil-dren. *Medical Anthropology Quarterly* 24(2): 199–219.
Hughes, Charles.
    1978    Ethnomedicine. In *Health and the Human Condition: Perspectives on Medical Anthropology*, ed. Michael Logan and Edward Hunt, 150–158. North Scituate, MA: Duxbury Press.
Hughes, Charles
    1996    Ethnopsychiatry. In *Medical Anthropology: Contemporary Theory and Method*, rev. ed., ed. Carolyn F. Sargent and Thomas M. John-son, 131–64. Westport, CT: Praeger.
Idler, Ellen, Stanislav Kasl, and Jon Lemki
    1990    Self-Evaluated Health and Mortality among the Elderly in New Haven, Connecticut and Iowa and Washington Counties, 1982–1986. *American Journal of Epidemiology* 31(1):91–103.
Illich, Ivan
    1975    *Limits to Medicine: Medical Nemesis, the Expropriation of Health*. London: Marion Boyars.
Institute of Medicine
    2002    *Speaking of Health: Assessing Health Communication Strategies for Diverse Populations*. Washington, DC: Institute of Medicine.
Interagency Forum on Child and Family Statistics
    2005    America's Children: Key National Indicators of Well-Being, 2005. www.childstats.gov/americaschildren/index.asp. Accessed July 19, 2005.

Janes, Craig, and O. Chuluundorj
2004    Free Markets and Dead Mothers: The Social Ecology of Maternal Mortality in Post-Socialist Mongolia. *Medical Anthropology Quarterly* 18(2):230–57.

Janzen, John
1978    *The Quest for Therapy in Lower Zaire.* Berkeley: University of California Press.
2001    *The Social Fabric of Health: An Introduction to Medical Anthropology.* New York: McGraw-Hill Humanities.

Jaye, Chrystal, Tony Egan, and Sarah Parker
2006    'Do as I Say, not as I Do': Medical Education and Foucault's Normalizing Technologies of Self. *Anthropology and Medicine* 13:141–55.

Johannessen, Helle
2007    Body Praxis and Networks of Power. *Anthropology and Medicine* 14:267–78.

Joralemon, Donald
1995    Organ Wars: The Battle for Body Parts. *Medical Anthropology Quarterly* 9(3):335–56.
2010    *Exploring Medical Anthropology.* 3rd ed. Boston: Allyn and Bacon.

Jordan, Brigette
1993    *Birth in Four Cultures: A Crosscultural Investigation of Childbirth in Yucatan, Holland, Sweden, and the United States.* 4th ed. Prospect Heights, IL: Waveland Press.

Joseph, C., B. Foxman, F. Leickly, E. Peterson, and D. Ownby
1996    Prevalence of Possible Undiagnosed Asthma and Associated Morbidity among Urban Schoolchildren. *Journal of Pediatrics* 129:735–42.

Justice, Judith
2000    The Politics of Child Survival. In *Global Health Policy, Local Realities,* ed. L. Whiteford and L. Manderson, 23–38. Boulder, CO: Lynne Rienner.

Katz, Claudio
2007    Socialist Strategies in Latin America. *Monthly Review* 59(4): 25–41.

Katz, Pearl
1999    *The Scalpel's Edge: The Culture of Surgeons.* Boston: Allyn and Bacon.

Kaufman, Sharon
2004    Dying and Death. In *The Encyclopedia of Medical Anthropology.* Volume 1, *Topics,* ed. Carol Ember and Melvin Ember, 244–52. New York: Kluwer Academic/Plenum.

Kelman, Sander
   1975    The Social Nature of the Definition Problem in Health. *Interna-tional Journal of the Health Services* 5:625–42.
Kendall, Carl
   1998    The Role of Qualitative Research in Negotiating Community Ac-ceptance: The Case of Dengue Control in El Progresso, Honduras. *Human Organization* 57:217–21.
   2005    Waste Not, Want Not: Grounded Globalization and Global Les-sons for Water Use from Lima, Peru. In *Globalization, Water, and Health: Resource Management in Times of Scarcity*, ed. Linda Whiteford and Scott Whiteford, 85–105. Santa Fe, NM: School of American Research Press.
Kim, Jim Yong, Joyce V. Millen, Alec Irwin, and John Gershaman, eds.
   2000    *Dying for Growth: Global Inequality and the Health of the Poor.* Monroe, ME: Common Courage Press.
Kim, Jongyoung
   2009    Transcultural Medicine: A Multi-Sited Ethnography on the Scientific-Industrial Networking of Korean Medicine. *Medical Anthropology* 28:31–64.
King, Gary
   1996    Institutional Racism and the Medical/Health Complex: A Con-ceptual Analysis. *Ethnicity and Disease* 6:30–46.
Klare, Michael T.
   2002    *Resource Wars: The New Landscape of Global Conflict.* New York: Henry Holt.
Klein, Herbert
   1992    *Bolivia: The Evolution of a Multi-Ethnic Society.* New York: Oxford University Press.
Kleinman, Arthur
   1980    *Patients and Healers in the Context of Culture: An Exploration of the Borderland between Anthropology, Medicine, and Psychiatry.* Berkeley: University of California Press.
   1988    *The Illness Narratives: Suffering, Healing, and the Human Condi-tion.* New York: Basic Books.
Kleinman, Arthur, Veena Das, and Margaret Lock, eds.
   1997    *Social Suffering.* Berkeley: University of California Press.
Kreiger, Nancy
   2005    *Health Disparities and the Body.* Boston: Harvard School of Public Health.

2007    Why Epidemiologists Cannot Afford to Ignore Poverty. *Epidemiology* 18(6):658–63.

Kreiger, Nancy, and S. Sidney
1996    Racial Discrimination and Blood Pressure: The CARDIA Study of Young Black and White Adults. *American Journal of Public Health* 86:1370–78.

LaBarre, Weston
1980    Anthropological Perspectives on Hallucination, Hallucinogens, and the Shamanic Origins of Religion. In *Culture in Context*, ed. Weston LaBarre. Durham, NC: Duke University Press.

Lambeck, Michael
2003    Irony and Illness—Recognition and Refusal. In *Irony and Illness*, ed. Michael Lambeck and Paul Antze, 1–20. New York: Berghahn Books.

Landy, David
1977    *Culture, Disease, and Healing: Studies in Medical Anthropology.* New York: Macmillan.

Lang, Joel
2006    Hot Debate over Hurricanes. *Hartford Courant*, October 15.

Larkin, Gerald
1983    *Occupational Monopoly and Modern Medicine.* London: Tavistock.

Last, Murray
1996    The Professionalization of Indigenous Healers. In *Medical Anthropology: Contemporary Theory and Method*, rev. ed., ed. Carolyn F. Sargent and Thomas M. Johnson, 374–95. Westport, CT: Praeger.

LeCompte, Margaret, and Jean Schensul, eds.
1999    *Ethnographer's Toolkit.* 6 vols. Walnut Creek, CA: AltaMira Press.

Leibing, Annette
2007    Much More than Medical Anthropology: The Healthy Body and Brazilian Identity. In *Medical Anthropology: Regional Perspectives and Shared Concerns*, ed. Francine Saillant and Serge Genest, 58–70. Malden, MA: Blackwell.

Levy, Barry, and Victor Sidel
2006    The Nature of Social Injustice and Its Impact on Public Health. In *Social Injustice and Public Health*, ed. Barry Levy and Victor Sidel, 5–21. Oxford: Oxford University Press.

Lock, Margaret
2002    *Twice Dead: Organ Transplants and the Reinvention of Death.* Berkeley: University of California Press.

2003    Medicalization and the Naturalization of Social Control. In *The Encyclopedia of Medical Anthropology*. Volume 1, Topics, ed. Carol and Melvin Ember, 116–25. New York: Kluwer Academic/ Plenum.

Lock, Margaret, and Vihn-Kim Nguyen
2010    *An Anthropology of Biomedicine*. Malden, MA: Wiley-Blackwell.

Lock, Margaret, and Nancy Scheper-Hughes
1996    A Critical-Interpretive Approach in Medical Anthropology: Rituals and Routines of Discipline and Dissent. In *Medical Anthropology: Contemporary Theory and Method*, rev. ed., ed. Carolyn F. Sargent and Thomas M. Johnson, 41–70. Westport, CT: Praeger.

Long, Debbi, Cynthia L. Hunter, and Sjaak van der Geest
2008    When the Field Is a Ward or a Clinic: Hospital Ethnography. *Anthropology and Medicine* 15:71–78.

Loustanunau, Martha O., and Elisa J. Sobo
1997    *The Cultural Context of Health, Illness, and Medicine*. Westport, CT: Bergin and Garvey.

Luborsky, Mark
1995    The Process of Self-Report of Impairment in Clinical Research. *Social Science and Medicine* 40:1447–59.

MacDonald, Malcolm
2002    Pedagogy, Pathology, and Ideology: The Production, Transmission, and Reproduction of Medical Discourse. *Discourse and Society* 13:447–67.

Macpherson, Cluny, and La'avasa Macpherson
1990    *Samoan Medical Belief and Practice*. Auckland, New Zealand: Auckland University Press.

Magdoff, Fred, and John Bellamy Foster
2010    What Every Environmentalist Needs to Know About Capitalism. *Monthly Review* 61(10): 1–30.

Magner, Lois
1992    *A History of Medicine*. New York: Marcel Dekker.

March of Dimes
2006    *The March of Dimes Global Report on Birth Defects: The Hidden Toll of Dying and Disabled Children*. Report 31-2008-05. Atlanta: March of Dimes.

Marshall, Patricia, and Abdallah Daar
  2000    Ethical Issues in Human Organ Replacement: A Case Study from India. In *Global Health Policy, Local Realities*, ed. Linda Whiteford and Lenore Manderson, 205–30. Boulder, CO: Lynne Rienner.
Marshall, Patricia, and Barbara Koenig
  1996    Bioethics in Anthropology. In *Medical Anthropology*, ed. Carolyn Sargent and Thomas Johnson, 349–73. Westport, CT: Praeger.
Martin, Emily
  1989    *The Woman in the Body: A Cultural Analysis of Reproduction*. Milton Keynes, UK: Open University Press.
Martyr, Phillippa
  2002    *Paradise of Quacks: An Alternative History of Medicine in Australia*. Paddington, Australia: Macleay.
Mattingly, Cheryl
  1998    In Search of the Good: Narrative Reasoning in Clinical Practice. *Medical Anthropology Quarterly* 12:272–97.
McClement, Susan
  1998    Symptom Distress in Children with Cancer: The Need to Adopt a Meaning-Centered Approach. *Journal of Pediatric Oncology Nursing* 15(1):3–12.
McClennon, James
  1997    Shamanic Healing, Human Evolution, and the Origin of Health. *Journal for the Scientific Study of Religion* 36:345–54.
McCombie, Susan
  1999    Folk Flu and Viral Syndrome: An Anthropological Perspective. In *Anthropology and Public Health*, ed. Robert Hahn, 27–43. Oxford: Oxford University Press.
McDade, Thomas
  2003    Life Event Stress and Immune Function in Samoan Adolescents: Toward a Cross-Cultural Psychoneuroimmunology. In *Social and Cultural Lives of Immune Systems: Contextualizing Psychoneuroimmunology, Embodying the Social Sciences*, ed. James Wilce, 170–88. New York: Routledge.
McElroy, Ann
  2003    Evolutionary and Ecological Perspectives. In *The Encyclopedia of Medical Anthropology*. Volume 2, *Cultures*, ed. Carol R. Ember and Melvin Ember, 31–37. New York: Kluwer Academic/Plenum.

McElroy, Ann, and Patricia Townsend
  2003   *Medical Anthropology in Ecological Perspective.* 3rd ed. Boulder, CO: Westview Press.
  2009   *Medical Anthropology in Ecological Perspective.* 5th ed. Boulder, CO: Westview Press.

McGarvey, Stephen
  2009   Interdisciplinary Translational Research in Anthropology, Nutrition, and Public Health. *Annual Review of Anthropology* 38:233–49.

McGlynn, Elizabeth, S. Asch, J. Adams, J. Keesey, J. Hicks, A. DeCristofaro, and E. Kerr
  2003   The Quality of Health Care Delivered to Adults in the United States. *New England Journal of Medicine* 348(26):2635–45.

McKenna, Brian
  2010   Take Back Medical Education—The "Primary Care" Shuffle. *Medical Anthropology* 29:6–14.

McKeown, Alice, and Gary Gardner.
  2009   Climate Change Reference Guide and Glossary. In *State of the World 2009: Confronting Climate Change*, ed. Linda Starke, 189–204. London: WorldWatch Institute.

McMichael, Tony
  2001   *Human Frontiers, Environments, and Disease.* Cambridge: Cambridge University Press.
  2003   Global Climate Change and Health: An Old Story Writ Large. In *Climate Change and Human Health: Risks and Responses*, ed. A. J. Michael, D. H. Campbell-Lendrum, C. F. Corvalan, K. L. Ebi, A. K. Githeko, J. D. Scheraga, and A. Woodward, 1–17. Geneva: World Health Organization.

McMichael, Tony, and Robert Beaglehole
  2003   The Global Context for Public Health. In *Global Public Health: A New Era*, ed. Robert Beaglehole, 1–23. Oxford: Oxford University Press.

McMullin, Juliet, and Diane Weinger
  2008   An Anthropology of Cancer. In *Confronting Cancer: Metaphors, Advocacy, and Anthropology*, ed. Juliet McMullin and Diane Weinger, 3–26. Sante Fe, NM: School for Advanced Research Press.

Mehrabadi, A.
   2005    Patents and Innovations in Biotechnology: From a Satellite Look-
           ing down at Our Use of Patents in the Great Planetary Scheme of
           Things. *Science Creative Quarterly* 1(April–June):22–33.
Mendenhall, Emily, Rebecca Seligman, Alicia Fernandez, and Elizabeth Jacobs
   2010    Speaking through Diabetes: Rethinking the Significance of Lay Dis-
           courses on Diabetes. *Medical Anthropology Quarterly* 24(2):220–39.
Mering, Otto von
   1970    Medicine and Psychiatry. In *Anthropology and the Behavioral and
           Health Sciences*, ed. Otto von Mering, 272–307. Pittsburgh, PA:
           University of Pittsburgh Press.
Michaels, David
   1988    Waiting for the Body Count: Corporate Decision Making and
           Bladder Cancer in the U.S. Dye Industry. *Medical Anthropology
           Quarterly* 2(3):215–32.
Moerman, Daniel
   2001    *Meaning, Medicine, and the "Placebo Effect."* Cambridge: Cam-
           bridge University Press.
Morales, Walter Queiser
   1992    *Bolivia: Land of Struggle.* Boulder, CO: Westview Press.
Morris, David B.
   1998    *Illness and Culture in the Postmodern Age.* Berkeley: University of
           California Press.
Mosack, Katie, Maryann Abbott, Merrill Singer, Margaret Weeks, and Lucy
           Rohena
   2005    If I Didn't Have HIV, I'd Be Dead Now: Illness Narratives of
           Drug Users Living with HIV/AIDS. *Qualitative Health Review*
           15(5):586–605.
Murdock, George Peter
   1980    *Theories of Illness: A World Survey.* Pittsburgh, PA: University of
           Pittsburgh Press.
Murphy, Robert
   1987    *The Body Silent.* New York: Holt.
Najman, Jake M.
   2003    Health and Illness. In *The Cambridge Handbook of Social Sciences
           in Australia*, ed. Ian McAllister, Steve Dowrick, and Riaz Hassan,
           536–53. Cambridge: Cambridge University Press.

Napier, A.
    2003    *The Age of Immunology: Conceiving a Future in an Alienating World.* Chicago: University of Chicago Press.
National Center for Health Statistics
    2002    *A Demographic and Health Snapshot of the U.S. Hispanic/ Latino Population.* Atlanta: Centers for Disease Control and Prevention.
Nations, Marilyn, and M. Amaral
    1991    Flesh, Blood, Souls, and Households: Cultural Validity in Mortality Inquiry. *Medical Anthropology Quarterly* 5:204–20.
Navarro, Vicente
    1986    *Crisis, Health, and Medicine: A Social Critique.* New York: Tavistock.
Nichter, Mark
    1989    *Anthropology and International Health: South Asian Case Studies.* Dordrecht: Kluwer Academic.
    1991    Ethnomedicine: Diverse Trends, Common Linkages: Commentary. *Medical Anthropology* 13:137–71.
    2008    *Global Health: Why Cultural Perceptions, Social Representations, and Biopolitics Matter.* Tucson: University of Arizona Press.
Nordstrom, Carolyn
    1998    Terror Warfare and the Medicine of Peace. *Medical Anthropology Quarterly* 12(1):103–21.
O'Connor, Bonnie Blair
    1995    *Healing Traditions: Alternative Medicine and Health Professions.* Philadelphia: University of Pennsylvania Press.
Olujic, Maria
    1998    Embodiment of Terror: Gendered Violence in Peacetime and Wartime in Croatia and Bosnia-Herzegovina. *Medical Anthropology Quarterly* 12(1):31–50.
O'Neill, Arthur
    1994    *Enemies Within and Without: Educating Chiropractors, Osteopaths, and Traditional Acupuncturists.* Bundoora, Victoria, Australia: La Trobe University.
Ortega, A., P. Gergen, A. Paltiel, H. Baucher, K. Belanger, and P. Leaderer
    2002    Impact of Site of Care, Race, and Hispanic Ethnicity on Medication Use for Childhood Asthma. *Pediatrics* 109(1):E1.

Ortiz de Montellano, Bernard
    1989    *Aztec Medicine, Health, and Nutrition.* New Brunswick, NJ: Rutgers University Press.

Pachter, Lee
    2006    Influences on Health Disparities. Paper presented at Role of Partnerships: Second Annual Meeting of Child Health Services Researchers. Agency for Healthcare Research and Quality, Rockville, MD.

Pachter, Lee, Susan Weller, Roberta Baer, and Robert Trotter
    2002    Asthma Beliefs and Practices in Mainland Puerto Ricans, Mexican-Americans, Mexicans, and Guatemalans: Consistency and Variability in Health Beliefs and Practices. *Journal of Asthma* 39(2):119–34.

Palsson, Gisli
    2007    *Anthropolology and the New Genetics.* Cambridge: Cambridge University Press.

Pandolfi, Mariella, and Gilles Bibeau
    2007    Suffering, Politics, Nation: A Cartography of Italian Medical Anthropology. In *Medical Anthropology: Regional Perspectives and Shared Concerns,* ed. Francine Saillant and Serge Genest, 122–41. Malden, MA: Blackwell.

Parker, Melissa
    2003    Anthropological Reflections on HIV Prevention Strategies: The Case for Targeting London's Backrooms. In *Learning from AIDS,* ed. George Ellison, Melissa Parker, and Catherine Campbell, 178–209. Cambridge: Cambridge University Press.

Parker, Richard
    2009    *Bodies, Pleasures, and Passions: Sexual Culture in Contemporary Brazil.* Nashville, TN: Vanderbilt University Press.

Parsons, Howard, ed.
    1977    *Marx and Engels on Ecology.* Westport, CT: Greenwood.

Paskal, Cleo
    2010    *Global Warming: How Environmental, Economic, and Political Crises Will Redraw the World Map.* New York: Palgrave Macmillan.

Payer, Lynn
    1988    *Medicine and Culture: Varieties of Treatment in the United States, England, West Germany, and France.* New York: H. Holt.

Petras, James, and Steve Vieux
    1992    Myths and Realities: Latin America's Free Markets. *International Journal of Health Services* 224:611–17.
Pfeiffer, James
    2005    Commodity Fetischismo, the Holy Spirit, and the Turn to Pentecostal and African Independent Churches in Central Mozambique. *Culture, Medicine and Psychiatry* 29:255–83.
Pickering, Andrew
    1995    *The Mangle of Practice: Time, Agency, and Science.* Chicago: University of Chicago Press.
Pirages, Dennis C., Paul J. Runci, and Robert H. Sprinkle
    2000    Human Populations in the Shared Environment. In *Ecosystem Change and Public Health: A Global Perspective*, ed. Joan L. Aron and Jonathan A. Patz, 165–87. Baltimore: Johns Hopkins University Press.
Pittock, A. Barrie.
    2009    *Climate Change: The Science, Impacts, and Solutions.* 2nd ed. Melbourne, Australia: CSIRO Publishing.
Pool, Robert, and Wenzel Geissler
    2005    *Medical Anthropology.* Maidenhead, England: Open University Press.
Porter, Roy
    1996    *The Greatest Benefit to Mankind: A Medical History of Humanity from Antiquity to the Present.* London: Fontana Press.
Price, Laurie
    1987    Ecuadorian Illness Stories: Cultural Knowledge in Natural Discourse. In *Cultural Models in Language and Thought*, ed. D. Holland and N. Quinn, 313–42. Cambridge; Cambridge University Press.
Proctor, Robert
    1995    *Cancer Wars: How Politics Shapes What We Know and Don't Know about Cancer.* New York: Basic Books.
Quesada, James
    1998    Suffering Child: An Embodiment of War and Its Aftermath in Post-Sandinista Nicaragua. *Medical Anthropology Quarterly* 12(1):51–73.
Quinland, Marsha
    2004    *From the Bush: The Front Line of Health Care in a Caribbean Village.* Belmont, CA: Wadsworth.

Rapp, Rayna
   2000    *Testing Women, Testing the Fetus.* London: Routledge.
Rasmussen, Susan
   2004    Tuareg. In *The Encyclopedia of Medical Anthropology.* Volume 2, *Cultures,* ed. Carol R. Ember and Melvin Ember, 1001–9. New York: Kluwer Academic/Plenum.
Ray, Celeste
   2001    Cultural Paradigms: An Anthropological Perspective on Climate Change. In *Global Climate Change,* ed. Sharon L. Spray and Karen L. McGlothin, 81–100. Lanham, MD: Rowman and Littlefield.
Read, Kenneth E.
   1955    Morality and the Concept of Person among the Pahuka-Gama. *Oceania* 25:253–82.
Rebhun, Linda-Anne
   1994    Swallowing Frogs: Anger and Illness in Northeast Brazil. *Medical Anthropology Quarterly* 8(4):360–82.
Reid, Janice
   1983    *Sorcerers and Healing Spirits: Community and Change in an Aboriginal Community.* Canberra: Australian National University Press.
Reis, Ria
   2000    The "Wounded Healer" as Ideology: The Work of *Ngoma* in Swaziland. In *The Quest for Fruition through Ngoma: Political Aspects of Healing in Southern Africa,* ed. Rijk van Dijk, Ria Reis, and Marja Spierenburg, 60–75. Athens: Ohio University Press.
Rekdal, Ole Bjorn
   1999    Cross-Cultural Healing in East African Ethnography. *Medical Anthropology Quarterly* 11:458–82.
Rivers, W. H. R.
   1927    *Medicine, Magic, and Religion.* London: Kegan Paul, Trench, Trubner.
Robbins, Paul
   2003    *Political Ecology: A Critical Introduction.* Malden, MA: Blackwell.
Robert Wood Johnson Foundation
   2005    *Characteristics of the Uninsured: A View from the States.* Princeton, NJ: Robert Wood Johnson Foundation.
Roberts, Charlotte, and Keith Manchester
   1995    *The Archaeology of Disease.* 2nd ed. Ithaca, NY: Cornell University Press.

Rödlach, Alexander
    2006    *Witches, Westerners, and HIV.* Walnut Creek, CA: Left Coast Press.

Roizen, Michael
    2001    *Real Age: Are You as Young as You Can Be?* New York: HarperCollins.

Romanucci-Ross, Lola
    1977    The Hierarchy of Resort in Curative Practices: The Admiralty Islands. In *Culture, Disease, and Healing: Studies in Medical Anthropology,* ed. David Landy, 481–87. New York: Macmillan.

Roney, James
    1959    Medical Anthropology: A Synthetic Discipline. *New Physician* 8(3):32–33, 81.

Rubel, Art, and Linda Garro
    1992    Social and Cultural Factors in the Successful Control of Tuberculosis. *Public Health Reports* 107:626–36.

Rubel, Arthur J., and Michael R. Hass
    1996    Ethnomedicine. In *Medical Anthropology: Contemporary Theory and Method,* rev. ed., ed. Carolyn F. Sargent and Thomas M. Johnson113–30. Westport, CT: Praeger.

Rubinstein, Robert
    1995    Narratives of Elder Parental Death: A Structural and Cultural Analysis. *Medical Anthropology* 9(2):257–76.

Ruyle, Eugene
    1977    A Socialist Alternative for the Future. In *Cultures of the Future,* ed. Magorah Maruyma and Arthur M. Harkins, 613–28. The Hague: Mouton.

Rylko-Bauer, Barbara, and Paul Farmer
    2002    Managed Care or Managed Inequality? A Call for Critiques of Market-Based Medicine. *Medical Anthropology Quarterly* 16(4):476–502.

Rylko-Bauer, Barbara, Merrill Singer, and John van Willigin
    2006    Reclaiming Applied Anthropology: Its Past, Present, and Future. *American Anthropologist* 108(1):178–90.

Saillant, Francine, and Serge Genest
    2007    Introduction to *Medical Anthropology: Regional Perspectives and Shared Concerns,* ed. Francine Saillant and Serge Genest, xviii–xxxiii. Malden, MA: Blackwell.

Sargent, Carolyn
   2006    Reproductive Strategies and Islamic Discourse: Malian Migrants Negotiate Everyday Life in Paris, France. *Medical Anthropology* 20(1):31–49.

Sargent, Carolyn, and Thomas Johnson, eds.
   1996    *Medical Anthropology: Contemporary Theory and Method.* Westport, CT: Greenwood.

Scheer, Jessica, and Mark Luborsky
   1991    The Cultural Context of Polio Biographies. *Orthopedics* 14:1173–84.

Scheid, Volker
   2002    *Chinese Medicine in Contemporary China: Plurality and Synthesis, Science and Cultural Theory.* Durham, NC: Duke University Press.

Scheper-Hughes, Nancy
   1992    *Death without Weeping: The Violence of Everyday Life in Brazil.* Berkeley: University of California Press.
   2000    The Global Traffic in Organs. *Current Anthropology*, 41(2):191–224.

Scheper-Hughes, Nancy, and Margaret Lock
   1987    The Mindful Body: A Prolegomenon to Future Work in Medical Anthropology. *Medical Anthropology Quarterly* 1(1):6–41.

Schrimshaw, Susan
   2001    Culture, Behavior, and Health. In *International Public Health*, ed. Michael Merson, Robert Black, and Anne Mills, 53–78. Gaithersburg, MD: Aspen.

Scott, Janny
   2005    Life at the Top in America Isn't Just Better, It's Longer. *New York Times*, May 16.

Shadbolt, Bruce, Jane Barresi, and Paul Craft
   2002    Self-Rated Health as a Predictor of Survival among Patients with Advanced Cancer. *Journal of Clinical Oncology* 20(10):2514–19.

Shapiro, Arthur
   1964    Etiological Factors in Placebo Effect. *Journal of the American Medical Association* 187(10):712–15.

Sharp, Leslie
   1995    Organ Transplantation as a Transformative Experience: Anthropological Insights into the Restructuring of the Self. *Medical Anthropology Quarterly* 9(3):357–89.

Singer, Merrill
    1996    A Dose of Drugs, a Touch of Violence, a Case of AIDS: Concep-
            tualizing the SAVA Syndemic. *Free Inquiry in Creative Sociology*
            24(2):99–110.
    2007    *Drugging the Poor: Legal and Illegal Drug Industries and the Struc-
            turing of Social Inequality.* Long Grove, IL: Waveland Press.
    2009    Beyond Global Warming: Interacting Ecocrises and the Critical
            Anthropology of Health. *Anthropology Quarterly* 82(3):795–820.
    2010a   *Interdisciplinarity and Collaboration in Responding to HIV and
            AIDS in Africa: Anthropological Perspectives. African Journal of
            AIDS Research* 8(4):379–87.
    2010b   Ecosyndemics: Global Warming and the Coming Plagues of the
            Twenty-first Century. In *Plagues and Epidemics: Infected Spaces
            Past and Present,* ed. Alan Swedlund and Ann Herring, 21–37.
            London: Berg.
Singer, Merrill, Carol Arnold, Maureen Fitzgerald, Lyn Madden, and Christa
Voight von Legat
    1984    Hypoglycemia: A Controversial Illness in U.S. Society. *Medical
            Anthropology* 8(1):1–35.
Singer, Merrill, and Hans Baer
    1995    *Critical Medical Anthropology.* Amityville, NY: Baywood.
    2007    *Killer Commodities: A Critical Anthropological Examination of Cor-
            porate Production of Harm.* Lanham, MD: AltaMira Press.
Singer, Merrill, and Scott Clair
    2003    Syndemics and Public Health: Reconceptualizing Disease in Bio-
            Social Context. *Medical Anthropology Quarterly* 17(4):423–41.
Singer, Merrill, Lani Davision, and Gina Gerdes
    1988    Culture, Critical Theory, and Reproductive Illness Behavior in
            Haiti. *Medical Anthropology Quarterly* 2(4):223–34.
Singer, Merrill, Pamela Erickson, Louise Badiane, Rosemary Diaz, Dugeidy
Ortiz, Traci Abraham, and Anna Marie Nicolaysen
    2006    Syndemics, Sex, and the City: Understanding Sexually Transmit-
            ted Disease in Social and Cultural Context. *Social Science and
            Medicine* 63(8):2010–21.
Singer, Merrill, Greg Mirhej, Susan Shaw, Hassan Saleheen, Jim Vivian, Erica
Hastings, Lucy Rohena, DeShawn Jennings, Juhem Narvarro, Alan H. B. Wu,
Andrew Smith, and Alberto Perez
    2005    When the Drug of Choice Is a Drug of Confusion: Embalming
            Fluid Use in Inner City Hartford, CT. *Journal of Ethnicity and
            Substance Abuse* 4(2):71–96.

Singer, Merrill, Glenn Scott, Scott Wilson, Delia Easton, and Margaret Weeks
2001    "War Stories": AIDS Prevention and the Street Narratives of Drug Users. *Qualitative Health Research* 11(5):589–611.

Singer, Merrill, Freddie Valentín, Hans Baer, and Zhongke Jia
1992    Why Does Juan Garcia Have a Drinking Problem? The Perspective of Critical Medical Anthropology. *Medical Anthropology* 14(1):77–108.

Singer, Philip
1977    Introduction: From Anthropology and Medicine to "Therapy" and Neo-Colonialism. In *Traditional Healing: New Science or New Colonialism*, ed. Philip Singer, 1–25. London: Conch Magazine.

Sloboda, Zili
1998    What We Have Learned from Research about the Prevention of HIV Transmission among Drug Users. *Public Health Reports* 113(Suppl. 1):194–204.

Smith, Michael
2003    *The Aztecs.* Malden, MA: Blackwell.

Smith-Nonini, Sandy
2010    *Healing the Body Politic: El Salvador's Popular Struggle for Health Rights from Civil War to Neoliberal Peace.* New Brunswick, NJ: Rutgers University Press.

Sobo, Elisa
1995    *Choosing Unsafe Sex: AIDS-Risk Denial among Disadvantaged Women.* Philadelphia: University of Pennsylvania Press.
2006    Profile of E.J. Sobo. SMA Website. www.medanthro.net/directory/entry.asp?ID=3049.

Sobo, E., and M. Loustaunau
2010    *The Cultural Context of Health, Illness and Medicine,* second edition. Santa Barbara, CA: Praeger.

Society for Medical Anthropology
2006    April Newsletter

Souza, Neusa Santos
1983    *Tornar-se Negro* [Becoming Black]. Rio de Janeiro, Brazil: Graal.

Speed, Shannon
2006    At the Crossroads of Human Rights and Anthropology: Toward a Critically Engaged Activist Research. *American Anthropologist* 108(1):66–76.

Spradley, James
1970    *You Owe Yourself a Drunk: An Ethnography of Urban Nomads.* Prospect Heights, IL: Waveland Press.

Spratt, David, and Philip Sutton.
   2008    *Climate Code Red: The Case for Emergency Action.* Melbourne, Australia: Scribe.
Stavrianos, L. S.
   1989    *Lifelines from Our Past.* New York: Pantheon.
Steensma, David
   2003    The Kiss of Death: A Severe Allergic Reaction to a Shellfish Induced by a Good-Night Kiss. *Mayo Clinic Proceedings* 78:221–22.
Stoller, Paul
   2008    Remissioning Life, Reconfiguring Anthropology. In *Confronting Cancer: Metaphors, Advocacy, and Anthropology,* ed. Juliet McMullin and Diane Weiner, 27–42. Sante Fe, NM: School of Advanced Research Press.
Stoner, Brad
   1986    Understanding Medical Systems: Traditional, Modern, and Syncretistic Health Care and Alternatives in Medically Pluralistic Societies. *Medical Anthropology Quarterly* 17(2):44–48.
Stopka, Thomas, Kristin Springer, Kaveh Khoshnood, Susan Shaw, and Merrill Singer
   2004    Writing about Risk: Use of Daily Diaries in Understanding Drug-User Risk Behaviors. *AIDS and Behavior* 8(1):73–85.
Strathern, Andrew, and Pamela J. Stewart
   1999    *Curing and Healing: Medical Anthropology in Global Perspective.* Durham, NC: Carolina Academic Press.
Strauss, Sarah, and Ben Orlove
   2003    Up in the Air: The Anthropology of Weather and Climate. In *Weather, Climate, Culture,* ed. Sarah Strauss and Ben Orlove, 3–14. Oxford: Berg.
Susser, Ida
   2009    *AIDS, Sex, and Culture: Global Politics and Survival in Southern Africa.* Malden, MA: Wiley-Blackwell.
Sutton, J.
   2004    Homebirth as an Alternative to the Dominant System of Hospital Birth in Australia. http://www.maternitycoalition.org.au.
Szasz, Thomas
   1973    *The Second Sin.* Garden City, NY: Anchor/Doubleday.
Tesh, S. N.
   1988    *Hidden Arguments: Political Ideology and Disease Prevention Policy.* New Brunswick, NJ: Rutgers University Press.

Thomas, R. Brooke
    1998    The Evolution of Human Adaptability Paradigms: Toward a Biology of Poverty. In *Building a New Biocultural Synthesis: Political-Economic Perspectives on Human Biology*, ed. Alan Goodman and Thomas Leatherman, 43–73. Ann Arbor: University of Michigan Press.
Thornton, Robert
    2008    *Unimagined Communities: Sex, Networks, and AIDS in Uganda and South Africa.* Berkeley: University of California Press.
Townsend, Peter
    1986    Why Are the Many Poor? *International Journal of Health Services* 16:1–32.
Trostle, James
    2005    *Epidemiology and Culture.* Cambridge: Cambridge University Press.
Trotter, Robert
    1996    *Multicultural AIDS Prevention Programs.* New York: Haworth Press.
Turner, Bryan
    1984    *The Body and Society.* London: Sage.
    1992    *Regulating Bodies: Essays in Medical Sociology.* London: Routledge.
Turner, Victor
    1968    *The Drums of Affliction: A Study of Religious Processes among the Ndembu of Zambia.* London: Hutchinson.
Turshen, Meredith
    1989    *The Politics of Public Health.* New Brunswick, NJ: Rutgers University Press.
UNAIDS
    2004    *Report on the Global AID Epidemic.* Geneva, Switzerland: Joint UN Programme on HIV/AIDS.
    2009    *AIDS Epidemic Update.* Geneva: Joint United Nations Programme on HIV/AIDS.
UNICEF
    2006    Childhood Interrupted in Darfur's Refugee Camps. www.unicef. org/sowc/index_30568.html. Accessed August 3, 2011.
Van der Geest, S., and S. Reynolds Whyte
    1988    *The Context of Medicines in Developing Countries: Studies in Pharmaceutical Anthropology.* London: Kluwer Academic.
Van Esterik, Penny
    1989    *Beyond the Breast-Bottle Controversy.* New Brunswick, NJ: Rutgers University Press.

Voeks, Robert, and Peter Sercombe
    2000    The Scope of Hunter-Gather Ethnomedicine. *Social Science and Medicine* 51:679–90.
Waitzkin, Howard
    2000    *The Second Sickness: Contradictions of Capitalist Health Care.* Lanham, MD: Rowman and Littlefield.
Weir, Michael
    2005    *Alternative Medicine: A New Regulatory Model.* Melbourne: Australian Scholarly Press.
Wennberg, Jack
    1999    *Dartmouth Atlas of Health Care.* Chicago: American Hospital Publishing.
Wermuth, Laurie
    2003    *Global Inequality and Human Needs: Health and Illness in an Increasingly Unequal World.* Boston: Allyn and Bacon.
Whelehan, Patricia
    2009    *The Anthropology of AIDS: A Global Perspective.* Gainesville: University of Florida Press.
White, Kevin
    2002    *An Introduction to the Sociology of Health and Illness.* London: Sage.
Whiteford, Linda, and Lenore Manderson, eds.
    2000    *Global Health Policy, Local Realities.* London: Lynne Rienner.
Whiteford, Linda, and Scott Whiteford
    2005    Paradigm Change. In *Globalization, Water, and Health: Resource Management in Times of Scarcity*, ed. Linda Whiteford and Scott Whiteford, 3–15. Santa Fe, NM: School of American Research Press.
Whiteford, Scott, and Linda Whiteford
    2005    Concluding Comments: Future Challenges. In *Globalization, Water, and Health: Resource Management in Times of Scarcity*, ed. Linda Whiteford and Scott Whiteford, 255–65. Santa Fe, NM: School of American Research Press.
Whitman, S., C. Williams, and A. Shah
    2004    *Sinai Health System's Improving Community Health Survey.* Report No. 1. Chicago: Sinai Urban Health Institute.
Wiesner, Dianne
    1989    *Alternative Medicine: A Guide for Patients and Health Professionals in Australia.* Kenthurst, Australia: Kangaroo Press.
Wilce, James
    2009    Medical Discourse. *Annual Review of Anthropology* 38:199–215.

Willis, Evan
  1989   *Medical Dominance: The Division of Labour in Australian Health Care.* St. Leonards, Australia: Allen and Unwin.
Wind, Gitte
  2008   Negotiated Interactive Observation: Doing Fieldwork in Hospital Settings. *Anthropology and Medicine* 15:79–89.
Winkelman, Michael
  2000   *Shamanism: The Neural Ecology of Consciousness and Healing.* Westport, CT: Bergin and Garvey.
Wohl, Stanley
  1984   *Medical Industrial Complex.* New York: Harmony Books.
Wolf, Eric
  1999   *Envisioning Power: Ideologies of Dominance and Crisis.* Berkeley: University of California Press.
World Health Organization
  1978a  *The International Classification of Diseases.* 9th rev. Ann Arbor, MI: Commission on Professional and Hospital Activities.
  1978b  *Primary Health Care.* Geneva: World Health Organization.
  1996   *World Health Report.* Geneva: World Health Organization.
  2000   World Health Organization Assesses the World's Health Systems. Press release. Geneva: World Health Organization.
  2006a  *Children's Environmental Health.* Geneva: World Health Organization.
  2006b  What Is the Evidence on Effectiveness of Empowerment to Improve Health? www.euro.who.int/data/assets/pdf_file/0010/74656/E88086.pdf. Accessed June 13, 2006.
Yelin, E., M. Nevitt, and W. Epstein
  1980   Toward an Epidemiology of Work Disability. *Milbank Memorial Fund Quarterly* 58(3):386–445.
Young, Allan
  1976a  Internalizing and Externalizing Medical Belief Systems: An Ethiopian Example. *Social Science and Medicine* 10:147–56.
  1976b  Magic as a Quasi-Profession: The Organization of Magic and Magical Healing among Amhara. *Ethnology* 14:245–65.
  1977   Mode of Production of Medical Knowledge. *Medical Anthropology* 2:97–124.
Zhang, Everett Yuehong
  2007   Switching between Traditional Chinese Medicine and Viagra: Cosmopolitanism and Medical Pluralism Today. *Medical Anthropology* 26:53–96.

# Source Material
# for Students

**MEDICAL ANTHROPOLOGY AND RELATED JOURNALS**

- *Anthropologies of African Biosciences* (aab.lshtm.ac.uk/blog)
- *Anthropology and Medicine* (www.tandf.co.uk/journals/carfax/13648470. html)
- *Anthropology in Action: Journal for Applied Anthropology in Policy and Action* (journals.berghahnbooks.com/aia/index.php)
- *Culture, Medicine and Psychiatry* (web.mit.edu/dumit/www/cmp.html)
- *Global Change and Human Health* (www.springerlink.com/content/ 106598/)
- *International Journal of Bio-Anthropological Practice* (sites.google.com/site/ ijbapractice/current-issue)
- *Journal of Complementary and Alternative Medicine* (www.liebertpub.com/ products/product.aspx?pid=26)
- *Journal of Ethnobiology and Ethnomedicine* (www.ethnobiomed.com/)
- *Journal of Human Ecology* (www.krepublishers.com/02-Journals/JHE/JHE -00-0-000-000-1990-Web/JHE-00-0-000-000-1990-1-Cover.htm)
- *Medical Anthropology and Bioethics* (en.tuva.asia/82-medical.html)
- *Medical Anthropology Quarterly* (www.medanthro.net/maq/index.html)
- *Medical Anthropology: Cross-Cultural Studies in Health and Illness* (www .tandf.co.uk/journals/titles/01459740.html)
- *Social Science and Medicine* (journals.elsevier.com/02779536/social-science -and-medicine/#description)

## MEDICAL ANTHROPOLOGY ORGANIZATIONS AND INSTITUTIONS

- Centre for Health and Society, University of Melbourne (Australia) (www
  .chs.unimelb.edu.au/)
- Durham University's Medical Anthropology Research Group (UK) (www
  .dur.ac.uk/anthropology/research/marg/)
- Institute of Medicine of the National Academies (www.iom.edu/)
- Medanthro Study Group (see www.h-net.org/~medanthro/)
- Medical Anthropology Network of the European Association of Social
  Anthropologists (www.easaonline.org/networks/medical/specint_applied
  .htm)
- The Medical Anthropology Working Group (Germany) (www.medical
  anthropology.de/)
- Society for Applied Anthropology (www.sfaa.net/)
- Society for Ethnomedicine (Germany) (www.agem-ethnomedizin.de/)
- Society for Medical Anthropology (www.medanthro.net/maq/index.html,
  and within this website, see medanth's "Coming to Terms" page: medanth
  .wikispaces.com/)

## MEDICAL ANTHROPOLOGY BLOGS

- AnthroGenetics Blog (anthrogenetics.wordpress.com/category/medical
  -anthropology/)
- Somatosphere: Science, Medicine, and Anthropology (www.somatosphere
  .net/2008/07/medical-anthropology-blog.html)
- Voices of Medical Anthropology (socmedanthro.wordpress.com/2010/
  01/07/who-are-we-in-the-public-imagination-carolyn-sargent/)

## MEDICAL ANTHROPOLOGY FILMS

A list of medical anthropology and related films is available at www.medanthro
.net/academic/films.html.

## UNIVERSITIES IN NORTH AMERICA WITH MEDICAL
## ANTHROPOLOGY GRADUATE PROGRAMS

Programs at these schools and what they have to offer the prospective student
can be searched individually.

- Boston University School of Medicine
- Brown University
- Case Western Reserve University
- City College of New York (CUNY)

- Columbia University
- East Carolina University
- Emory University
- Harvard University
- McGill University
- Michigan State University
- Northwestern University
- Rensselaer Polytechnic Institute
- San Diego State University
- Southern Methodist University
- State University of New York (SUNY), Binghamton
- University of Alabama
- University of Alberta
- University of Arizona
- University of Buffalo
- University of California, San Diego
- University of California, San Francisco
- University of Colorado, Denver
- University of Connecticut
- University of Hawaii
- University of Iowa
- University of Kansas
- University of Kentucky
- University of Manitoba
- University of Massachusetts
- University of Memphis
- University of Michigan
- University of Missouri, Columbia
- University of Montana
- University of North Carolina, Chapel Hill
- University of Pennsylvania
- University of Pittsburgh
- University of South Florida
- University of Toronto
- University of Washington
- Washington State University
- Wayne State University
- Yale University
- York University

## ENCYCLOPEDIAS

Encyclopedia of Medical Anthropology (www.springer.com/west/home/generic/search/results?SGWID=4-40109-22-173660355-0)

Ethnic Diseases Sourcebook (www.omnigraphics.com/product_view.php?ID=229)

The Gale Encyclopedia of Alternative Medicine (www.gale.com/servlet/BrowseSeriesServlet?region=9&imprint=000&cf=es&titleCode=GEACME&dc=null&dewey=null&edition=)

## ONLINE MEDICAL ANTHROPOLOGY TUTORIALS

Medical Anthropology: How Illness Is Traditionally Perceived and Cured around the World (anthro.palomar.edu/medical/default.htm)

Medical Anthropology Web (www.uic.edu/classes/osci/osci590/tableof contents.htm)

# Index

# About the Authors

**Merrill Singer** is a professor of anthropology and senior research scientist at the Center for Health, Intervention, and Prevention at the University of Connecticut. He has conducted medical anthropology research on a range of issues in the United States, Brazil, China, and the U.S. Virgin Islands and has developed and implemented various projects designed to prevent the spread of HIV/AIDS that have contributed to a measurable drop in local HIV incidence. He is the author, coauthor, or editor of twenty-four books, including *Unhealthy Health Policy*, *Killer Commodities*, and *The War Machine and Global Health*.

**Hans Baer** is a lecturer in the School of Social and Environmental Enquiry and the Centre for Health and Society at the University of Melbourne, Australia. He has studied complementary and alternative healing systems in the United States, Britain, and Australia. His books include *Encounters with Biomedicine: Case Studies in Medical Anthropology*, *Toward an Integrative Medicine*, and *Medical Anthropology and the World System*.